Displacement in Isabel Allende's Fiction, 1982–2000

Hispanic Studies: Culture and Ideas

Volume **54**

Edited by
Claudio Canaparo

PETER LANG
Oxford · Bern · Berlin · Bruxelles · Frankfurt am Main · New York · Wien

Mel Boland

Displacement in Isabel Allende's Fiction, 1982–2000

PETER LANG
Oxford · Bern · Berlin · Bruxelles · Frankfurt am Main · New York · Wien

Bibliographic information published by Die Deutsche Nationalbibliothek.
Die Deutsche Nationalbibliothek lists this publication in the Deutsche National-
bibliografie; detailed bibliographic data is available on the Internet
at http://dnb.d-nb.de.

A catalogue record for this book is available from the British Library.

Library of Congress Cataloging-in-Publication Data:

Boland, Mel, 1975-
 Displacement in Isabel Allende's fiction, 1982-2000 / Mel Boland.
    pages cm. -- (Hispanic Studies: Culture and Ideas ; 54)
 Includes bibliographical references and index.
 ISBN 978-3-0343-0932-5 (alk. paper)
1. Allende, Isabel--Criticism and interpretation. 2. Displacement (Psychology) in
literature 3. Spanish literature--History and criticism. I. Title.
 PQ8098.1.L54Z59 2013
 863'.64--dc23
                        2013004372

Cover illustration: 'La Pampa' © Claudia del Río, 2013.

ISSN 1661-4720
ISBN 978-3-0343-0932-5

© Peter Lang AG, International Academic Publishers, Bern 2013
Hochfeldstrasse 32, CH-3012 Bern, Switzerland
info@peterlang.com, www.peterlang.com, www.peterlang.net

All rights reserved.
All parts of this publication are protected by copyright.
Any utilisation outside the strict limits of the copyright law, without the
permission of the publisher, is forbidden and liable to prosecution.
This applies in particular to reproductions, translations, microfilming,
and storage and processing in electronic retrieval systems.

Contents

Acknowledgements — vii

Preface — 1

CHAPTER 1
An Introduction to Displacement in Isabel Allende's Fiction — 3

CHAPTER 2
Local Development and Displacement: Esteban Trueba's Experiences in Las Tres Marías in *La casa de los espíritus* — 35

CHAPTER 3
Appearance, Disappearance and Displacement: A Carnivalesque Reading of *De amor y de sombra* — 71

CHAPTER 4
Displacing Language: Secondary Orality and Silence in *Eva Luna* and *Cuentos de Eva Luna* — 103

CHAPTER 5
Cultural Displacement in *El plan infinito*, *Hija de la fortuna* and *Retrato en sepia* — 133

Conclusion — 185

Bibliography — 191

Index — 201

Acknowledgements

I am very grateful to my colleagues in Spanish at NUI Galway, under the stewardship of Professor Diarmuid Bradley on my arrival in September 2001 and succeeded by Professor Bill Richardson. Particular thanks are due to Kate, Lorraine, Lorna, Begoña, Karen and Pilar, for their interest, conversations and support. I would also like to thank the NUI Galway Millennium Fund for assistance with the cost of publication.

Thanks also to all my friends for their support and for helping me keep my feet on the ground, especially Paul, Niamh, Gráinne, David, Claire and Matt.

With much love, I thank my dear family: my sisters Claire (with Alan, Matt, Millie and Scott, of course!) and Anita, and my brothers, Martin, Eamonn, Junior, Michael, Colm (well, the 3Cs, Colm, Ciara and Chloe!) and Paul. I reserve special thanks for Paul for all his help – you couldn't ask for a better brother!

This book would not have been completed without my wonderful, caring and endlessly supportive father, Tom. Thank you Tom for everything you do for me.

Above all, I dedicate this book to the memory of my dear mother, Marie, whom we lost in February 2008. Her kindness, her love for life and her way of making everyone feel so special will always bring a smile to my face rather than a tear to my eye. I miss you so much, and I hope you would be proud of me. This is for you, Mar xxx

Preface

Isabel Allende's work is suffused with experiences of, and references to, displacement, and her personal experiences of exile and migration have informed character development and the thematic content of her fiction. Allende's first foray into the world of fiction was the now globally and critically acclaimed *La casa de los espíritus* [*The House of the Spirits*] in 1982, a fictionalized panorama of twentieth-century Chilean society. *La casa de los espíritus* was written by Allende in self-imposed exile, and the reflections on and interrelations between personal, national and universal histories continue to inform her writing today.

This study examines the relevance of the concept of displacement to the seven works of fiction by Allende published between 1982 and 2000. This discussion comprises five chapters: in Chapter 1, displacement is introduced and traced through Allende's fiction in broad terms. In Chapter 2, the relevance of displacement to the development of the character of Esteban Trueba in *La casa de los espíritus* is explored through his relationship with inhabitants on his family's country estate, Las Tres Marías, and it is argued that Trueba's trajectory in the novel is underscored by a constant awareness of social and geographical displacement. In Chapter 3, appearance, disappearance and displacement are explored in Allende's second novel, *De amor y de sombra* [*Of Love and Shadows*], which was published in 1984. A carnivalesque reading of the text, informed by the work of Russian literary theorist, Mikhail Bakhtin, is used to suggest that this novel displays an underlying coherence, and highlights rampant subversive activity, a key element in Allende's fiction. In Chapter 4, oral language and silence are examined in *Eva Luna* [*Eva Luna*] (1987) and the short-story spin-off collection, *Cuentos de Eva Luna* [*The Stories of Eva Luna*] (1989), and it is argued that Allende reinstates the primacy of oral language through written language in *Eva Luna*, while she illustrates the power of silence and reticence in *Cuentos de Eva Luna*. In Chapter 5, the question of cultural displacement is examined through an analysis of three novels, published following Allende's relocation to the United States: that is, *El plan infinito* [*The Infinite Plan*] (1991), *Hija de la fortuna* [*Daughter of Fortune*] (1999) and *Retrato en sepia* [*Portrait in Sepia*] (2000). In this chapter, relationships between the individual and the community, as well as the variety of reflections of inner and outer conflicts experienced by characters, are explored.

This study argues that the recurring motif of displacement in Allende's writings illustrates the writer's concerted, nuanced engagement with issues of identity and a search for belonging. Allende's fiction moves beyond the confines of Latin America into a more international setting, and reflects her own experiences of displacement. Her fiction explores cross-cultural concerns of key relevance to contemporary global society. Moves in Allende's fiction towards the treatment of global concerns are juxtaposed with the growing importance of the individual, as a sense of displacement becomes increasingly internalized and indeed embraced by characters in her work.

CHAPTER 1

An Introduction to Displacement in Isabel Allende's Fiction

> In spite of Allende's obvious talents, there is not a single ounce of originality in the 300 pages of [*Retrato en sepia*]; one may read on, enthralled, but one never gets lost in another world in the way one does with the best books.
>
> — ILAN STAVANS[1]

> I am an eternal foreigner; the daughter of diplomats, a refugee, an immigrant. I have started from scratch in a new place with a new language several times, so I am not attached to objects.
>
> — ISABEL ALLENDE[2]

Introduction: Unoriginal Sin?

At first glance, critic Ilan Stavans's scathing description of Chilean author Isabel Allende's sixth novel, *Retrato en sepia* [*Portrait in Sepia*],[3] published in 2000, may appear to be a strange point of departure for an examination of Allende's fiction, but his comment is apposite for a number of reasons:

---

1   Ilan Stavans, 'Do you remember?', *The Times*, 5 October 2001, <http://www.timesonline.co.uk/tol/incomingFeeds/article766336.ece> [accessed 18 June 2012].
2   Isabel Allende, *The Guardian*, 14 April 2008, Section G2, p. 14, <http://www.guardian.co.uk/theguardian/2008/apr/14/features.g2> [accessed 23 July 2012].
3   Isabel Allende, *Retrato en sepia* (Barcelona: Plaza & Janés, 2000). Further references will appear parenthetically in the text.

first, Stavans is one of many critics who consider Allende's works a qualified success; while he acknowledges positive features such as her ability to tell stories, he nevertheless cites a lack of originality as one of the key failings of this novel. In Stavans's eyes, the novel is engaging, but lacks an original, compelling or radically different perspective on the quest by the protagonist, Aurora del Valle, to decipher the meaning of the nightmares from her childhood and to forge a place for herself in Chilean society. Other commentators have also made reference to the relative degree of originality in *Retrato en sepia* as well as in other, if not all, works of fiction by Allende. Some argue that the recognizable features of her fiction are in fact quite positive: for example, in her review of the novel, Helen Falconer describes *Retrato en sepia* as 'trademark Allende', which she understands to be 'a family saga crowded with brilliant personalities, outlined then coloured in with such artistic care that we can't help but imagine them as drawn from life'.[4] However, many other critics follow the line of argument propounded by Stavans and view this novel as merely further evidence that Allende's writing is formulaic and wholly predictable in terms of plot and character development: for example, María de la Cinta Ramblado-Minero states that 'the trajectory of Aurora [in *Retrato en sepia*] is a repetition of the experience of previous characters, from the original ones in *La casa de los espíritus* [*The House of the Spirits*], to Aurora's own maternal grandmother, Eliza, in *Hija de la fortuna* [*Daughter of Fortune*]'.[5] She coins the term 'Allendian' (p. 177) to describe what she identifies as recurring features throughout Allende's work. In an overview of critical approaches to Allende's work published up to 2002, Beth Jorgenson also cites repetition as a feature of her fiction; she states that 'the potential for

---

4   Helen Falconer, 'Colouring the Family Album', *The Guardian*, 17 November 2001 <http://www.guardian.co.uk/books/2001/nov/17/fiction.isabelallende> [accessed 15 June 2012].

5   María de la Cinta Ramblado-Minero, *Isabel Allende's Writing of the Self: Trespassing the Boundaries of Fiction and Autobiography* (Lewiston, NY: Edwin Mellen, 2003), p. 177. See also Claire Lindsay's discussion of critical views on Allende in her *Locating Latin American Women Writers: Cristina Peri Rossi, Rosario Ferré, Albalucía Angel, and Isabel Allende* (New York: Peter Lang, 2003), pp. 113–20.

pleasure [in Allende's work] is limited to the real but easy pleasure of the familiar, and has not to date provided the more challenging reward of an encounter with the new and the unexpected'.[6] However, it is perhaps in Harold Bloom's introduction to a collection of essays on Allende where some of the most pointed criticism of the similarities to be found between her works can be discerned: Bloom summarily dismisses her work, and argues that 'rereading her is simply not possible'.[7] While he does acknowledge her 'humane political and social stances' (p. 2), he shares Ramblado-Minero's concerns regarding characterization when he explains how he struggles to differentiate between characters such as Nívea, Clara, Blanca and Alba in *La casa de los espíritus*. Bloom's uncertainty on the status of Allende's fiction leads him to wonder whether her novels are 'permanent works of literary art' or rather 'popular romances for our age of Ideology and Information' (p. 2). Bloom's introduction is a damning precursor to a work which endeavours to illustrate the depth and underlying complexity to be found in Allende's writing and highlights the critical polarity that surrounds Allende and her work.

Despite the body of critical work adopting a sceptical view of the nature and content of Allende's fiction, it is nevertheless undeniable that her works have had a significant and enduring impact on the Latin American, and indeed global, literary scene. Furthermore this impact has been, and continues to be, the subject of much criticism and commentary in studies on contemporary Latin American literature: Efraín Kristal, for example, suggests that Allende has made a crucial, central contribution when he explains that '[a]fter the initial "Boom," a second wave of worldwide interest in the Latin American novel was generated, almost single-handedly at first, by Isabel Allende, whose critical and commercial success opened the way

---

6   Beth Jorgenson, '"Un puñado de críticos": Navigating the Critical Readings of Isabel Allende's Work', in *Isabel Allende Today*, ed. by Rosemary G. Feal and Yvette E. Miller (Pittsburgh: Latin American Literary Review, 2002), pp. 128–46 (p. 142).
7   Harold Bloom, 'Introduction', in *Isabel Allende*, ed. by Harold Bloom (Broomall, PA: Chelsea House, 2003), pp. 1–3 (p. 2).

for the recognition of women writers'.[8] Attempts to categorize Allende's work within Latin American literary movements have also been frequent, with many critics identifying her work as belonging to the Post-Boom wave of writing: for example, Raymond Leslie Williams argues that Allende's 'fast-moving plots and accessible works make her the post-Boom writer par excellence',[9] while Donald L. Shaw devotes an entire chapter to Allende's work in *The Post-Boom in Spanish American Fiction*.[10] The continuing critical indecision surrounding Allende's place in the literary scene is a useful point of departure for the present study, which addresses primarily the concerns raised by critics such as Bloom, Stavans and Ramblado-Minero about issues of repetition and originality in Allende's fiction. It is argued here that it is only through careful reading – and rereading – of her work that subtle differences in her approaches to issues can be discerned. The present discussion focuses on seven works of fiction published by Allende between 1982 and 2000, and the recurring motif of displacement is employed as a way of examining her approach to characters and themes. Admittedly, these seven texts represent only a selection of Allende's ever-expanding body of work, but within this time period, which begins with the publication of *La casa de los espíritus* in 1982 and concludes with the release in 2000 of *Retrato en sepia*, it is argued that a clear evolution can be traced in Allende's approach to plot and character.[11] Furthermore, *Retrato en sepia* in a sense functions as an intertextual bridge between her 1999 novel *Hija de la fortuna* and *La casa de los espíritus*, and thus its arrival in

---

8   Efraín Kristal, 'Introduction', in *The Cambridge Companion to the Latin American Novel*, ed. by Efraín Kristal (Cambridge: Cambridge University Press, 2005), pp. 1–22 (p. 9).
9   Raymond Leslie Williams, *The Columbia Guide to the Latin American Novel Since 1945* (New York: Columbia University Press, 2007), p. 62.
10 Donald L. Shaw, *The Post-Boom in Spanish American Fiction* (Albany: State University of New York Press, 1998).
11 Isabel Allende, *La casa de los espíritus*, 12th edn (Barcelona: Plaza & Janés, 2004). Further references will appear parenthetically in the text.

An Introduction to Displacement in Isabel Allende's Fiction

2000 closes a narrative circle in Allende's writing, and invites a review of her fiction produced to that point.[12]

The focus on displacement in this study is proposed for the following reasons: first, we argue that an analysis of displacement in Allende's fiction highlights the author's concerted exploration of the relationship between individuals and communities in her work. This approach is used as a means of revisiting and reappraising both characters and themes in texts which have already garnered significant critical attention, such as Esteban Trueba's relationship with the inhabitants of his family's country estate in *La casa de los espíritus*, to be broached in Chapter 2, and issues relating to communication and communities in both *Eva Luna* [*Eva Luna*] and in her short-story collection *Cuentos de Eva Luna* [*The Stories of Eva Luna*], examined in Chapter 4.[13] It will be argued that it is through the foregrounding of experiences of displacement that the uniqueness in Allende's writing is to be found; while it would be futile to contend that similarities between characters' trajectories in these texts are not readily apparent, as suggested earlier by Ramblado-Minero, this analysis instead highlights the subtle differences between characters as a way of arguing that Allende's fiction is multi-layered and indeed remains a relatively untapped corpus of work in critical terms.

Second, an examination of Allende's fiction within this period through the prism of displacement aims to reconcile two apparently contradictory trends which have emerged in her writing: on the one hand, the settings of her fiction have moved beyond the recognizably national confines of

---

12   Isabel Allende, *Hija de la fortuna*, 3rd edn (Barcelona: Plaza & Janés, 1999). Further references will appear parenthetically in the text. Much of the global success of this novel may in fact be attributed to the selection of its English-language translation, *Daughter of Fortune*, in February 2000 as part of US chat show host Oprah Winfrey's hugely successful book club (Oprah's Book Club). For further information, see Ana Patricia Rodríguez's article '"Did Isabel Allende Write This Book for Me?": Oprah's Book Club Reads *Daughter of Fortune*' in *The Oprah Affect*, ed. by Cecilia Konchar Farr and Jaime Harker (Albany: State University of New York Press, 2008), pp. 189–210.
13   Isabel Allende, *Eva Luna*, 5th edn (Barcelona: Plaza & Janés, 1993). All subsequent references will be to this edition.

Chile in *La casa de los espíritus* and *De amor y de sombra* [*Of Love and Shadows*] into a more international setting from the publication of *Eva Luna* onwards; on the other hand, questions of inner conflict and identity appear to have gained in importance, with characters especially in her later fiction questioning both their respective individuality and their affiliations to various communities with whom they come into contact, including communities in exile.[14] This study looks at how, beyond the more international landscapes of Allende's fiction written since her move to the United States in 1988, it is the relationship with self and indeed the *embracing* of a sense of displacement that form part of the originality to be found in later works such as *Retrato en sepia*.

Third, in considering this fiction, this analysis aims to illustrate the relevance and importance of three works of fiction by Allende which have received relatively scant critical attention, that is, *De amor y de sombra* (1984), *Cuentos de Eva Luna* (1989) and *El plan infinito* [*The Infinite Plan*] (1991).[15] These texts are examined in Chapters 3, 4 and 5 respectively in order to gauge their place and importance in Allende's literary output. For a variety of reasons, these texts have often been neglected by critics: for example, the relative merits of *De amor y de sombra* as an independent text are often ignored in favour of a comparative analysis between this text and *La casa de los espíritus*; *Cuentos de Eva Luna* is often discounted by virtue of being a short-story collection and *El plan infinito* is often criticized for being overly ambitious in attempting to chart the dramatic changes in the United States of the mid- to late twentieth century.[16] This analysis seeks to locate each text within Allende's *oeuvre* and, in particular, to highlight the significance of *Cuentos de Eva Luna* in relation to her exploration of the relationship between self and community.

---

14   Isabel Allende, *De amor y de sombra*, 8th edn (Barcelona: Plaza & Janés, 1995). All subsequent references will be to this edition.
15   Isabel Allende, *El plan infinito* (Barcelona: Plaza & Janés, 1991). Subsequent references will appear parenthetically in the text.
16   To cite just one example, Karen Castellucci Cox's *Isabel Allende: A Critical Companion* (Westport, CT: Greenwood, 2003) completely ignores *Cuentos de Eva Luna*. Further critical discussion of these texts may be found in their respective chapters.

Fourth, Allende's position in the context of contemporary Latin American studies will be considered towards the conclusion of this discussion, and it will be shown how an analysis of the thematic content of her later fiction, with its increasing focus on negotiating cultural difference, raises various issues about the feasibility of continuing to describe her fiction within strictly Latin American parameters. First, however, it is important to establish the scope of displacement for the purposes of this analysis.

Displacement: A Point of Departure

The selection of the polysemous term *displacement* as a common thread here necessarily requires some justification: first, the basic sense which provides a springboard for the present discussion may be found in a definition offered by Angelika Bammer, who, in an introduction to a critical collection on the topic, describes displacement as 'the separation of people from their native culture either through physical dislocation (as refugees, immigrants, migrants, exiles, or expatriates) or the colonizing imposition of a foreign culture'.[17] Both parts of this definition highlight the important interplay between culture and displacement: on the one hand, there is a very visible and physical form of dislocation through the movement of people from their homeland to another place, while on the other, the sense of displacement is less apparent, but equally influential, through enforced political changes which may have significant social and psychological repercussions, despite the lack of any obvious geographical relocation of people. This basic dichotomy of visible and invisible displacement offered above by Bammer, moreover, can be broken down further: political upheaval in a country may lead to the enforced movement or migration of people from

---

17 Angelika Bammer, 'Introduction', in *Displacements: Cultural Identities in Question*, ed. by Angelika Bammer (Bloomington: Indiana University Press, 1994), pp. xi–xx (p. xi).

one part of a country to another, yet this group of people may end up being prevented from crossing the border into another country, owing perhaps to problems with documentation or to an unwillingness on the part of the prospective host country to grant them entry. This situation, which has been reported with increasing frequency in the media in the twenty-first century, is known as *internal displacement*, and those who find themselves in a type of limbo, within their own national borders, but unable to escape, have been referred to as *internally displaced persons* (IDPs).[18] Indeed, it is not merely changes in political regime that may effect a form of enforced movement within the borders of a country: policy changes instituted by a government may also trigger movement, which is known as *development-induced displacement*.[19] Another frequent cause of internal displacement is environmental change, with natural disasters often causing sudden mass movements of people.[20] Of course, political and environmental factors are

18   The concept of internal displacement is of growing relevance in global affairs, and concerted efforts have been made to identify, name and highlight not only the problem of internal displacement, but also those who suffer from being trapped within their own national borders. For a rigorous introduction to the concept, as well as a fascinating snapshot of how lobbying proceeds in a supranational organization such as the United Nations, see Thomas G. Weiss and David A. Korn's *Internal Displacement: Conceptualization and its Consequences* (London: Taylor & Francis, 2006).
19   In the run-up to the Beijing Summer Olympics in 2008, there was much controversy surrounding the enforced relocation of citizens from lands which were to be redeveloped for the hosting of the games. An official document relating to the relocation process, which seeks to explain the Chinese Government's views, 'Briefing on the relocation project for Olympic venues', can be found at <http://en.beijing2008.cn/news/official/preparation/n214253222.shtml> [accessed 4 July 2012]. The Geneva-based Centre on Housing Rights and Evictions (COHRE), on the other hand, presents a much grimmer picture of the relocation process in the report 'One World, Whose Dream? Housing Rights Violations and the Beijing Olympic Games'. The full report is available to be read online at the following URL: <http://www.cohre.org/store/attachments/One_World_Whose_Dream_July08.pdf> [accessed 9 July 2012].
20   Examples of climate-induced displacement are plentiful, but the Hurricane Katrina situation of August 2005 in New Orleans, Louisiana, is a key example of displacement

equally relevant to situations of exile, or *external displacement*, which is the term used in contradistinction to situations of internal displacement mentioned above. A cursory glance at coverage of contemporary global affairs suffices to show the range of conflicts throughout the world that have forced people to move away from their homes and relocate in order to escape a dangerous or threatening situation and to search for asylum in neighbouring countries, from the significant waves of migration throughout the twentieth century through to ongoing conflicts this century in Sudan and Israel, to cite but two examples.[21] In addition, contemporary debates on globalization examine the impact of the practices of multinational companies on economies and communities worldwide.[22]

Situations of internal and external displacement have been commonplace in Latin America, especially since colonial times. Since the beginning of the twenty-first century alone, there has been widespread reporting on the internally displaced people (IDPs) of Colombia, owing to the continuing civil war there:[23] in a report which looks at public policy on forced

---

affecting a developed country. The US government's slow response to the plight of many of their own citizens created a media furore. For further discussion, see *Natural Disaster Analysis After Hurricane Katrina: Risk Assessment, Economic Impacts and Social Implications*, ed. by Harry W. Richardson, Peter Gordon and James E. Moore (Cheltenham: Edward Elgar, 2009).

21 For a recent discussion of the problems of internal displacement in Sudan, see Munzoul Assal's 'Rights and Decisions to Return: Internally Displaced Persons in Post-war Sudan' in *Forced Displacements: Whose Needs are Right?*, ed. by Katarzyna Grabska and Lyla Mehta (Basingstoke: Palgrave Macmillan, 2008), pp. 139–58. In relation to Israel, Kim Chernin's *Everywhere a Guest, Nowhere at Home: A New Vision of Israel and Palestine* (Berkeley, CA: North Atlantic Books, 2009) provides a very personal perspective on the impact of the creation of the Israeli state in 1948 and subsequent conflicts.

22 The organization *Human Rights Watch* provides a comprehensive and regularly updated website at <www.hrw.org>, with further information regarding displacement and migration.

23 An important UN Refugee Agency report on the plight of internally displaced people in Colombia, entitled *Colombia. Internal Displacement – Policies and Problems*, is available online at <http://www.unhcr.org/refworld/docid/44bf463a4.html> [accessed 7 January 2009].

displacement in Colombia, Marta Inés Villa states that '[e]n la actualidad hay más de tres millones de desplazados internos en Colombia y cerca de 300.000 colombianos han buscado refugio en países vecinos, como Ecuador, Venezuela y Panamá, y en países más distantes, como Estados Unidos de Norteamérica, Canadá y Costa Rica' [*there are currently more than 3 million internally displaced people in Colombia and around 300,000 Colombians have sought refuge in neighbouring countries, such as Ecuador, Venezuela and Panama, and in more distant countries, such as the United States, Canada and Costa Rica*].[24] In Bolivia, the fractured nature of society and uneven distribution of wealth and resources have become more pronounced through recent political wrangling over the acceptance of the new constitution, approved in January 2009 by the government of Evo Morales. Regional calls for autonomy and challenges to attempts to reform the linguistic, social and economic situation of the country are played out in a territory whose inhabitants are constantly on the alert, given the ever-present threat of natural disasters, as witnessed already on numerous occasions this century. Displacement may also be usefully examined diachronically in this context, through the various waves of colonization and migration in Latin America, and the concomitant reconfigurations of the sociopolitical landscape.[25] In relation to the history of Chile, Allende makes reference to several significant examples in her 2003 memoir, *Mi país inventado* [*My Invented Country*]; she discusses the plight of indigenous populations there over the last two centuries, and in particular the displacement of the indigenous Mapuche tribe. In addition, she describes the arrival of the British in the

---

24 Marta Inés Villa, 'Políticas públicas sobre el desplazamiento forzado en Colombia: Una lectura desde las representaciones sociales', in *Las migraciones en América Latina: políticas, culturas y estrategias*, ed. by Susana Novick (Buenos Aires: Catálogos, 2008), pp. 229–48 (p. 230). All translations into English are by me.

25 For a comprehensive overview of Latin American history since colonial times, see Marshall C. Eakin, *The History of Latin America: Collision of Cultures* (New York: Palgrave Macmillan, 2007). Mario Sznajder and Luis Roniger offer a more specific examination of Latin American history in relation to exile in *The Politics of Exile in Latin America* (Cambridge: Cambridge University Press, 2009): the section 'Spanish America: Practices of Expulsion' (pp. 41–5) includes extensive reference to displacement or 'destierro'.

nineteenth century, the impact of neo-colonialism and the controversial measures introduced through government policies which sought to encourage immigration from Europe throughout the nineteenth and twentieth centuries. Allende strongly believes that Chile's 'política de inmigración ha sido abiertamente racista' [*immigration policy has been openly racist*].²⁶ In relation to British expatriates resident in Chile, she notes how their descendants, despite never having set foot in Britain, continued to live in a form of splendid isolation: 'tenían a mucha honra hablar castellano con acento y enterarse de las noticias por periódicos atrasados que venían de allá' (p. 60) [*they took great pride in speaking accented Spanish and learning about the news from old newspapers which came from Britain*].²⁷

Changes throughout the Chilean political landscape of the twentieth century, particularly since the 1973 political coup in which General Augusto Pinochet played a crucial role, often led to situations of self-imposed exile for figures who subsequently went on to achieve global acclaim as writers; apart from Allende herself, many other prominent Chilean writers, including Ariel Dorfman, Antonio Skármeta and José Donoso, have considered questions of displacement at various stages in their writing, with their literature often providing a space in which estrangement and isolation during and after experiences of totalitarian regimes are explored.²⁸

---

26   Isabel Allende, *Mi país inventado* (Barcelona: Areté, 2003), p. 58.
27   Allende examines in great detail the tensions and dynamics in the relationship between British expatriate siblings Jeremy and Rose Sommers, who have moved to Valparaíso, Chile, in *Hija de la fortuna*; see Chapter 5 for further discussion of this.
28   A 2007 documentary film, *A Promise to the Dead: The Exile Journey of Ariel Dorfman*, directed by Peter Raymont, charts Dorfman's experiences of the coup and his return to Chile following the death of Pinochet. In many ways, key issues addressed in this documentary, such as memory and exile, are equally pertinent to investigating Allende's work. Skármeta's *El baile de la victoria* (Barcelona: Planeta, 2003) sketches a love story in post-Pinochet Chile, where the spectre of the dictatorship still haunts the lives of the protagonists. Donoso's *La desesperanza* (Barcelona: Seix Barral, 1986) is set in the midst of the Pinochet regime and uses the death of celebrated poet Pablo Neruda's wife, Matilde Urrutia, as a springboard for the examination of protagonist Mañungo Vera's efforts to resettle in Chile following an extensive period living in Paris.

Allende's own experiences of displacement have been well documented, and she has spoken widely, and in great detail, about her decision to leave Chile and move to Caracas, Venezuela in 1975, two years after the Pinochet coup. While it is not the intention of this study to replicate the extensive treatment already given elsewhere to the specific issue of exile as a feature of Allende's life and work, it is nevertheless instructive to mention some of Allende's comments, owing to their relevance to the focus of this discussion.[29] For example, the second epigraph to this chapter highlights Allende's belief that she has always felt that she was different, and that travel and movement have defined her life. Her peripatetic past has consequently made her privilege memory over place and possibly spurred her on to become a writer: '[m]aybe because I have been a displaced person all of my life, I need to carry with me my roots and my memories and that is why [memory] is so important for me. Maybe that's why I write. I wouldn't be a writer otherwise.'[30] If writing, then, is a means of grounding Allende's experiences, then it is also a process that has helped her gain a clearer understanding of her homeland, albeit at a distance: she argues that 'being an outsider is the best position for a writer,'[31] given that it has afforded her the advantage of detachment from her home environment and has granted her perspective. This is confirmed in another interview, when she states that '[t]he fact that I have had to put distance between my country and myself has made my country clearer to me.'[32] John Rodden, who has collated a number of Allende's interviews given since her rise to prominence in the nineteen eighties, suggests that Allende's current personal circumstances, as a Californian resident and US citizen, have greatly

---

29 For a comprehensive discussion of Allende's life, see the introductory chapter in Linda Gould Levine's *Isabel Allende* (New York: Twayne, 2003), pp. 1–17.
30 In interview with Cristen Reat, 'Self-Portrait in Sepia', in *Conversations with Isabel Allende*, revised edn, ed. by John Rodden (Austin: University of Texas Press, 2004), pp. 281–90 (p. 282).
31 In interview with Jennifer Benjamin and Sally Engelfried, 'Magical Feminist', in *Conversations*, pp. 185–99 (p. 194).
32 In interview with Elyse Crystall, Jil Kuhnheim, and Mary Layoun, 'An Overwhelming Passion to Tell the Story', in *Conversations*, pp. 115–30 (p. 105).

influenced her writing, and he argues that she now 'possesses a "double perspective" from living in the United States and writing from her Latin American past'.[33] The question of cultural displacement will be examined in Chapter 5 in relation to the three novels she has written since her move to the United States.

As can be inferred from Allende's comments and documented experiences, the implications of geographical displacement on identity are far-reaching: Bammer suggests that 'our sense of identity is ineluctably, it seems, marked by the peculiarly postmodern geography of identity: both here *and* there and neither here *nor* there'.[34] The relationship between identity and displacement has been investigated in many fields of enquiry, including philosophy and psychoanalysis.[35] Indeed, the various tensions that are created through the experience of displacement, between past and present circumstances, public and private spheres, and a sense of one's individuality being in opposition to a sense of community, are all significant elements broached by Allende through her fiction. While certain critics mentioned in the opening stages of this chapter suggest these experiences of displacement, and in particular, external displacement, have an all-too-familiar ring to them, it is worth bearing in mind critic Sophia McClennen's comments on the question of the exilic condition: she argues that each instance of exile maintains its own uniqueness, and that '[the exiles'] experience of displacement, decentering and disempowerment is grounded in the particularity of their experience and cannot be categorized as merely symbolic of the

33 John Rodden, 'Introduction', in *Conversations*, pp. 1–42 (p. 14).
34 Angelika Bammer, 'Introduction', in *Displacements: Cultural Identities in Question*, ed. by Angelika Bammer (Bloomington: Indiana University Press, 1994), pp. xi–xx (p. xii).
35 Work by philosophers Søren Kierkegaard and Martin Heidegger has foregrounded displacement both as an intrinsic part of self and a necessary rite of passage to be experienced and recognized in order to gain a greater understanding of self. For a discussion of the links between displacement and intellectual exile in Kierkegaard, see Poul Houe's 'Place and Displacement in Kierkegaard: Place and Displacement of Kierkegaard', *Edda*, 97 (1997), 358–63. A comprehensive approach to Heidegger's work on displacement is provided by Miguel de Beistegui's *Thinking with Heidegger: Displacements* (Bloomington: Indiana University Press, 2003).

condition of the outsider or as representative of linguistic *différance*.[36] In Allende's case, while internal displacement has not been a significant feature documented in her life, attempts to communicate the experience and impact of external displacement are pervasive, and two main aspects of Allende's biography are of importance here, especially in reference to language issues: first, her move to Venezuela and second, her current place of residence, that is, California. With her move to Venezuela, for example, in 1975, it would appear from the outset that language would not prove to be a militating factor in attempts at integration, owing to the shared Spanish language of her homeland Chile and her new adopted home. However, as she explains in *Mi país inventado*, even the process of integration into a new land where one's language is also spoken can be complicated by cultural differences.[37] Experiences of linguistic diversity and attempts at communication feature strongly throughout Allende's fiction, and questions on the tensions between oral, written language and silence will be explored in Chapter 4. A more obvious example of language and displacement can be found in relation to Allende's move in 1988 to California, where she married her second husband, William Gordon. Allende's experience in the United States has led to her increased fluency in English; however, she chooses to continue writing fiction in Spanish. While perfectly comfortable speaking English, as can be attested by the numerous interviews and talks which she has given, Allende nevertheless feels that there remains a type of cultural barrier, as is evidenced from meeting up with friends in California with her husband. She explains in *Mi país inventado*:

---

36 Sophia A. McClennen, *The Dialectics of Exile: Nation, Time, Language, and Space in Hispanic Literatures* (West Lafayette, IN: Purdue University Press, 2004), p. 20. McClennen's mention of Jacques Derrida's term *différance* is, of course, another philosophical avenue worthy of investigation; though not examined in this discussion, Derrida's exploration of the interplay between language and translation is also quite explicitly linked to displacement. For further information, see Leslie Hall's *The Cambridge Introduction to Jacques Derrida* (Cambridge: Cambridge University Press, 2007).

37 *Mi país inventado*, p. 162. Here Allende recounts the simple tale of trying to order a coffee at the bar, and the cultural differences between Chileans and Venezuelans.

Entiendo el idioma [inglés], pero no tengo las claves. En las ocasiones en que nos juntamos con amigos, puedo participar poco en la conversación, porque no conozco los acontecimientos o la gente de los cuales hablan, no vi las mismas películas en mi juventud, no bailé al son de la guitarra epiléptica de Elvis, no fumé marijuana ni salí a protestar contra la guerra del Vietnam. (p. 213)

[*I understand English, but I don't have the keys to the language. When we meet up with friends, I play very little part in conversations, because I am not familiar with the events or people they are talking about; I didn't see the same movies in my youth, nor did I dance to the sound of Elvis's epileptic guitar, smoke marihuana or take to the streets to protest against the Vietnam war.*]

Both examples cited above, though apparently of little import, are crucial issues to be broached in Chapter 5, as questions on the nature and process of integration into new communities, the recognition of multilingual and multicultural diversity, the attempts to retain and at times to recover cultural heritage and the experiences of cultural displacement all become increasingly prominent in Allende's fiction. Furthermore, while Allende herself does not write fiction in English, her personal experiences of lacking cultural references may also be identified through her characters' experiences of displacement in her fiction.[38]

Overview of Texts Examined

This section provides an overview of Allende's work to date, describes in broad terms the seven texts under discussion here and the focus to be adopted in each of the subsequent chapters. As has been mentioned in this discussion already, Allende's arrival on the literary scene was heralded by the release of her first novel, *La casa de los espíritus*, in 1982. This work was

---

38   In a sense, this perceived cultural barrier has finally been overcome by Allende through the extensive research she engaged in while preparing for the writing of her North American novels, the focus of Chapter 5 in this study.

based on a letter which Allende had begun writing in Caracas, Venezuela when she received the news that her grandfather was dying back in Santiago. *La casa de los espíritus* has been described by Lloyd Davies as 'a testament to [former Chilean president] Salvador Allende's enduring efforts to bring about change'.[39] In the novel, Allende conflates fact and fiction, and provides an elaborate and exuberant account of the vicissitudes of the four generations of the fictional Trueba and Del Valle families within the ostensibly factual framework of events that transpired in twentieth-century Chilean history. Towards the conclusion of the novel, emphasis is placed on the political turmoil and uncertainty after the overthrow by General Augusto Pinochet of the democratically-elected Socialist government led by Allende's father's cousin, Salvador Allende, in 1973, and the resulting military dictatorship. It is worth mentioning that at no stage in the text does Allende refer specifically to Chile, despite the numerous allusions to events in Chilean history; Stephen M. Hart neatly describes the novel as an 'imaginative projection of Chilean reality rather than a thetic statement about that reality'.[40]

La casa de los espíritus remains the touchstone for any examination of Allende's fiction, and it is a real challenge to encapsulate the breadth of critical work produced on the text, especially since it has been used as a point of comparison with works as diverse as African-American author Toni Morrison's *Beloved* and Chinese-American author Maxine Hong Kingston's *The Woman Warrior*.[41] It is, however, the comparison with Gabriel García

---

39   Lloyd Davies, *La casa de los espíritus* (London: Grant & Cutler, 2000), p. 20.
40   Stephen M. Hart, '*The House of the Spirits* by Isabel Allende', in *The Cambridge Companion to the Latin American Novel*, pp. 270–82 (p. 275). Alicia Galaz-Vivar Welden traces references to Chile in detail in 'Chile en el discurso referencial de *La casa de los espíritus*' in *Narrativa Hispanoamericana Contemporánea: Entre la vanguardia y el posboom*, ed. by Ana María Hernández de López (Madrid: Pliegos, 1996), pp. 265–77.
41   The articles referred to are P. Gabrielle Foreman, 'Past-On Stories: History and the Magically Real, Morrison and Allende on Call', *Feminist Studies*, 18 (1992), 369–88 and Ruth Y. Jenkins, 'Authorizing Female Voice and Experience: Ghosts and Spirits in Kingston's *The Woman Warrior* and Allende's *The House of the Spirits*', *Melus*, 19 (1994), 61–73.

Márquez's *Cien años de soledad* [*One Hundred Years of Solitude*] which has generated much debate.[42] Apart from comparative work, *La casa de los espíritus* has been extensively analysed in relation to issues such as the representation of patriarchy, the nature of magic realism in the text and the matrilineal thread within the novel.

La casa de los espíritus highlights the narrative dovetailing of two characters whose lives are shaped by experiences of displacement: Esteban Trueba, the domineering, self-made man who is burning with desire to regain a sense of aristocratic privilege which he feels his family has lost through his father's profligacy, and his granddaughter Alba, who is herself exploring the past through her notebooks and the written accounts left by her grandmother, and Esteban's wife, Clara. This dynamic text examines relationships within a variety of families, and explores the complicated impact of tradition on the present, the conflict between public and private spheres and the latent power found in and on the margins of mainstream society. Displacement suffuses the narrative: Trueba's relationship with his mother and sister is complex and paradoxical, as he depends on them yet also appears to despise them. His own later efforts to establish and bequeath a legacy of patriarchy are rejected by his wife Clara and children Blanca, Nicolás and Jaime, whose actions somewhat ironically parallel his own rejection of his sister Férula and mother Ester. His endeavours to establish rural and urban seats of power lead to his losing control over both, and there is rampant subversive activity, from the forbidden relationship between his daughter, Blanca, and the rebellious Pedro Tercero García near his country estate Las Tres Marías, through to his son Jaime and granddaughter Alba's efforts to remove the guns stockpiled in the basement of the house in the city. The presence of magical realism, pervasive in the early parts of the text, and evidenced by Clara's powers of telekinesis and clairvoyance as well as her spiritual gatherings, attended by the Mora sisters, becomes significantly less obvious as the plot progresses, and the resilience of the

---

42 Extensive treatment of this issue can be found in Robert Antoni's 'Parody or Piracy: The Relationship of *The House of the Spirits* to *One Hundred Years of Solitude*', *Latin America Literary Review*, 32 (1988), 16–28.

human spirit becomes more privileged over the world of spirits towards the end of the text. Memory and oblivion also play key roles in the text, and the selective nature of Trueba's memory returns to haunt him at various junctures, the most telling event perhaps being the arrival into the city of Esteban García, an illegitimate grandson who is also fuelled by a belief that he has been denied what is rightly his. García becomes an important figure in the military dictatorship that holds power at the close of the novel, and he wreaks revenge on Trueba's family by raping Alba and having her tortured. Ultimately, Trueba, who has been socially marginalized, must rely on the help of another marginal figure, Tránsito Soto, a prostitute who has important contacts with the new dictatorial regime and whom he had first encountered during his early days in the rural estate of Las Tres Marías. She successfully intercedes with the authorities on Trueba's behalf for Alba's safe return.

Chapter 2 of this discussion focuses on *La casa de los espíritus* and in particular on Esteban Trueba's representation. Through an examination of his relationship with the inhabitants of his family's country estate, Las Tres Marías, this discussion argues that he is actually a permanently displaced character throughout the text; apparent accomplishments in terms of power and patriarchal progress merely serve to undermine him further as he is blind to the defiant actions of his family members and his employees. He endeavours to recover an apparent past of privilege, and his paradoxical relationship with his mother and sister is mirrored in his relationships with his wife Clara and their children. The critical framework for this exploration of Trueba's character is somewhat unconventional, in that recent analyses of local development and displacement in the field of Development Studies will be applied to the text. Trueba's interaction with the local inhabitants of the land which surrounds his family's country estate in Las Tres Marías is examined in order to assess the relative success of Trueba's engagement with the local community.

Allende's second novel, *De amor y de sombra*, was published in 1984. The text continues closely in the vein of *La casa de los espíritus*, in the sense that it too is a novel which is set in Chile but which does not directly name this country. Allende has explained on several occasions that *De amor y de sombra* has a clear factual basis:

An Introduction to Displacement in Isabel Allende's Fiction 21

[*De amor y de sombra*] se basa en un hecho acontecido en Chile, en la localidad de Lonquén, a 50 kilómetros de Santiago. En unos hornos abandonados de cal se encontraron 15 cadáveres de campesinos, asesinados durante el Golpe Militar. Este descubrimiento se hizo a través de la Iglesia Católica, en el año 1978, cuando yo estaba ya en Venezuela.[43]

[[*Of Love and Shadows*] *is based on a factual event in Chile, in Lonquen, around 30 miles outside of Santiago. The corpses of fifteen country people, who had been killed during the military coup, were found in abandoned limestone ovens. This discovery was made by the Catholic Church, in 1978, when I was still living in Venezuela.*]

The text is a fictionalized representation of this event, with Lonquén renamed as Los Riscos. The discovery of these missing people, or *desaparecidos*, provides the backdrop for a novel which also charts the political awakening of a young, upper-class journalist named Irene Beltrán. Her collaborative, clandestine work with photographer and former clinical psychologist Francisco Leal somewhat unexpectedly leads to love. However, they also face a future in enforced exile because of their pivotal roles in exposing the military dictatorship's unsuccessful efforts to cover up the murder of alleged subversives. One of those found murdered is Evangelina Ranquileo, a fifteen-year-old girl who had experienced mysterious and seemingly inexplicable trance-like states and had publicly embarrassed Lieutenant Juan Dios de Ramírez, a high-ranking official, when she attacked him during one of these trances. Irene and Francisco witness this attack when they are covering Evangelina's story for the magazine on which they work together. They begin to investigate Evangelina's disappearance on behalf of her adopted family, and visit hospitals, police stations and detention centres. Their growing involvement in the investigation, as well as the discovery of Irene's subsequent covert recording of a conversation with Sergeant Rivera, arouses suspicion in military circles, and Irene is shot and

---

43   Michael Moody, 'Entrevista con Isabel Allende', *Discurso literario*, 4.1 (1986), 41–53 (p. 43). A detailed description of the Lonquén incident may be found in Ascanio Cavallo, Manuel Salazar and Oscar Sepúlveda's 'Silencio en los hornos' in *La historia oculta del régimen militar: Chile 1973–1988* (Santiago de Chile: Grijalbo, 1997), pp. 219–27.

seriously injured. Irene manages to pull through, but both she and Francisco find themselves forced into assumed identities in order to escape out of the country and begin a new life together elsewhere.

De amor y de sombra is a very pointed effort on Allende's part to tell the tale of the Lonquén *desaparecidos* and she draws heavily on court reports and interviews conducted with relatives of the victims as a basis for her text. This novel is less ambitious than *La casa de los espíritus* in the sense that the story revolves principally around a relatively small cast of characters and is not infused with magically real elements, which were so prominent throughout much of her first novel, aside from Evangelina's trances. Chapter 3 concentrates on *De amor y de sombra* and shifts the focus of the overall discussion from local to national level, by identifying the changes experienced both directly and indirectly by the protagonists who are living under a military dictatorship. While for many critics the text fails to replicate the heady mix of magical realism and political concerns so prominent in *La casa de los espíritus*, this study seeks to illustrate its crucial importance in Allende's development of theme and character through a carnivalesque reading of the text. This chapter draws on the work of Russian literary theorist Mikhail Bahktin and, through an analysis of appearance, disappearance and displacement, it aims to illustrate how underground efforts once again serve to undermine authorities. Furthermore, the analysis also suggests that Allende's presentation of subversion differs subtly from the underground elements which were apparent in her first novel; she highlights the presence of dissenting voices even from within the military, including Sergeant Rivera; Evangelina's adoptive brother, Pradelio Ranquileo and Irene's fiancé, Captain Gustavo Morante. The carnivalesque highlights social disorder and an overriding sense of confusion and uncertainty in the text, and it is argued that this paradoxically helps to uncover the underlying coherence in the work. Irene's growing political awareness leads to her loss of innocence, and her determined efforts alongside Leal illustrate the importance of the journey which she has undertaken away from the relative comfort of her life as a journalist and into a harsh world in which torture and terror are pervasive. Irene ironically gains political enlightenment by entering the world of shadows.

Eva Luna, published in 1987, was Allende's third novel, and marks a shift in setting for her work, with its implicit backdrop being Allende's adopted country of Venezuela. Through the parallel stories of an Austrian immigrant, Rolf Carlé, and a young girl, the eponymous Eva Luna, the quest for survival in the midst of hardship and a series of life-changing displacements feature strongly. Political issues which were prominent in Allende's earlier novels continue to play a subtle, but nevertheless important role in understanding the backgrounds of characters, and the backdrop to the novel contains resonances of the Venezuelan dictatorship of Juan Vicente Gómez, who ruled the country between 1908 and 1935 and on whom Allende modelled El Benefactor, the dictator of the opening chapters of the novel.[44] *Eva Luna* is presented, by and large, from the perspective of the eponymous heroine. Eva is the daughter of an Indian gardener from a local tribe, and Consuelo, who conceives while trying to save the life of the gardener, who is dying after having been bitten by a snake. The novel is a *Bildungsroman*, and charts Eva's development through constant displacement, as she works with a variety of masters and mistresses in a text that resonates with the picaresque tradition. Following the death of Eva's mother, Consuelo, who would tell Eva stories to distract her from the harshness of their impoverished existence, living and working in the house of the eccentric Professor Jones, Eva remains temporarily under the protection of the African cook, La Madrina. With the death of Professor Jones, the seven-year-old Eva is sent away to work with different masters and earn a living. Her experiences are generally negative, although she does befriend another cook, Elvira, in her first new house, and she strikes up a close friendship with her. Following a disagreement with her mistress, Eva runs away, and has a chance meeting with a young street child, Huberto Naranjo, which leads to her meeting a diverse group of colourful characters. Eva later meets Naranjo again, having lived with other masters, and is taken in by La Señora, a local madame. She also meets an Italian transvestite, Melesio, whose friendship becomes crucial to her professional development

---

44 For further discussion of the historical basis of this novel see José Otero, 'La historia como ficción en "Eva Luna" de Isabel Allende', *Confluencia*, 4 (1988), 61–7.

in her adult years. Eva is a strong, creative and resilient woman, somewhat reminiscent of Allende herself. Eva relies upon her ability to tell stories in order to survive on the streets and with different employers. Ultimately, she uses her love of words to carve out a career for herself when she becomes a scriptwriter for a *telenovela* [*soap opera*].

Storytelling in the text is not merely a means of making a living for Eva as it also beguiles the men she encounters, and it serves as a form of solace for Rolf Carlé, whose story is narrated in alternate chapters. Eva is encouraged to devote herself to writing by Melesio, who is now Mimí, having undergone gender reassignment surgery to become a woman. Allende charts the circumstances which led to Rolf's move to South America, with particular reference to his traumatic childhood experiences, from the constant torment at the hands of his cruel father and local schoolteacher, Lukas, through to his inability to protect his mother and his subsequent feelings of guilt when a group of schoolboys exact revenge on his father's hardline discipline in school by murdering him. Rolf and Eva's stories intertwine towards the end of the text as Rolf is making a film on Naranjo, and works as a photographer in the television company which is to broadcast Eva's *telenovela*. Eva and Rolf later become involved in helping to secure the release of political prisoners from the penal colony of Santa María, and Eva uses this incident as the substance of the *telenovela* she writes. The narrative carefully links up the tales of Eva and Rolf and the importance of the written word is given prominence throughout the text. Popular culture, in terms of the *telenovela*, is seen as a way of defying official versions of history and events, while the ending of the text illustrates how Allende herself appears keen to defy readers' expectations by blurring the difference between novel and *telenovela* at the conclusion.

Cuentos de Eva Luna appeared in 1989 and is Allende's first, and thus far only, excursion into the genre of the short story. In loose terms, it may be considered a spin-off collection from *Eva Luna*, with Eva as implied narrator. In addition, Eva and Rolf appear both in the framing prologue to the twenty-three stories and in the final story of the collection, 'De barro estamos hechos'. Issues from Rolf's childhood, as explained in detail in *Eva Luna*, resurface in this final story and, indeed, remain relatively unresolved, but in general much of the collection is not concerned with their story, and instead focuses on a variety of carefully constructed vignettes of life in Latin America. While Allende draws on a diverse range of themes throughout the collection, she has explained that '[t]odos [los cuentos] son de amor, ése es el hilo que los une' [*all of the stories are about love; this is the common thread*].[45] Arguably, however, the interplay between communication and displacement appears to be more evident than love in this collection: from the opening tale, 'Dos palabras' [*'Two Words'*], one of the many deceptively simple stories in the book, Allende explores the consequences of geographical displacement and the latent power of language and gesture, skilfully illustrating within the constraints of ten pages a love story involving the wordsmith Belisa Crepusculario (the links between Belisa and Isabel are readily apparent in Allende's anagrammatical insertion of her first name into the text) and the feared outlaw known only as El Coronel [*The Colonel*]. Beneath the tale of his bid to become a presidential candidate, Allende raises a wide range of issues, and invites reflection on the nature and power of oral and written language, the pervasiveness of illiteracy in Latin America, the question of official and lost histories and the reciprocal impact of mainstream events on the margins. This depth to the short stories is an abiding feature of much of the collection: for example, 'Tosca' [*'Tosca'*] explores one woman's fascination with a man she meets by chance who shares her love of classical music, but at the same time subtly investigates the interplay of high and low culture, and the form of cultural imperialism practised by Tosca when she follows this man, a doctor named Leonardo Gómez, to the depths of the jungle and endeavours to educate the locals on operatic performances. 'Lo más olvidado del olvido' [*'Oblivion's Most Forgotten Thing'*] recounts another chance encounter, on this occasion between two exiles who discover they share much more than the country which they have left behind, and recall their tortured pasts and sense of loss. 'De barro estamos hechos' [*'Of Clay We are Made'*], as mentioned earlier, charts the devastating impact of a local natural disaster on a small rural community, and subsequently on

---

45   Celia Correas Zapata, *Isabel Allende: Vida y espíritus* (Barcelona: Plaza & Janés, 1998), p. 106.

Rolf Carlé, and the resurgence of childhood memories he had sought to escape from through his move from Austria to South America.

Chapter 4 broaches the interplay between silence and language in both *Eva Luna* and *Cuentos de Eva Luna*. The settings of these texts is less identifiably Chilean but continues to be recognizably South American, and thus the focus of the overall discussion reflects the move away from national to international concerns by looking at the more universal questions of communication and communities. The focus is first on links between oral and written language in *Eva Luna*, and it is argued that, while the development of Eva's skills in writing short stories and *telenovela* scripts is important, it is the issue of what has been described by theorist Walter J. Ong as *secondary orality* that is of greater significance to her professional success. It will be argued that oral communication displaces written communication in the text, and that the power of the spoken word (the actors in the *telenovela*), refracted through the written word (the *telenovela* script) illustrates the ultimate primacy of oral language in the text. The second part of the discussion examines the four stories outlined in the previous paragraph from *Cuentos de Eva Luna*, that is, 'Dos palabras', 'Tosca', 'Lo más olvidado del olvido' and 'De barro estamos hechos', and explores the various forms of silence that feature in these stories. The discussion contends that silence is pervasive throughout the collection, and identifies the various types of silence and its effects on the characters involved. Concluding comments in this chapter explore the apparent gaps throughout *Cuentos de Eva Luna*, which could be considered a failure on Allende's part to provide readers with a fuller explanation of certain key elements, such as the two words which Belisa gives to El Coronel in 'Dos palabras'. This discussion argues that these gaps may be considered alternatively as part of Allende's narrative strategy, which serves on the one hand to privilege the inherent power of oral language by refusing to commit these elements to writing, thereby encouraging the reader to fill in these apparent omissions and, on the other, to suggest the positive force of silence and to use silence to highlight traumatic events which are often not openly articulated. Allende's deliberate displacement of speech is in line with much of the open-endedness of the tales in the collection.

Cuentos de Eva Luna was written at a time of great change in Allende's life, and perhaps, given the personal circumstances, the short-story genre provided her with an outlet to continue writing. Allende moved to California following a whirlwind romance with a man who was later to become her second husband, William Gordon, whom she met on a book tour. The tale of Gordon's childhood provides the basis for the characterization of Gregory Reeves, the protagonist of her fourth novel, *El plan infinito*, published in 1991. This switch of narrative setting from Latin America to the United States is a significant change in her writing. *El plan infinito* is an ambitious text, and endeavours to capture the sense of opportunity and angst of the times, through the experiences of Reeves. Reeves is born into a peripatetic family, and they travel throughout the United States. Gregory's father, Charles Reeves, gives presentations on 'El plan infinito', his understanding of the nature of reality. The family are forced to settle down when Charles falls seriously ill and they settle in a Latino *barrio* of Los Angeles. However, Gregory struggles to adapt to a sedentary lifestyle, and is bullied by the older Latino boys and subsequently raped by a young boy named Martínez. As the story moves forward a number of years, it is revealed that Gregory stands up for his close friend Carmen Morales by challenging Martínez to race against a train. Martínez dies when he is killed by the oncoming train. The novel charts other key experiences in Reeves's life, from his move to university in Berkeley, through to his unsuccessful marriage with Samantha Ernst, a tour of duty in Vietnam, his work as a lawyer and second marriage to Shanon, an employee of his. Throughout the novel, Reeves agonizes over an inability to understand the various misfortunes that befall him, and he seeks refuge in a variety of addictions. His inability to relate to his children ultimately leads to an anxiety attack. Reeves must rely on help from old friends and from the therapist Ming O'Brien in order to begin making sense of his experiences.

Hija de la fortuna, Allende's fifth novel, was published in 1999, eight years after *El plan infinito*, and returned to a similar backdrop and cultural concerns.[46] The search for self and the quest for both personal and collective identity resurface as prominent themes in *Hija de la fortuna*, and most of the action switches between Chile and California, two key landscapes in the author's life. Rodden describes the novel as 'a study in border culture, challenging readers to ponder the complexities of temporal as well as geographical borders: how the life of a young Latina possesses countless parallels in the nineteenth and twenty-first centuries'.[47] *Hija de la fortuna* spans three continents, Asia, Europe and the Americas, and includes a diverse range of cultural and language choices. Displacement features strongly: an infant girl is abandoned in the garden of a British aristocratic family, (Miss) Rose and Jeremy Sommers, siblings who have emigrated to the port of Valparaíso, Chile, in the middle of the nineteenth century. The child is found on the doorstep in a soap crate, wrapped in a man's sweater, perhaps the only clue to her parentage. The childless, unmarried Miss Rose decides to keep this child, whom she names Eliza. This is in spite of the protestations of her brother, who is heavily preoccupied with maintaining his business, the *Compañía Británica de Importación y Exportación* [*The British Import and Export Company*]. Rose maintains her role of chatelaine in her brother's home and also raises Eliza with the help of her local maid, Mama Fresia. The novel charts Eliza's growth and development, exploring

---

46 After publishing Reeves's story in *El plan infinito*, Allende moved into the world of non-fiction when she wrote *Paula* (Barcelona: Plaza & Janés, 1994), a family memoir, during the sudden illness and later loss of her daughter. Paula was stricken by porphyria, a rare blood condition, while in Madrid, and Allende charts her daughter's illness and family history through this text. This work was hugely successful for its frankness and subject matter, and Allende has explained that the book had a hugely cathartic effect. All royalties from the book were, and still are, donated to a foundation which seeks to continue her daughter's work in ensuring economic opportunities for women throughout the world. Her next work was *Afrodita: cuentos, recetas y otros afrodisíacos* [*Aphrodite: Stories, Recipes and other Aphrodisiacs*] (Barcelona: Plaza & Janés, 1997), and provided Allende with another key step in recovering her narrative voice. She produced this work with friends and family. It is a humorous, exuberant and genre-confounding work celebrating love, sex and food, and heralded Allende's return to feeling passionate about life.

47 John Rodden, 'Technicolored Life', in *Society*, March/April 2005, 62–5 (p. 63).

how, as an adolescent, she falls in love with Joaquín Andieta, a poor local boy, and an employee of her reluctant adoptive father Jeremy Sommers. Andieta's sudden departure from Valparaíso, in his quest to find fortune in the promised land of Gold Rush California, leaves Eliza distraught and she resolves to be reunited with him. A significant part of the novel is devoted to Eliza's attempts to find Andieta, first by travelling as a stowaway aboard the *Emilia* boat bound for California so as to escape without her family realizing, and then journeying around the Californian wastelands disguised as a young man and renamed Elías Andieta, assuming the surname of her lover and pretending to be his brother. Eliza is aided in her perilous journey by Tao Chi'en, a Chinese physician who was forced onto a ship sailing from Hong Kong to Chile to work as a cook, and who helps to smuggle her onto the second voyage of the *Emilia* ship from Chile to California. Their growing friendship and their respective self-discoveries in California form the basis for the development of the plot. According to critic Linda Gould Levine, *Hija de la fortuna* 'removes itself from twentieth-century reality and returns to the tumultuous era of the nineteenth century when legends were created, passion and greed were unleashed, and diverse ethnic groups struggled to shape a new life for themselves in America'.[48]

Retrato en sepia picks up a number of threads from *Hija de la fortuna* and draws links between various cultures and continents. The tale is narrated by the adult Aurora del Valle, the granddaughter of Eliza Sommers and Tao Chi'en, and develops from two principal landscapes, North America and Chile. Aurora is born Lai-Ming, the Chinese for Aurora, and is raised in Chinatown, San Francisco by her maternal grandparents following the death of her mother, Lynn, in childbirth. Lai-Ming is born into a multicultural and multilingual world and lives there until the age of five, when she is abruptly removed to live with her paternal grandmother, the successful Chilean businesswoman, Paulina del Valle, in Nob Hill, San Francisco. Paulina demands that she only be known as Aurora in her house, which is part of the businesswoman's attempts to erase all Chinese facets of Aurora's identity. *Retrato en sepia* charts the adult Aurora's struggles to overcome

---

48   Linda Gould Levine, *Isabel Allende* (New York: Twayne, 2003), p. 135.

the barriers which have isolated her from her childhood memories and prevented her from recovering a key part of her unique multicultural heritage. María Claudia André succinctly describes the text as Aurora's 'search to decipher the meaning behind unintelligible mysteries of her childhood and the psychological implications behind her recurrent nightmares'.[49] In a similar way to Eliza's story in *Hija de la fortuna*, key elements in the story of Aurora's life are described retrospectively, from her move to Santiago with Paulina, through to her later travels in Europe, her unhappy marriage with Diego Domínguez in Chile and, after leaving him, her subsequent love affair with Paulina's former physician, Iván Radovic, a Chilean national and son of an immigrant of Balkan descent. The quest for her suppressed Chinese heritage proceeds throughout the narrative, and she is aided by the sporadic reappearance of important people from her early years, including her biological father, Matías, who had previously disowned her, and her grandmother Eliza, who had made a pact with Paulina not to return while Paulina was alive.

Chapter 5 looks at the interplay between culture and displacement, drawing on *El plan infinito*, *Hija de la fortuna* and *Retrato en sepia* to examine a (re)engagement with local communities in Allende's fiction written in North America and how these novels present a subtle analysis of the challenges faced by those endeavouring to integrate into communities. In these texts, it will be argued that Allende provides a mosaic of cultural displacements, and illustrates the uniqueness of the expatriate experience through Gregory Reeves, the British Sommers family and Jacob Todd, the rejection of privilege through Eliza and the hidden marginality of Aurora. All these characters are linked through a shared sense of cultural displacement, including the resolute efforts of the British expatriates to remain isolated from the local people and to follow the customs – and sometimes seasons – of their homeland. It is argued that displacement plays a crucial role in understanding Reeves's different experiences, and that Allende

---

49   María Claudia André, 'Breaking through the Maze: Feminist Configurations of the Heroic Quest in Isabel Allende's *Daughter of Fortune* and *Portrait in Sepia*', in *Isabel Allende Today*, pp. 74–91 (p. 75).

carefully presents a web of displacements in Reeves's life that relate back to incidents in his youth and to the ways in which he has been a target of displacement activity, exemplified through his sister's sudden rejection of him following her abuse at the hands of their father, and Reeves's brutal rape at the hands of a local Latino boy. The patterns of frustration and revelation in his adult life, from his failed marriage, the discovery of his sister's abuse, his inability to communicate with his children and the fear that he may be genetically predisposed towards abuse, lead to him indulging in a range of activities to avoid facing up to reality, seeking comfort through camaraderie in the Vietnam war, or through materialism on his return to the United States and his work as a lawyer.

The character of Jacob Todd/Freemont highlights the question of a fabricated existence, in which Jacob endeavours to invent and subsequently reinvent himself in Chile and in California respectively. The introduction of the Chinese community into Allende's fiction is also explored through a character analysis of Tao Chi'en, and this discussion examines his complex and troubled relationship with his own culture, and his resistance to parochial tendencies within his own community. Eliza's exploration of gendered displacement and imitation will also be broached, while Allende's characterization of Aurora, and her search for a fuller understanding of her past, raises important questions about the nature of appearance and ethnicity in Allende's work and the concept of the displaced self. Some concluding comments look at how the characters in these novels appear to embrace their experiences of displacement.

While the present study deals in detail with fiction written by Allende up to and including *Retrato en sepia*, Allende has continued to be prolific, and since the release of *Retrato en sepia*, she has written another trilogy, this time aimed at teenagers. The novels are *La ciudad de las bestias* [*City of the Beasts*] (2002), *El reino del Dragón de Oro* [*Kingdom of the Golden Dragon*] (2004) and *El bosque de los pigmeos* [*Forest of the Pygmies*] (2005), respectively. She has also written a backstory to the legendary bandit, *Zorro* [*Zorro*] (2005) and described the experiences of Inés Suárez in *Inés del alma mía* [*Inés of My Soul*] (2006). Allende has also written *Mi país inventado* (2003) and *La suma de los días* [*The Sum of Our Days*] (2007), which are two memoirs. Her 2009 novel, *La isla bajo el mar* [*The Island Beneath the Sea*], examines the struggles of a young slave girl named Zarité on the island of Saint Domingue in the eighteenth century, while her 2011 novel, *El Cuaderno de Maya* [*Maya's Notebook*] explores Californian teenager Maya Vidal's efforts to escape addiction and revisit her roots by spending time on the remote island of Chiloé, off the coast of Chile.[50] While, to date, critical work on these works remains quite limited, Philip Swanson has examined both *La ciudad de las bestias* and *Zorro* and their relevance to the question of magical realism.[51] Other critics have also made reference to Allende's trilogy of children's fiction and its relationship to magical realism.[52] Interestingly, it is in Allende's memoirs where information regarding her foray into the world of children's literature can be garnered. For example, in *La suma de los días*, written as if it were a form of dialogue with her deceased daughter, Paula, Allende explains how she found inspiration for what was to become *La ciudad de las bestias* following a trip to the Amazon. Allende states that '[l]a imaginación se me despierta al salir del ambiente conocido y confrontar otras formas de existencia, gentes diferentes, lenguas que no domino, vicisitudes imprevisibles' [*my imagination is sparked when I leave a familiar environment and face new forms of existence, different people, languages I cannot speak and unexpected difficulties*], which suggests that Allende finds displacement to be a rich source of creativity.[53] She proceeds to explain in detail the characters of this novel, the bases for these characters in reality, and she draws inspiration from every story she encounters on her trips, even going so far as to experiment with a local drug, *ayahuasca*, and to use that unsettling experience of displacement for literary purposes.

---

50 Isabel Allende, *La isla bajo el mar* (Barcelona: Plaza & Janés, 2009); Isabel Allende, *El Cuaderno de Maya* (Barcelona: Plaza & Janés, 2011).
51 Philip Swanson, 'Magic Realism and Children's Literature: Isabel Allende's *La Ciudad de las Bestias*', in *A Companion to Magical Realism*, ed. by Stephen M. Hart and Wen-Chin Ouyang (Woodbridge: Tamesis, 2005), pp. 168–80. See also Swanson's 'Z/Z: Isabel Allende and the Mark of Zorro', *Romance Studies*, 24 (2006), 265–77.
52 Don Latham, 'The Cultural Work of Magical Realism in Three Young Adult Novels', *Children's Literature in Education*, 38 (2007), 59–70.
53 Isabel Allende, *La suma de los días* (Barcelona: Plaza & Janés, 2007), p. 57.

The overview provided of the texts to be explored in this discussion highlights how Allende has drawn extensively upon her diverse life experiences in the exposition of her fiction. First, though, this study returns to the local and domestic level, and to how one of Allende's most discussed characters, Esteban Trueba, in what remains Allende's most celebrated text, *La casa de los espíritus*, endeavours to recover a past of privilege by rebuilding his family's country estate.

CHAPTER 2

Local Development and Displacement: Esteban Trueba's Experiences in Las Tres Marías in *La casa de los espíritus*

Introduction

This chapter looks in detail at Isabel Allende's 1982 novel *La casa de los espíritus*, and focuses in particular on the somewhat strained relationship between Esteban Trueba and the community of campesinos living on his family's country estate, and former model of patriarchal power, Las Tres Marías. This analysis draws on recent research carried out in the field of Development Studies, and in particular on the recognition of local communities and local knowledge; four key issues raised in relation to this research, to be elaborated upon in due course, provide the basis for an exploration of Trueba's personal trajectory through the novel. Here it is argued that Trueba's approach to developing Las Tres Marías, when compared to real-life examples taken from Development Studies, is fundamentally flawed and inextricably linked with displacement. The threat of displacement – that is, eviction from the estate – for non-compliance and Trueba's unrelenting unwillingness to accept the campesinos as equals – or at times even as humans – sow the seeds for future problems in his relationship with them and, indeed, with his own family. An interesting, additional form of displacement in the text is also found in the character of Trueba himself; it is also suggested in this chapter that he constantly battles against his own fundamental sense of societal displacement and of not truly belonging anywhere. His efforts at self-development and self-improvement proceed through a form of self-displacement and subsequently through the concerted development of the country estate. Unlike previous critical approaches, which have tended to foreground Trueba's patriarchal nature and his attempts to establish and subsequently maintain his hold on personal and public status, this analysis is instead restricted to the episodes in Las Tres Marías in order to illustrate the inherent complexity of Trueba's character, and it aims to show that, in spite of his apparently successful attainment of social status and privilege, he remains peripheral and ultimately powerless to contain constant efforts to undermine him. His increasing awareness of this permanent peripherality colours his presence as both character and contributory narrator and, crucially, provides scope within the text for Trueba to undergo a type of humbling transformation towards the latter stages of the text. His role as narrator is also examined in the conclusion in order to consider and indeed counter the views of certain critics that Allende has, in a sense, missed out on an opportunity to apportion a form of intratextual justice for Trueba's wanton behaviour by not having him face any formal punishment. This discussion argues that Allende deliberately eschews any crude presentation or exploration of justice, preferring instead to dismantle Trueba's fragile sense of power subtly and systematically, and in this way she illustrates his slow realization, as he grows older, of his ultimate and seemingly inescapable marginality.

Trueba is a complex and ambivalent character, and this has been reflected in the many commentaries on his role and nature in *La casa de los espíritus*. A small selection of critics' comments suffices to illustrate the problematic nature of his character: for example, Nora Glickman suggests that 'Trueba es el doble grotesco del régimen militar, atrapado en su propia red de abusos y extorsiones, expresados en su violencia física y en su anticomunismo histérico' [*Trueba is the grotesque double of the military regime; he is trapped in his own net of abuse and extortion, articulated through physical violence and his hysterical anticommunism*].[1] This

---

[1] Nora Glickman, 'Los personajes femeninos en *La casa de los espíritus*', in *Los libros tienen sus propios espíritus*, ed. by Marcelo Coddou (Mexico: Universidad Veracruzana, 1986), pp. 54–60 (p. 56).

explanation draws together the main threads of his character, where violence, entrapment and a fear of unfamiliar ideology determine and limit his interaction in both personal and professional spheres. However, Gabriela Mora also quite rightly points out some of Trueba's positive traits: 'es trabajador incansable, se arrepiente de sus acciones violentas, y en su vejez se doblega a la ternura por el amor a su nieta.' [*he is a tireless worker, regrets his violent actions and in his old age softens through his love for his granddaughter*][2] Trueba's character is further nuanced by his intermittent contributions throughout the text as a first-person narrator, in contradistinction to the narration provided directly by his granddaughter Alba, and indirectly by his wife Clara and daughter Blanca. Trueba has been considered the quintessential patriarch by many critics: for example, René Campos suggests he is 'la figura masculina en cuyos atributos (padre, patrón, oligarca, senador del Partido Conservador) se reconoce toda una historia de dominación' [*the male figure in whom an entire history of domination is recognized through his roles (father, boss, oligarch, Conservative Party Senator)*].[3]

While displacement is a feature that critics such as Mario Rojas have briefly alluded to in previous studies, explaining how Trueba is a 'figura patriarcal [...] desplazada a la periferia' [*patriarchal figure [...] displaced to the margins*],[4] this treatment of displacement is rather limited, referring specifically to his position within the family home, a mere facet of the overall displacement which is here argued to permeate his character.

2 Gabriela Mora, 'Ruptura y perseverancia de estereotipos en *La casa de los espíritus*', in *Los libros tienen sus propios espíritus*, pp. 71–8 (p. 76).
3 Rene Campos, '*La casa de los espíritus*: mirada, espacio, discurso de la otra historia', in *Los libros tienen sus propios espíritus*, pp. 21–8 (p. 22).
4 Mario A. Rojas, '*La casa de los espíritus* de Isabel Allende: un caleidoscopio de espejos desordenados', in *Los libros tienen sus propios espíritus*, pp. 83–90 (p. 84).

Community Development and the Local in Development Studies

In broad terms, the field of Development Studies explores the ways in which efforts to tackle economic and social disparities across the world are devised, undertaken and coordinated. Within the field, issues outlined in Chapter 1 of the present discussion, such as internal, external and development-induced displacement, are of crucial importance.[5] Another key concern in Development Studies is the question of local, and typically rural communities and the attempts that are made at national and international level to improve living conditions and to share technological advances in order to help impoverished and disadvantaged communities become more self-sufficient or to become productive.

While there has been much analysis of displacement in this field, particularly in relation to how environmental disasters or newly installed regimes enforce wholesale movement from places of origin, experts have in recent years begun to pay particular attention to the territorial unit known as the *local*, which has been understood as a distinctive unit with its own cultural practices, perspectives and needs.[6] Community development has been extensively examined diachronically, and in the context of Latin America, studies on colonial programmes of social development have been closely examined.[7] The sensitivity to local practices and power relations within the local community has re-emerged as a significant point

---

5   Vandana Desai and Robert B. Potter's *The Companion to Development Studies*, 2nd edn (London: Hodder Education, 2008) is an excellent introduction which contains one hundred and fifteen thumbnail sketches from experts in the field.
6   Part 3 ('Rural development') of Desai and Potter's book looks in detail at issues related to local development.
7   Mark A. Burkholder and Lyman L. Johnson offer a detailed description of Latin American colonial life, in relation to social organization, restrictions on social mobility and the challenges of economic development. See their *Colonial Latin America*, 5th edn (New York: Oxford University Press, 2003) and in particular Chapter 6 (pp. 182–211), which examines 'The Social Economy: Societies of Caste and Class'.

Local Development and Displacement

of interest in synchronic studies on developing nations, with negotiation, participation and engagement becoming key features of any successful programme which focuses on local development.

A seminal article co-authored by Giles Mohan and Kristian Stokke identifies four key trends in development thinking and practice which help to illustrate the growing prominence of the local:[8]

1 *Decentralization* (pp. 250–2): Described by Mohan and Stokke as 'a fluid and flexible discourse that can be utilised by different ideological interests' (p. 250), decentralization is explored in relation to a variety of economic models. The authors note how decentralization has become a feature of international agencies such as the World Bank, which actively encourages a move away from strongly centralized structures of governance, and seeks to develop deregulation and delegation of responsibility to lower levels of governance. Within this system, the role of local citizens has been highlighted along with a move towards more democratic forms of local government, with the example of Mahbabul Karim's work on non-governmental organizations (NGOs) in Bangladesh cited in support of this (p. 252).

2 *Local knowledge and participatory development* (pp. 252–4): This has had a huge impact in Development Studies, and has led to a paradigm shift in the field. In essence, the suggestion is that local communities and local knowledge often provide a more effective basis for development projects rather than the arrival of outsiders and formal scientific knowledge. A key feature in the valorizing of local knowledge in certain areas of development is *visualization*, described as 'various mapping exercises whereby locals relate

---

[8] Giles Mohan and Kristian Stokke, 'Participatory Development and Empowerment: The Dangers of Localism', *Third World Quarterly*, 21 (2000), 247–68. This article highlights the importance of the local, although its focus is also on the apparent risks in adopting an approach that merely focuses on the local as a homogenous unit and is consequently ignorant of local diversity, local hierarchical units and the interaction between the local and the national.

aspects of their lives through spatial representations, usually on the ground, using local materials such as pebbles and sticks' (p. 253).[9] Mohan and Stokke also highlight some problems in relation to this approach, such as the temptation to categorize local knowledge as homogenous in character and, by implication, the failure to recognize diversity within local communities. In addition, they highlight how 'many aid-receiving governments who have paid lip service to participation are now doing so because they are aware that, since it has become a discourse of Western donors, they ignore it at their financial peril' (p. 254).

3 *Social capital and local development* (pp. 255–8): Social capital, a term coined by Robert Putnam to describe the connections that are built up through social networks, is explored in Development Studies to suggest that the local networks and interactions are in themselves a crucial resource for local development. Mohan and Stokke describe social capital as 'the sociocultural "glue" which binds communities together and ensures both political and economic progress' (p. 255), but also explore the selectivity of the concept and at times the failure of theorists in the area to acknowledge the other, long-standing concepts that may be brought to bear on the relative economic success of an area, such as class relations and conflict. In addition, they also note the 'tendency to ignore the state's role in enabling or destroying social capital' (p. 257), implying that while the importance of the local is made apparent in studies, the continuing impact of the nation-state must also be considered in the evaluation of the respective social capital in a local community.

4 *Social movements* (pp. 258–63): In this section, Mohan and Stokke identify shifts in the field of alternative development and focus on the emergence of radical democracy and the question of

---

9 The communities referred to are pre-literate, and issues of orality and secondary orality, to use theorist Walter J. Ong's terms, will be examined in Chapter 4 of the present discussion.

participation to suggest that locally based movements could challenge power structures and enable engagement with the state. This section draws on the work of anthropologist Arturo Escobar, who looks at the defence of local interests and the increasing relevance of culture in collective struggles in the 1970s and 1980s. Mohan and Stokke also note that 'most cases are characterized by a growing complexity of alliances and conflicts between collective actors in civil society and actors within the state' (p. 260), and in this way draw out the subtleties and complexities in the attempted incorporation of new demands by social movements within pre-existing paradigms of local and state governance. Their discussion also uses the example of the Zapatistas to illustrate the way in which locally based groups have *scaled up*, that is, have moved beyond the strictures of the local to interact with other national and international social movements.

In some concluding comments, Mohan and Stokke note that their exploration of the local is not 'an outright rejection of the local as a basis for empowerment' but rather that studies, groups and political projects 'will have to overcome binary opposites such as local/global and state/civil society in order to be relevant' (p. 264). The four categories outlined by Mohan and Stokke in their comprehensive overview of the position of the local in Development Studies, that is, decentralization, participatory development, social capital and social movements, will be used as a springboard for the analysis of Trueba's interactions with the *campesinos* of Las Tres Marías, given that it is the local which is indeed a key place from which Trueba desires to launch his quest for a privileged place in society.

(Self-)Decentralization and (Self-)Development: Tracing Trueba's Roots/Routes of Discontent

In tracing Esteban Trueba's desire for a privileged place in society, his own views on home and family and the circumstances leading to his return to the country estate of Las Tres Marías provide not only a necessary basic appreciation of what is driving him but also compelling evidence of the paradoxical nature of his search for social status. Trueba's concept of home is coloured by his negative experiences of impoverishment, a childhood of privation and a profoundly ambivalent relationship with his dying mother, Doña Ester, and his overbearing elder sister, Férula. At the opening of the novel, he seems to have actively sought out a means of creating as much distance as possible from his mother and his sister; indeed a form of decentralization has taken place in his own life, as he ekes out a miserable, isolated existence in the mines in the north of the unnamed country. This distancing from family, however, also entails a necessary displacement from his fiancée, Rosa del Valle, whom he has actually only met on one occasion. Trueba dutifully and diligently endeavours to provide a financially secure future for himself and Rosa, and he consciously sacrifices his present with her in order to achieve this. This sense of geographical displacement, however, is only one element in Trueba's situation at the outset: he is doubly displaced in the text, given that his self-imposed experience of geographical displacement is the by-product of a stronger feeling of enforced societal displacement, with the loss of familial prestige following the death of his father, who had apparently drunk away what little wealth the family had once enjoyed. Trueba's objectives are clear: he determines to regain the aristocratic status once held by his family, and to forge his own future, with an established and recognized place in society. He appears willing to do whatever is necessary, even if he must spend a prolonged period of time away from the city to attain his goal. A sense of urgency drives him on, and this is intimated when he explains how he feels that 'quedaba poca vida por delante para labrarme un futuro y tener la posición deseada' [*I had very little life left to forge a future for myself and achieve the position I desired*].¹⁰ He draws a direct link between progress and proximity to Rosa in the centre, by suggesting that his failure to be successful would only delay his return to her: 'cada minuto de ocio era un siglo más lejos de Rosa' (p. 31) [*each idle moment left me a century further away from Rosa*]. The sense of social displacement which colours his actions and drives him forward, however, is interestingly not from direct childhood experience, a time about which he merely recalls 'frío, soledad y un eterno vacío en el estómago' (p. 32) [*cold, loneliness and an eternal emptiness in my stomach*]. A faded memory of lost prestige is something he appears to have inherited rather than experienced first-hand, which would suggest that the financial situation of the Trueba family was already precarious before his birth.

Despite Trueba's desire to keep his family at a distance, his personal and professional self-development is actually aided both directly and indirectly by his family: he admits how, for example, in his efforts to woo Rosa, 'Férula me ayudó a acercarme a la familia del Valle, descubriendo remotos parentescos entre nuestros apellidos y buscando la oportunidad de saludarnos a la salida de misa' (p. 34) [*Férula helped me get close to the del Valle family by discovering distant links between our surnames and by seeking out opportunities to greet them after mass*]. Furthermore, the mine concession which he receives in his first attempt to fashion a future away from his blood relatives is only given to him thanks to a loan on the strength of the 'prestigio del apellido de mi madre' (p. 35) [*prestige of my mother's surname*]. It is somewhat paradoxical that his quest to retrieve the lost glory of his family's aristocratic past involves rejecting his mother, Doña Ester, who is wasting away from a degenerative disease, for he is also dependent upon her, given that it is through his mother's side of the family that his aristocratic stock can be traced.¹¹ Interestingly, it is Férula who reminds

---

10   Isabel Allende, *La casa de los espíritus*, 12th edn (Barcelona: Plaza y Janés, 2004), p. 31. Further references will appear parenthetically in the text. This quotation also appears heavily laced with tragic irony, when considered in relation to what occurs to his fiancée Rosa.

11   Margarita Saona makes an interesting point about Trueba's surname, arguing that 'el apellido verdaderamente encumbrado no era Trueba, sino el de ella, que ni se

him of their aristocratic heritage: 'le recordaba que por el lado de la madre llevaba el apellido más noble y linajudo del Virreinato de Lima' (p. 56) [*she reminded him that, on their mother's side, he had the most noble, blue-blooded surname from the Viceroyalty of Lima*]. If matrilineality is a crucial element in the development of female characterization in *La casa de los espíritus*, then it is equally important in understanding the roots of Trueba's sense of societal displacement in the novel.

Thus, the early part of the novel establishes a sharp contrast between Trueba's conceptualization of home and its reality. For him, home is an ideal or abstraction, a future reality which will reflect past privilege and a return to a position of power. The route to power and privilege for Trueba, however, appears to be something which will not occur overnight: this is hinted at through an early incident in the coffee shop of the Hotel Francés, where Trueba treats himself to an expensive coffee with his first hard-earned wage: in his excitement, he stirs the coffee too vigorously, and unwittingly smashes the glass cup in the process. His embarrassment at this incident is compounded by the reaction of the domineering Férula, who chastises him for his profligacy and who attributes the accident to divine intervention: 'eso te pasa por gastar el dinero de las medicinas de mamá en tus caprichos. Dios te castigó' (pp. 54–5) [*that's what you get for spending Mum's medicine money on your whims. God punished you*]. Férula cruelly invokes a formidable combination of sisterly and divine authority, and she also reminds Trueba of their ailing mother, all of which serve to increase his sense of guilt at his self-indulgent actions, as well as the personal embarrassment caused by the incident itself. It also reinforces his social gaucheness and confirms the power that Férula wields over him, even as an adult, and this seems to fuel his desire to move as far away from his family as possible.

Trueba is abruptly forced to return to the city when he hears of the sudden death of his fiancée, Rosa, an innocent victim of poisoning probably

---

menciona, ni sería transmitido a los hijos de Esteban' (p. 56) [*the truly distinguished surname was not Trueba but rather his mother's, which is not mentioned or passed on to Esteban's children*]. For further discussion see *Novelas familiares: figuraciones de la nación en la novela latinoamericana contemporánea* (Rosario: Beatriz Viterbo, 2004).

meant for her father, Severo del Valle, who was running for election. His brief return to the family home on the occasion of Rosa's funeral determines an alternative course of action in his efforts to gain wealth; he turns his attention to his family's dilapidated country estate of Las Tres Marías, 'una tierra de nadie, un roquerío sin ley' (p. 59) [*a no-man's-land, a lawless rocky place*], in the words of a local man whom Trueba meets and who escorts Trueba to the estate. Trueba considers Las Tres Marías an escape route from the increasingly suffocating atmosphere engendered and wilfully sustained by Férula, who 'lo envolvía en la red invisible de la culpabilidad y de las deudas de gratitud impagas' (p. 53) [*wrapped him up in her invisible net of guilt and debts of gratitude still unrepaid*]. He sets out on a campaign of recovery and recognition of his family's aristocratic past: his desire to reappropriate the past and his family's identity also entails a physical reappropriation and reconstruction of Las Tres Marías.

Thus a key means of understanding Trueba is through the concept of decentralization: Trueba's quest for wealth and a life of privilege with Rosa initially involves the conscious move away from the city in an effort to strike it rich by searching for gold in the mines of the north. Rosa's sudden death causes him to rethink his strategy and by implication his rationale for his actions and he determines to make a fortune in the former site of his family's prestige.

Local Knowledge and Participatory Development: Displacing the García Family?

In Robert Chambers's discussion of participatory research and development, he identifies three different uses of the term 'participation': (1) as a cosmetic label used by authorities 'to make whatever is proposed appear good'; (2) a 'co-opting practice, to mobilize local labour and reduce costs'; and (3) 'an empowering process which enables local people to do their own analysis, to take command, to gain in confidence, and to make their own decisions'.[12] At first glance, it would appear that, in the case of Trueba's early interactions with the local inhabitants of Las Tres Marías, it is the second of these descriptions that is most apposite: Trueba resolves to stamp his authority on the estate's inhabitants from the outset, with displacement crudely presented as the only viable alternative for them to working under him: '[a]l que no le guste la idea [de trabajar], que se vaya de inmediato' (p. 62) [*anyone who doesn't like the idea [of working] can leave immediately*]. The response of Pedro Segundo García, who later acts as a crucial intermediary between the campesinos and Trueba, is significant: '[n]o tenemos donde ir, siempre hemos vivido aquí. Nos quedamos' (p. 62) [*we've nowhere else to go; we've always lived here. We'll stay*]. The country estate becomes a means for Trueba to exercise his self-appointed authority, and he works side by side temporarily with the workers merely in an effort to create greater distance between them and him. For the workers, the redevelopment of the estate is the price they have to pay to remain on the land where they have always lived. Indeed, following the successful combined efforts of all involved, it is with pride that Trueba can declare that his 'vecinos más próximos quedaban a una buena distancia a lomo de caballo' (p. 65) [*closest neighbours were a good distance away on horseback*].

During Trueba's first-person narrative, he highlights what he sees as the positive impact of his return, with men, women and children all apparently becoming involved and engaged in the development and maintenance of the estate: he provides the men with basic carpentry and plumbing skills, and teaches them out of some manuals which he has purchased. In this sense, Trueba appears interested in passing on what is typically called *exterior knowledge* in the field of Development Studies, though interestingly the suggestion is that perhaps he too is only learning the skills as he goes along, with the manuals as the essential source of knowledge. He also employs local women as servants in the redeveloped house, and has a school built in the estate, although he struggles to find a teacher in the initial stages.

---

12   Robert Chambers, 'Paradigm Shifts and the Practice of Participatory Research and Development', in *Power and Participatory Development*, ed. by N. Nelson and S. Wright (London: Intermediate Technology, 1998), pp. 30–42 (p. 30).

Local Development and Displacement 47

As is explained, '[c]ada hombre, mujer, anciano y niño que pudiera tenerse en sus dos piernas, fue empleado por el patrón, ansioso por recuperar en pocos meses los años de abandono' (p. 70) [*every man, woman and child who could stand on their own two feet was employed by the boss, who was anxious to make good the years of neglect in the space of a few short months*]. Trueba is ostensibly concerned with local development and education, and his endeavours bear clear and sustained rewards:

> En el transcurso de los diez años siguientes, Esteban Trueba se convirtió en el patrón más respetado de la región, construyó casas de ladrillo para sus trabajadores, consiguió un maestro para la escuela y subió el nivel de vida de todo el mundo en sus tierras. (pp. 73–4)
>
> [*Over the course of the following ten years, Esteban Trueba became the most respected boss in the region, building brick houses for his workers, getting a teacher for the school and increasing the quality of life of everyone on his lands.*]

However, on closer inspection, the productive estate which reflects the dynamic success of Trueba may be juxtaposed with the social status quo that he is determined to maintain through whatever means necessary. One key problem that can be detected in Trueba's approach to his interaction with the campesinos is tellingly revealed during his first-person narrative: in essence, he considers the local people as unsocialized children, who have little knowledge and who grow increasingly dependent upon him: '[s]i vamos al fondo de las cosas, no sirven ni para hacer los mandados, siempre lo he dicho: son como niños' (p. 76) [*if we're honest about it, they're not even good at running errands. I've always said it – they're like children*]. He casts himself in the role of a father figure, and takes it upon himself not only to provide knowledge, but also to determine exactly how much the locals should learn: 'no era partidario de que adquirieran otros conocimientos, para que no se les llenara la cabeza con ideas inapropiadas a su estado y condición' (p. 70) [*He wasn't in favour of them acquiring other skills, so that their heads would not be filled with ideas unbecoming of their state and station*]. He believes himself now indispensable to the campesinos, and is blind to the abject poverty and the damaging impact of his actions, preferring to believe that his arrival has helped to establish a delicate balance and that his return to the city would be ruinous for them: '[s]in mí estarían perdidos, la prueba es que cuando doy vuelta la cara, se va todo al diablo y empiezan a hacer burradas' (p. 75) [*they'd be lost without me. The proof is when I turn my head, everything goes to hell and they start doing stupid things*]. He presents himself in an almost Messianic light, and deludes himself into believing in his own indispensability, repeatedly suggesting that he is a conduit for a greater good. He suggests that the value of the estate has doubled and that 'si quisiera venderlo, podría irme a Europa a vivir de mis rentas' (p. 75) [*If I wanted to sell it, I could go to Europe and live off the returns*], which is a strikingly paradoxical suggestion, given his apprehension about what he terms the '[i]deas bolcheviques' (p. 75) [*Bolshevik ideas*] emanating from that continent.

It would also appear to be the case that the possibility of employing visualization, mentioned by Mohan and Stokke earlier as a strategy used in development projects as a means of encouraging local participation, would also be unsuccessful, as the locals struggle to conceive of the world in miniature on Trueba's map: 'no podían imaginar el mundo del tamaño de un papel suspendido en el pizarrón, ni a los ejércitos reducidos a la cabeza de un alfiler' (p. 72) [*they could not conceive of a world the size of a piece of paper hanging on the blackboard, nor armies reduced to the size of a pinhead*]. Trueba's careful husbandry of land and resources also extends to the campesinos, when he asks local veterinary surgeons to check not only the animals, but also the locals.

Indeed, beneath the veneer of progress, Trueba's steely determination to perpetuate social stasis and his refusal to treat the locals as possible agents of self-advancement are manifest: the locals are maintained in a financial limbo, as Trueba refuses to pay them money and instead hands out tokens which can be used in the local shop which he has established and tightly controls. Furthermore, while he apparently provides employment opportunities for women on the estate, he also exploits them to fill the emotional void in his life by raping them at will, thereby creating rancour and mistrust in the community through his actions, which go unpunished.

In a way, the complex combination of open rejection and selective reliance which characterizes his relationship with his mother and sister may arguably also be true of his interactions with the campesinos. His determination to restrict social mobility and ensure social stasis only succeeds with the crucial intervention of the one form of local knowledge that Trueba does value in the community, that is, the selfless help that he receives from Pedro García, the wise, elderly bastion of the local García family unit: Pedro García's key intervention in ridding the estate of a plague of insects by talking to them is juxtaposed with the unsuccessful application of exterior scientific knowledge provided by the outsider Mr Brown. The other key example follows the earthquake which reduces the estate to ruins and almost kills Trueba in the process. All exterior medical knowledge provided by practitioners from urban areas fails to help Trueba and, again, Pedro García silently steps forward and resets Trueba's bones. Trueba does acknowledge the importance of García to his life, but nevertheless seems less interested in this knowledge unless as a last resort. The García dynasty is displaced as Trueba's determination to continue acquiring wealth and status continues unabated.

Thus, the possibility of participatory development in Las Tres Marías is never truly entertained by Trueba owing to his infantilization and dehumanization of the local people who have lived there all their lives. Trueba uses local knowledge only as a last resort, and his imposition of financial and social limitations on the rural community sows seeds of discord. Allende subtly and ironically employs the language of cultivation to suggest the real impact of Trueba's arrival on the local community:

> siguió *labrando* su prestigio de rajadiablos, *sembrando* la región de bastardos, *cosechando* el odio y *almacenando* culpas que no le hacían mella, porque se le había curtido el alma y acallado la conciencia con el pretexto del progreso. (p. 74, emphasis added)
>
> [*he continued* working on *his prestige as a hellraiser,* sowing *the region with bastard children,* reaping *hatred and* storing up *sins that had no effect on him, because he used the excuse of progress to keep his conscience quiet and his heart had hardened.*]

Social Capital: Establishing and Disrupting Social Networks

In Development Studies the concept of social capital, and the interlinked term of social networks, has become a crucial gauge of local interaction and of the relative success of local projects. As outlined in the previous section, Trueba has little understanding of or interest in the nature of the rural community, and thus it would appear from the outset that social networks would play an insignificant role in understanding Trueba's sense of displacement in the text. However, social networks actually become a useful way of seeing both Trueba's attempts to consolidate power in both rural and urban settings, and how this sense of power also becomes gradually eroded as his family begin to undermine him, and as national events begin to impinge upon the running of the estate.

In public life Trueba continues to find ways to reinforce his newly acquired position of power, and he joins a landlord consortium. Echoing his first comments on arrival at Las Tres Marías, Trueba again threatens the locals with displacement if they fail to comply with his wishes, on this occasion in order to ensure a political status quo is maintained: at a party for the local people it is revealed that 'si salían el candidato conservador, tendrían una bonificación, pero si salía cualquier otro, se quedarían sin trabajo' (p. 80) [*if the Conservative candidate won, they would get a bonus; however, if any other candidate won, they would lose their jobs*]. Trueba toasts the success of the Conservatives with the following speech, which is heavily tinged with tragic irony in the context of later political change in the country:

> aquí el Partido Conservador gana limpiamente y no se necesita a un general para que haya orden y tranquilidad, no es como esas dictaduras regionales donde se matan unos a otros, mientras los gringos se llevan todas las materias primas. (p. 81)
>
> [*here the Conservative Party wins cleanly and we do not need a general for there to be order and peace. It is not like those regional dictatorships where they kill each other, while the gringos make off with all the raw materials.*]

Local Development and Displacement 51

As Trueba endeavours to establish a second locus of power in the city, Las Tres Marías becomes of less interest to him. He leaves the estate in the capable hands of Pedro Segundo García and returns to the city, where he marries Clara. On his return to the estate, his perception of what he has achieved there and his success at establishing social stasis appear to be of little consequence to him:

> Miraba las vacas inexpresivas rumiando en los potreros, la lenta faena de los campesinos repitiendo los mismos gestos cada día a lo largo de sus vidas, el inmutable marco de la cordillera nevada y la frágil columna de humo del volcán y se sentía como un preso. (p. 109)
>
> [*He looked at the inexpressive cows chewing the cud in the fields, the campesinos working slowly, repeating the same gestures every day of their lives, the never-changing picture of the snowy mountain range and the fragile column of smoke billowing from the volcano and he felt trapped.*]

This sense of not belonging on the estate is heightened by the decision to take the entire family there for a period. Indeed, his relationship with his family progressively worsens during their summers on the estate. During their first stay there as a family, Trueba grows increasingly jealous of the closeness between his sister Férula and Clara, and it is noted that Férula's passion for Clara 'se parecía más a la [pasión] de un marido exigente que a la de una cuñada' (p. 138) [*resembled more a demanding husband's rather than that of a sister-in-law*]. The distance between Trueba and Clara becomes more pronounced: '[s]entía a su mujer cada vez más alejada, más rara e inaccesible' (p. 139) [*he felt his wife more and more distant from him, stranger and more inaccessible*]. The physical inaccessibility is paralleled on an emotional level: he admits that 'estaba consciente de que la mujer que reposaba a su lado no estaba allí, sino en una dimensión desconocida a la que él jamás podría llegar' (p. 142) [*he was aware that the woman who slept by his side was not there, but rather in an unknown dimension which he would never be able to access*]. Unable, however, to vent his fury at his wife, Trueba instead transfers this onto Férula and blames her:

> Se convenció de que la culpa de todo la tenía Férula, que había sembrado en su mujer un germen maléfico que le impedía amarlo y que, en cambio, robaba con caricias prohibidas lo que le pertenecía como marido. (p. 142)
>
> [*He became convinced that it was Férula who was to blame for everything; she had sown in his wife an evil seed which stopped her from loving him. Férula, on the other hand, stole forbidden caresses with Clara, caresses which were rightfully his as her husband.*]

His later dismissal of Férula from the estate irrevocably severs the one remaining link with his own family.

The sense of political change in the country, with the arrival of a new Socialist candidate, prompts Trueba to strengthen his own social network and to cement links with other landowners against this perceived threat of the reconfiguration of the political landscape. He simplifies the debate on land ownership by considering it a question of effort over equality of opportunity: 'no hay un solo patrón en toda la zona que no esté de acuerdo, no vamos a permitir que vengan a predicar contra el trabajo honrado, el premio justo para el que se esfuerza' (p. 183) [*there isn't a single landowner around who doesn't agree. We're not going to allow them to come here and preach against honest labour, the just reward for those who make the effort*]. Alongside this strategic rapprochement, Trueba seeks to solidify his established position by befriending the enigmatic outsider, Jean de Satigny. Trueba sees this friendship as an 'adquisición social' (p. 196) [*social acquisition*] which also serves the purpose of increasing rancour amongst his social equals: '[l]os caballeros envidiaban la suerte de Esteban Trueba' (p. 196) [*the gentlemen were jealous of Esteban Trueba's luck*]. Yet the welcoming of de Satigny into his family life and as a business partner further disrupts the fragile network that Trueba has sought to establish and maintain and creates further, apparently irreconcilable divisions between Trueba and his own family. In addition to the unsuccessful chinchilla business that de Satigny had sought to establish with Trueba, de Satigny's revelation to Trueba of the secret trysts that had been occurring between his daughter, Blanca, and the rebellious Pedro Tercero García, son of Trueba's intermediary with the locals, Pedro Segundo García, leads to perhaps Trueba's most disastrous act. The fragile position in society that Trueba has established is threatened by this relationship and he attacks both his daughter, for her affair, and his wife, Clara, for her insolence. His attempts to maintain social stasis cause irrevocable change to his family life:

> Clara no volvió a hablar a su marido nunca más en su vida. Dejó de usar su apellido de casada y se quitó del dedo la fina alianza de oro que él le había colocado más de veinte años atrás. (p. 214)

> [*Clara never spoke to her husband again during her lifetime. She stopped using her married name and took off the delicate gold ring which he had placed on her finger over twenty years before.*]

In one fell swoop, Clara condemns Trueba to a marriage without communication and displaces Trueba's putative patriarchal power by rejecting their figurative and literal marital bonds. Following this act, Trueba must thereafter rely on his children as intermediaries between him and Clara.

Trueba's fragile social network and increasingly tenuous links with his family are ironically threatened even further by another relation of his, even though Trueba refuses to acknowledge the affiliation: the appearance of Esteban García, one of his illegitimate grandchildren, marks not only a significant turn in the plot, but also serves to reinforce Trueba's displacement in the novel. Esteban García's first name establishes a clear link with his grandfather, yet his surname also reinforces his distance from Trueba and his sense of belonging within the García family, and, by implication, within the local community. His actions, however, illustrate the potent mix of the suppressed voice of the campesino and the ruthless, aspiring aristocrat. From the outset, it is noticeable that García is driven by a sense of social displacement similar to that experienced and expressed by Trueba at the beginning of the novel. García feels that a failure on the part of Trueba to acknowledge him has prevented him from enjoying success in life: he bitterly notes that 'si su padre hubiera nacido en el lugar de Blanca, Jaime o Nicolás, habría heredado Las Tres Marías y podría haber llegado a Presidente de la República, de haberlo querido' (p. 202) [*if his father had been born in Blanca, Jaime or Nicolás's place, he would have inherited Las Tres Marías and he might have even become President of the Republic, if he had wanted to*]. Trueba and García are inextricably linked by blood ties and a nagging sense of feeling they have been denied what they feel is rightfully theirs: as Lloyd Davies explains, García 'might be seen [...] as the shadow who imitates Esteban Trueba's gestures and copies his voice from afar'.[13]

Trueba, however, continues to be blinded by rage, and, rather than blame his situation on his own actions, he apportions blame to a third party, much in the same way as he had earlier blamed Férula for his failure to connect with Clara: 'Pedro Tercero García tenía toda la culpa de lo que había pasado' (p. 216) [*Pedro Tercero García was completely to blame for what had happened*]. His search for Pedro, following the revelation of his ongoing relationship with Blanca, is actually aided by Esteban García, who leads him to the subversive's hideout. Trueba later recounts how his reaction and subsequent attack on Pedro surprised even himself: 'estaba como en otro mundo, confundido y aterrado de mi propia violencia' (p. 217) [*I felt I was in another world, confused and frightened at my own violence*]. The desire for societal acceptance and fear of social displacement consume Trueba and drive his actions. He drags de Satigny to the city, and marries Blanca off to him as a means of avoiding any public disgrace: 'la mejor forma de evitar el escándalo era saliéndole al encuentro con una boda espectacular' (p. 228) [*the best way to avoid scandal was to meet it head on with a spectacular wedding*]. Trueba is aware of the fragility of the position he has attained in society, and he employs a form of internal displacement by sending the couple north, rather than have his daughter banished socially from city life.

In spite of his anger at his granddaughter Alba for not using her father's surname, it is with her that Trueba becomes closest in his family, and '[l]a presencia de su nieta en la casa dulcificó el carácter' (p. 281) [*his granddaughter's presence mellowed his character*]. However, he is unable to prevent her from exploring the house, and Alba becomes yet another member of the family to undermine his authority. Although forbidden from entering the basement, 'Alba se deslizaba de cabeza por una claraboya y aterrizaba sin ruido en aquel paraíso de los objetos olvidados' (p. 284) [*Alba slipped head first through the skylight and landed noiselessly in that paradise of forgotten things*]. Trueba's relationship with his own children, however, 'no hacía más que empeorar con el tiempo' (p. 290) [*merely deteriorated with time*].

---

13   Lloyd Davies, *La casa de los espíritus* (London: Grant & Cutler, 2000), p. 72.

He endeavours to explain to Alba the need to have a landlord by saying 'se necesita alguien que piense por ellos, que tome las decisiones, que los ayude' (p. 299) [*they need somebody to think for them, to make decisions, to help them*], and he is determined to bequeath her Las Tres Marías: '[Trueba] tenía la idea de que ninguno de sus tres hijos merecía heredarlo y que a su nieta la dejaría asegurada con Las Tres Marías' (p. 324) [*Trueba thought that none of his three children deserved to inherit it and he would leave his granddaughter set up for the future with Las Tres Marías*].

The move of figures from the country estate to the city impacts on Trueba's life in significant ways: Esteban García visits Trueba's house, and seems to focus all his anger on Alba, whose position in the family, in his eyes, should rightfully be his. Mindful of how he had earlier been refused a reward for leading Trueba to Pedro Tercero García, Esteban García seethes with repressed rage as he reminds himself of his state of displacement, which has led to ignominy and anonymity:

> todo aquello podría haber sido suyo, si hubiera nacido de origen legítimo, como tantas veces se lo explicó su abuela, Pancha García [...] [s]u abuela [...] no le permitió olvidar que era diferente de los demás, porque en sus venas corría la sangre del patrón. (p. 300)

> [*all of that could have been his, if he had been born legitimate, as his grandmother, Pancha García had explained to him on so many occasions. She would not let him forget that he was different to the rest, because the blood of the landlord coursed through his veins.*]

Trueba becomes increasingly obsessed with politics following Clara's death. However, the culmination of his political endeavours is tinged with ridicule, as is suggested when it is revealed that '[e]ra fanático, violento y anticuado, pero representaba mejor que nadie los valores de la familia, la tradición, la propiedad y el orden' (p. 323) [*he was fanatical, violent and old-fashioned, but he represented family values, tradition, propriety and order better than anybody else*]. The traditional values that Trueba had fought for throughout his life are parodied when they are cast alongside his increasingly volatile behaviour. Despite the changing political climate, he refuses the offer of a post in a foreign consulate and resolves to remain in the country: '¡[d]e aquí no salgo ni muerto, Excelencia!' (p. 324) [*I'll never leave here,*

Your Excellency, not even when I'm dead!]. Trueba rejects this escape route and resolves to remain in his country. Little does Trueba realize that this rejection of the offer of exile is his last real chance to escape the impending changes that serve to disrupt all networks he had sought to establish and maintain.

Thus the concept of social networks is a useful means of examining Trueba's growing problems after the second rebuilding of Las Tres Marías (following the earthquake which had reduced the estate to rubble). His disillusionment with Las Tres Marías and his renewed interest in the city following his rejection of Férula and the death of his mother alert Trueba to the potential importance of establishing strategic alliances. His failure to recognize the important social network existing in Las Tres Marías on his arrival stores up future problems for Trueba, as he instead strives to consolidate rural and urban power. His connections with outsiders such as de Satigny highlight his inability to see beyond the appearance of social status, and the results of his disruptive activity in Las Tres Marías begin to become apparent in the growing importance of two members of the rural García family in national affairs which will forever undermine Trueba's own social network.

Social Movements: Local and National Change

As outlined in Chapter 1 of the present discussion, there is an appreciable shift in the plot of *La casa de los espíritus* when national events begin to impinge upon the lives of Esteban Trueba and the inhabitants of Las Tres Marías. The surprise victory of the Socialists in the elections creates major changes within the country as a whole and in the life of Trueba, whose fragile hold on political status swiftly slips away. Displaced from his powerful position of senator, Trueba decides to convene meetings with other Conservatives on the city outskirts. Despite Trueba's initial suggestions regarding the most appropriate methods to be employed in order to

Local Development and Displacement 57

overthrow the new Socialist government, he soon changes his mind, feeling that underhand actions are instead called for:

> Al principio, el largo ejercicio de la democracia lo limitaba en su capacidad para poner trampas al gobierno, pero pronto abandonó la idea de jorobarlo dentro de la ley y aceptó el hecho de que la única forma de vencerlo era empleando los recursos prohibidos. (p. 367)

> [*At first, the lengthy exercise of democracy restricted his ability to set traps for the government; yet he soon abandoned the idea of ruining things through legal means and accepted that the only way to defeat it was by using forbidden means.*]

Trueba attempts to use his landlord status in Las Tres Marías as a means of reasserting some sense of societal place, but even here he finds himself thwarted by the solidarity amongst the campesinos, who have been buoyed by the election results. Trueba is tied up by the workers, but not mistreated, and he humiliates himself when he is shown on television later that evening, raving at the apparent injustice of the situation. It is now Trueba who appears to be like an animal, and not the campesinos:

> Esa noche todo el país pudo ver en sus pantallas al máximo representante de la oposición amarrado, echando espumarajos de rabia y bramando tales palabrotas que tuvo que actuar la censura. (p. 375)

> [*That night the whole country could witness on their screens the leader of the Opposition tied up, spluttering with rage and bellowing out so many swearwords that the censor's office had to act.*]

The reconfiguration of the political landscape is also reflected in one of the locals, the dissident, Pedro Tercero García, reluctantly taking up a position in government. It is Pedro Tercero who helps to extricate Trueba from his embarrassing incarceration. However, on his release, Trueba embarks on an even more vigorous campaign to undermine the Socialists and to restore the Conservatives to power. The arrival of one of Clara's friends, Luisa Mora, hints at further impending changes on the political landscape, suggesting he will merely enjoy a Pyrrhic victory: she predicts that Trueba 'estará en el bando de los ganadores, pero el triunfo no le traerá más que sufrimiento y soledad' (p. 383) [*will be on the winning side, but victory will only bring suffering and loneliness*]. Trueba, however, fails to heed this warning.

The apparent return of the Conservatives to power, orchestrated in secret by Trueba and his cohorts during the Socialists' period in office, affords him a brief moment of celebration. However, things have noticeably changed, and this is suggested by the stark contrast between the putative restoration of societal place enjoyed by Trueba and the abject torture suffered by his son Jaime, who has been arrested by the military, who have suddenly attained a menacingly powerful presence in political affairs:

> En la gran casa de la esquina, el senador Trueba abrió una botella de champán francés para celebrar el derrocamiento del régimen contra el cual había luchado tan ferozmente, sin sospechar que en ese mismo momento a su hijo Jaime estaban quemándole los testículos con un cigarrillo importado. (p. 390)

> [*In the great corner house, Senator Trueba opened a bottle of French champagne to celebrate overthrowing the regime which he had fought so vigorously against, never once suspecting that, at that very moment, his son Jaime's testicles were being burnt with an imported cigar.*]

The ironic juxtaposition of imported goods, the French champagne and the cigar, illustrates Trueba's blindness to his son's fate and to the fate of the country at large. This image in many ways realizes Luisa Mora's earlier premonition about the consequences of changes in political power in the country. However, Trueba gradually becomes aware that his belief that things have returned to normal is erroneous, and that he has no part to play in the new government. Displacement has once again returned to haunt Trueba, and the awareness of this is heightened by the guilt which he feels. He has nobody to turn to, and feels of little use to anybody, admitting that 'la situación se me estaba escapando' (p. 395) [*I was losing control of things*]. His place in his family and on the political landscape appears in even greater jeopardy now than when the Socialists held power:

> Empecé a pensar que me había equivocado en el procedimiento […] me sentía cada vez más solo, porque ya nadie me necesitaba, no tenía a mis hijos y Clara, con su manía de la mudez y la distracción, parecía un fantasma. Incluso Alba se alejaba cada día más. (p. 396)

Local Development and Displacement   59

> [*I began to think that my way of acting had been wrong [...] I felt more and more alone, because nobody needed me any more, I didn't have my children and Clara, with her absentmindedness and silences, seemed like a ghost. Even Alba was drifting away.*]

In one final, desperate attempt to assert power, validate his place in rural society and recover control of his land, Trueba returns to Las Tres Marías. He mistakenly assumes that 'era necesario un período de dictadura para que el país volviera al redil del cual nunca debió haber salido' (p. 405) [*a dictatorial period was needed, so that the country would return to the fold which it never should have left*], and he endeavours to assuage his anger by gaining revenge on the campesinos who had earlier held him captive on his own land:

> Sin pensarlo dos veces, se fue al campo con media docena de matones a sueldo y pudo vengarse a sus anchas de los campesinos que se habían atrevido a desafiarlo y a quitarle lo suyo. (p. 405)
>
> [*Without thinking twice about it, he headed to the countryside with half a dozen paid heavies and could wreak revenge at his ease on the campesinos who had dared challenge him and try and take away what was his.*]

Initially, it appears that Trueba will cling to the first sense of authority he achieved over the campesinos of Las Tres Marías. He wreaks revenge summarily, making good his original threat of displacement, and reinforcing his original, dehumanizing view of the locals: 'despidió a todos los inquilinos con la advertencia de que si volvía a verlos rondando por la propiedad, sufrirían la misma suerte que los animales' (p. 405) [*he dismissed all the tenants with a warning that, if he were to see them hanging around the estate again, they would face the same fate as the (slaughtered) animals*]. Yet the orgy of violence and rage that consumes him later gives way to intense feelings of contrition, his outlandish actions disgusting ultimately even himself: '[a]squeado, el patrón regresó a la capital sintiéndose más viejo que nunca. Le pesaba el alma' (p. 405) [*disgusted with himself, the landlord headed back to the capital, feeling older than ever. His heart weighed heavy*]. Trueba begins to reflect on all he has done, and he even offers the campesinos an opportunity to return to the land, which they do not do. He despairs at the changing state of his country: '[h]undido en su poltrona, como un anciano acabado, lo vieron llorar calladamente. No lloraba por la pérdida del poder. Estaba llorando por su patria' (p. 406) [*slumped in his armchair, like a washed-up old man, they watched him sob quietly. He wasn't crying over the loss of power. He was crying for his country*]. Trueba's lament for his country is accompanied by a sense of intense solitude; displaced from political power, he is unaware of a further loss of authority soon to be experienced with the arrival of the military, who significantly have begun to disrupt and displace previous configurations of the geography and the history of the country when it is revealed how they '[a]comodaron los mapas, porque no había ninguna razón para poner el norte arriba, tan lejos de la benemérita patria, si se podía poner abajo, donde quedaba más favorecida' (p. 402) [*they redrew the maps, because there was no reason to have north up, so far away from their beloved country, if it could be down, where it looked better*].

One of Trueba's final efforts to undo some of the damage he has caused is to help his daughter, Blanca, and Pedro Tercero García, flee into exile. A sense of reconciliation is intimated with both Blanca, whom he had viciously assaulted on hearing of her illicit relationship, and Pedro Tercero García, the man he had once vowed to destroy for his apparent insubordination and who later released Trueba from his brief period of imprisonment in Las Tres Marías:

> Entonces abrió los brazos y los dos hombres, en un apretado nudo, se despidieron, libres al fin de los odios y los rencores que por tantos años les habían ensuciado la existencia. (p. 413)

> [*Then he opened his arms and the two men hugged each other tightly and said goodbye, free at last from all the hatred and rancour which had soured their existences for so many years.*]

His ultimate return to a state of societal displacement appears to be now accepted stoically by him, and this acceptance of marginality gives him the freedom to help others and to recognize the hurt he had caused. His acts of redemption, through which he prioritizes his family over the newly installed military authorities, go some way to undoing some of the damage

Local Development and Displacement 61

he has caused. However, Trueba's one remaining bastion of authority, the corner house in the city, falls when his house is stormed by the military towards the end of the novel:

> [Esteban] [n]unca se imaginó, sin embargo, que vería irrumpir en su casa, al amparo del toque de queda, una docena de hombres sin uniformes, armados hasta los dientes, que lo sacaron de su cama sin miramientos y lo llevaron de un brazo hasta el salón, sin permitirle ponerse las pantuflas o arroparse con un chal. (p. 420)
>
> [*Esteban never imagined, however, that he would see a group of men, armed to the teeth and in plain clothes, burst into his house under the cover of curfew. He never thought they would drag him unceremoniously from bed and drag him by the arms into the living room, without allowing him to put on slippers or wrap up in a shawl.*]

Trueba's desperate spiralling into displacement culminates in the seizing of Alba and in his inability to help. Behind these actions is the figure of Esteban García, who has in a sense usurped Trueba's place in society through his acrimonious acquisition of political power. Trueba is left alone at home, a 'figura patética' (p. 422) [*pathetic figure*] who recalls his sense of isolation not merely in the mines as he sought to forge a future with Rosa but also after the first reconstruction of the mansion in Las Tres Marías during his return there. Yet his growing realization of the severity of his earlier actions, and his act of kindness in assisting Blanca and Pedro Tercero García to escape to Canada, are repaid through the help he receives from the prostitute Tránsito Soto, who is decisive in securing Alba's release from captivity. His heartfelt plea to Tránsito illustrates both his reliance on her powerful position on the margins because of her relationship with the military and the opposite trajectories of their lives since their first encounter in the brothel named El Farolito Rojo [*The Red Lantern*]:

> si no fuera porque estoy en el límite de mis fuerzas, después de haber agotado todos los recursos, no hubiera venido a molestarla a usted, por favor, Tránsito, en nombre de nuestra vieja amistad, apiádese de mí, soy un pobre viejo destrozado, apiádese y busque a mi nieta Alba antes que me la terminen de mandar en pedacitos por correo, sollocé. (p. 441)

> [*I wouldn't have come to trouble you, Tránsito, if it wasn't for the fact that I've explored and exhausted all avenues. In the name of our long-standing friendship, have pity on me – I'm a poor broken old man, have pity on me and find my granddaughter Alba before they end up mailing her back to me piece by piece – I wept.*]

Tránsito secures the release of Alba, and Trueba succeeds in spending his last moments with her, displaced from power but reunited with his one remaining relative still in the country. The brutal quelling of the Socialist movement in the text leads to cataclysmic change in the country, but the one positive ghost from Trueba's past, Tránsito Soto, repays Trueba's faith in her and allows him to spend his final moments in the company of Alba.

Conclusion: Displacement and the Ghosts of Trueba's Past

In a discussion of the past, Marshall Berman has said that 'we yearn to grasp [the past], but it is baseless and elusive; we look back for something solid to lean on, only to find ourselves embracing ghosts'.[14] Allende herself has stated that '[h]istory itself is a ghost to be confronted, exorcized, used, overcome'.[15] These quotations provide a useful basis for reviewing Esteban's trajectory through *La casa de los espíritus*.

As illustrated throughout this chapter, Trueba's character depends fundamentally on a highly selective appropriation of the past, and it is figures from his past that determine his actions: his desire to reconstruct the architecture of aristocracy, provided by the memory of his mother's lineage and the reconstruction of Las Tres Marías, is threatened by natural

---

14 Marshall Berman, *All That Is Solid Melts into Air: The Experience of Modernity* (London: Verso, 1983), p. 333.
15 Allende in 'Magical Romance/Magical Realism: Ghosts in US and Latin American Fiction', in *Magical Realism: Theory, History, Community*, ed. by Lois Parkinson Zamora and Wendy B. Faris (Durham, NC: Duke University Press, 1995), pp. 407–550 (p. 503).

Local Development and Displacement 63

forces – including earthquakes and insect plagues – and by a growing political awareness of the potential for change on the part of the campesinos. Through his role as contributory narrator in the text, Trueba highlights his efforts at becoming a self-made man by dint of hard work and determination. His early dynamism is paradoxically replicated through the later actions of both his family – legitimate and illegitimate – and his employees: his family ultimately rejects the rigid patriarchal strictures he strives to impose through their constant subversive activity and jeopardizes Trueba's social status, from Blanca's relationship with Pedro Tercero García through to Clara's independence, his son Nicolás's outlandish actions and his other son Jaime's rejection of the Trueba surname and covert friendship with high-ranking officials in the Socialist government. Indeed, Trueba's own initial dynamism and determination to achieve social station is followed almost immediately by an attempt to impose and perpetuate social stasis, preventing workers from having basic entitlements such as wages. His aggressive tactics automatically create a social chasm between Trueba and the inhabitants; he unsuccessfully endeavours to bridge this gap through his subsequent dealings with the campesinos. All apparent concessions are steeped in convoluted terms, or offered to satisfy his wife, Clara, and opportunities for self-improvement and self-development are systematically restricted, couched in language that confuses and serves to perpetuate the hegemonic discourse espoused by Trueba. Indeed, Trueba's obsession with outside threats, including the imported Socialist thinking, blinds him to the threats from within, be it from his family, his employees or even his own political party. He is instead more interested in being, as Philip Swanson notes, 'the source and centre of everything.'[16] The rise of the Socialists to power perhaps ironically shows Trueba at his dynamic best, as he rouses the Conservatives into action from their position of marginality. However, even during his attempts to garner support, he is continually undermined by his own family, such as when Alba and Jaime remove weapons to the

---

16   Philip Swanson, 'Tyrants and Trash: Sex, Class and Culture in *La casa de los espíritus*', in *Isabel Allende*, ed. by Harold Bloom (Philadelphia, PA: Chelsea House, 2003), pp. 109–32 (p. 115).

countryside and house political refugees in forgotten corners of the corner house in the city. The campesinos from Las Tres Marías also taste limited independence during the Socialists' time in power, and although their rebelliousness is harshly punished by eviction, it is Trueba who suffers, left on an empty estate that in many ways reflects his isolation on first arriving at Las Tres Marías and foreshadows his emptiness towards the end of the novel. With the intervention of the military comes an apparent opportunity to regain power, but this proves to be temporary and ultimately illusory. Las Tres Marías is returned to him but both his house in the city and his granddaughter are violated.

Indeed, it could be argued that Trueba's character is both based on and restricted by the ghosts of his past. Throughout the text, he comes face to face with a range of ghosts, from the spectral and imaginative souls that populate the house during Clara's séances, through to the figurative ghosts of his past, those people who return in search of repayment for past indiscretions, in particular, his illegitimate grandson Esteban García. The past may be irresistible for Trueba – the inspiration for his actions and the source of his sense of social displacement – but the ghosts of the past are ineluctable. His search for societal place involves geographical and temporal displacement, from family, home and city. His retreat into the past, however, is ultimately unsuccessful, given that the acquisition of societal place comes at a heavy cost, since he finds that his ideas and his actions are consistently undermined by his family. His initial rejection of his own sister and family is mirrored subsequently through his wife and his children's rejection of his intolerance and hypocrisy. Engaged in a constant jostling for power with his wife Clara, Trueba strives to achieve a firmer sense of place through his political endeavours. However, he finds himself further undermined in the domestic sphere by the actions and affection of his sister Férula toward Clara, and subsequently by the relationship that develops between his daughter Blanca and Pedro Tercero García.

His failure to acknowledge his past indiscretions and his unwillingness to engage in a meaningful way with the campesinos in Las Tres Marías indirectly lead to the arrival into the city of Esteban García, who is unwittingly set on the path of displacing Trueba by being provided with the financial support to embark on a career in the police force.[17] The brutal legacy of Trueba's prior actions is apparent when his great corner house, the putative emblem of his status and the heart of central, patriarchal authority, is ransacked, and his granddaughter Alba is violently snatched away from him. Yet a sense of resolution and understanding fills the final chapters of the novel, when Trueba becomes reconciled with his past and present. Interestingly, it is also in the final stages that a sense of reconciliation with Clara is intimated.

Trueba's final attempt to retain some vestige of authority and authenticity may be traced through his position as narrator-protagonist. Alba reveals that 'mi abuelo tuvo la idea de que escribiéramos esta historia' (p. 450) [*my grandfather had the idea that we should write this story*]. Trueba encourages Alba to write the story in order to remember her family's past, should she herself have to leave her homeland: 'podré llevarme las raíces conmigo si algún día tengo que irme de aquí' (p. 450) [*I can take my roots away with me if someday I have to leave here*]. Beyond this, of course, is an attempt through Trueba's contributions to incorporate his own memories of events and perhaps a desire to justify his actions. Whatever the hidden intentions of Trueba's desire to have the family tale recorded may be, it is clear that through the content of his discourse, when juxtaposed with the matrilineal narrative by Alba, Clara and Blanca, Trueba once again becomes displaced and undermined: in his role as first-person narrator, for example, he appears to undermine himself through his somewhat contradictory views of changes to the status quo, and he displays a very tangible fear of the importation of European ideas, which are presented by him in a reductive, other-worldly form. Fear of Europe does not extend to architecture, however, and he desires to create a domestic space that mimics

---

17   Stephen M. Hart discusses the idea of politicized ghosts in a comparative study which includes the English translation of *La casa de los espíritus*, and he draws attention to the privileging of the feminine in the text. For further information, see 'Magical Realism in the Americas: Politicised Ghosts in *One Hundred Years of Solitude*, *The House of the Spirits*, and *Beloved*', *Journal of Iberian and Latin American Studies*, 9 (2003), 115–23.

European designs, an indication, in Swanson's eyes, of 'Trueba's obsession with "civilization"'.[18]

As Doris Meyer explains, 'Allende's ingenious blending of the two narrative voices not only clearly situates the female voice within the context of a *machista* culture but it also displaces and subverts the power of that culture.'[19] Thus, Trueba is for one final time displaced in the text, and the presentation of his story, which seeks to explain his path to power and authority from his own perspective, merely serves to illustrate the perpetual prevalence of displacement in his personal and professional life and after his death through the insertion of his words in the text. Alba's decision to include her grandfather's own perspective allows her to fulfil one of his dying wishes while simultaneously showing Trueba's extensive contributions to his own demise. Davies notes that 'Esteban's discourse of authority and power, unrestrained at the outset, appears subdued and tempered by female values at the conclusion.'[20] His discourse is paradoxically both preserved and dismantled through its presentation alongside the polyvocal narrative penned by Alba, Clara and Blanca. Trapped by his dependence on matrilineality in the text, Trueba ultimately becomes a discordant and distant echo of patriarchy as, in Swanson's opinion, 'a productive female line displaces a circle of sterile male activity'.[21] (p. 121). His efforts to justify his actions are thwarted by their juxtaposition with a comparative perspective and by their assimilation into a text that is matrilineal. Marcelo Coddou suggests that this presentation of Trueba from both first and third person perspectives:

---

18   Swanson, p. 116.
19   Doris Meyer, '"Parenting the Text": Female Creativity and Dialogic Relationships in Isabel Allende's *La casa de los espíritus*' in *Isabel Allende*, ed. by Harold Bloom (Philadelphia: Chelsea House, 2003), pp. 31–42 (p. 34).
20   Davies, p. 102.
21   Swanson, p. 151.

desvía [...] el relato de lo que, de otro modo, habría sido sólo 'autobiografía' – de Trueba – y permite mantener [un] centro de equilibrio ideológico, desde el cual ofrecer una perspectiva valorizadora del mundo.[22]

[*changes the course of [...] a story which otherwise would have been purely 'autobiographical' (Trueba's story) and allows [Allende] to maintain an ideological centre of equilibrium, from which to offer an evaluative perspective of the world.*]

However, there is a further layer to Trueba's own contribution in the text: his final recognition of displacement also offers an affirming potential for reunion with his wife Clara after his death. It is noticeable that towards the end of his life, divested of power and prestige, he becomes able to see the spirit of his dead son Jaime and to communicate with Clara. Critics have noted this change in Trueba's character: Davies argues that 'Esteban's own shift from belligerent authoritarianism towards tolerance of alien personal and political values lends credence to the possibility of a different mode of behaviour which might at first appear to be hopelessly idealistic'.[23] Davies is suggesting here that the shift in Trueba's discourse is more compelling when read within the overall context of a shift in the text towards solidarity. In terms of Trueba's contribution to the writing of the tale, Patricia Hart argues that his 'written narration [...] is part of his spiritual regeneration'.[24] She continues, saying that he 'manages through his writing to arrive at a much-needed absolution that enables him to die in peace'.[25] Thus, within the text, the evolution of his character through different forms of displacement also succeeds in illustrating Trueba's recognition of his failings and his final efforts to undo in some way the damage which he has caused.

The complex mix between the overall presentation of Trueba and the message that is transmitted by Allende has inevitably frustrated critics:

---

22   Marcelo Coddou, '*La casa de los espíritus*: De la historia a la Historia' in *Los libros tienen sus propios espíritus*, ed. by Marcelo Coddou (Mexico: Universidad Veracruzana, 1986), pp. 7–14 (p. 11).
23   Davies, p. 101.
24   Patricia Hart, '"Magic Books" and the Magic of Books', in *Isabel Allende*, ed. by Harold Bloom (Philadelphia, PA: Chelsea House, 2003), pp. 5–22 (p. 16).
25   Ibid., p. 19.

one of the strongest criticisms of Trueba's characterization is presented by Mora, who suggests that in spite of his actions, '[l]a visión conciliadora en que se asienta el fundamento ideológico de la obra, termina, no obstante, otorgándole una larga vida y una muerte feliz' [*however, the conciliatory vision on which the ideological basis of the novel rests ends up granting him a long life and a happy death*].[26] The suggestion here is that Trueba is apparently saved from punishment by the ideology underpinning Allende's writing. However, there is arguably compelling evidence to suggest that Trueba is subjected to a degree of punishment in the text. Juan Manuel Marcos and Teresa Méndez-Faith correctly note one of the clearest examples of intratextual justice for Trueba when they explain how he 'sufre la humillación del vejamen a que lo someten los nuevos amos y de arrastrarse hasta Tránsito Soto para pedirle la libertad de su nieta' [*suffers humiliation at the hands of the new leaders and has to drag himself to Tránsito Soto to ask her to help free his granddaughter*].[27] Furthermore, while Trueba is responsible for encouraging Alba to write the tale, and to incorporate his own contributions, the juxtaposition of both perspectives undermines Trueba and his words serve to lock him into a presentation that highlights his faults and the systematic dismantling of his fragile sense of personal and public power. In this way, Allende seems to avoid a one-dimensional characterization of Trueba, thereby calling into question José Miguel Oviedo's assertion that her approach to characterization in the novel appears to be essentially Manichean: 'la autora no quiere que corramos el riesgo de confundir a los villanos con los héroes (o heroínas)' [*the author does not want us to run the risk of confusing villains with heroes (or heroines)*].[28] It is precisely the nuances and subtle changes in Trueba that refute this claim, as his gradual loss of power, which he had striven to achieve, leads to him becoming dependent on other marginal figures such as the dissident Miguel and the

---

26 Mora, p. 76.
27 Juan Manuel Marcos and Teresa Méndez-Faith, 'Multiplicidad, dialéctica y reconciliación del discurso en *La casa de los espíritus*', in *Los libros tienen sus propios espíritus*, pp. 61–70 (p. 69).
28 José Miguel Oviedo, *Historia de la literatura hispanoamericana 4. De Borges al presente* (Madrid: Alizana, 2001) p. 395.

prostitute Tránsito Soto to secure the future of his family line through the survival of Alba. His own voice, which sought to promote patriarchy despite his unavoidable dependence on his mother's aristocratic past, eventually becomes subsumed within the matrilineal narrative, where it is preserved but perpetually undermined through its insertion in the text.

Throughout the text, Allende deftly interweaves issues of geographical and social displacement, projecting the complexities and aspirations of Trueba by showing his attempts to overcome a nagging sense of marginalization through the redevelopment of his family's country estate. Despite the apparent acquisition of power and privilege through his questionable exploits, Trueba ultimately finds that his family, through their own rebelliousness and unwillingness to conform, have inherited traits which he himself displayed throughout his early years. His recognition of his failings and his gradual reconciliation with family members towards the end of the text are only achieved through an awareness of his loss of status and of the importance of family, and it is perhaps the only positive ghost from his past, Tránsito Soto, who allows him to die in peace, secure in the knowledge that Alba is safe.

The next chapter switches focus from local to national events by exploring the impact of the imposition of a military dictatorship in the society presented in Allende's second novel, *De amor y de sombra*.

CHAPTER 3

Appearance, Disappearance and Displacement: A Carnivalesque Reading of *De amor y de sombra*

> All the images of carnival are dualistic; they unite within themselves both poles of change and crisis.
> — MIKHAIL BAKHTIN[1]

Introduction

This chapter moves away from the focus on local and rural events to an examination of the impact of national events on citizens with the arrival of a military dictatorship in Allende's 1984 novel *De amor y de sombra*. Drawing on work by Russian literary theorist Mikhail Bakhtin, the aim of this chapter is to view Allende's second novel through a carnivalesque lens. Particular attention is paid to the tensions between authorities and citizens; these tensions are examined through the questions of appearance, disappearance and societal displacement. This chapter contends that Allende provides a nuanced reading of changes which affect all citizens in a totalitarian regime, and that, by tracing carnivalesque features, the fundamental coherence which underpins the text can be clearly illustrated.

As mentioned in Chapter 1, *De amor y de sombra* is often compared unfavourably with *La casa de los espíritus*, and studies which focus exclusively on the text are few and far between: critics who have broached the

---

1   Mikhail Bakhtin, *Problems of Dostoevsky's Poetics* (Minneapolis: University of Minnesota Press, 1984), p. 126.

text are divided on the question of coherence, which may be due in some part to the challenge of locating the novel within a particular genre. Linda Gould Levine, for example, believes that Allende 'blends fiction with fact [in *De amor y de sombra*] to create a powerful work that straddles several literary genres and situates itself in the middle of testimonial literature, a police novel fraught with suspense, and a tender story of love'.[2] However, other critics are not so kind, and find that this melding of genres leads to an uneven result: for example, Karen Castellucci Cox argues that that the text is guilty of 'periodically capitulating to a passionate sentimentality that does not ring true when juxtaposed with gruesome acts of unchecked cruelty'.[3] The attempt on Allende's part to write a text that illustrates the extent of injustice experienced under a military dictatorship while also simultaneously developing a love story has led others to dismiss the text as an unhappy marriage of irreconcilable elements: for example, Gabriela Mora suggests that female characterization is confused, since 'el retrato se resiente de falsedades y contradicciones' [*their portrayal suffers from falsehoods and contradictions*].[4] Monique J. Lemaitre, for her part, questions the political coherence of *De amor y de sombra*, and argues that:

> [el texto] contiene elementos importantes de denuncia, pero también parece abogar por una solución dentro del 'status quo' que establece una diferencia entre los grupos sociales que crecieron con niñera y aquellos que crecieron sin ella.[5]
>
> [*[the text] contains important elements of protest but also seems to champion a solution within the status quo, which establishes a difference between social groups raised with nannies and those raised without nannies.*]

---

2   Linda Gould Levine, *Isabel Allende* (New York: Twayne, 2003), p. 39.
3   Karen Castellucci Cox, *Isabel Allende: A Critical Companion* (Westport, CT: Greenwood, 2003), p. 49.
4   Gabriela Mora, 'Las novelas de Isabel Allende y el papel de la mujer como ciudadana', *Ideologies and Literature*, 2.1 (1987), 53–61 (p. 58). Part of this quotation will be used in the conclusion to this chapter.
5   Monique J. Lemaitre, 'Deseo, incesto y represión en "De amor y de sombra"', in *Critical Approaches to Isabel Allende's Novels*, pp. 97–107 (p. 105).

Lemaitre appears to be suggesting that the testimonial features of the text are in some way undermined by the failure on Allende's part to suggest a radical or revolutionary alternative model to the dictatorial regime presented in the text. The present discussion explores the validity of this suggestion by examining the instances of subversive activity within the model presented by Allende. To do so, it is to the question of what is understood by the term *carnivalesque* that this discussion turns.

Carnivalesque Displacement in *De amor y de sombra*

Russian literary theorist Mikhail Bakhtin's contributions to the development of critical theory have been examined and applied extensively; this discussion draws on arguments made in his discussion of medieval carnival, which was explored in his book *Rabelais and his World*.[6] Working from medieval carnival as the culture of the marketplace and folk humour, Bakhtin examines the nature of this temporary festival through issues such as role-reversal, disguise, masks and the general mixing of upper and lower classes. It is during these festivities that, as Bakhtin notes, 'all hierarchical rank, privileges, norms and prohibitions disappear' (p. 10). Within this period, status and social stasis give way temporarily to a form of social levelling, granting people the possibility of acting differently, be it above or below their perceived station. The aspect of carnival that is of particular relevance to this discussion is, however, not the festivity itself, but more the reconfiguration of roles in society brought about during this period: admittedly, there are few, if any, overt references to carnival, festivity or folk humour in *De amor y de sombra*, the one possible exception perhaps being Hipólito Ranquileo, who works occasionally as a clown with a circus

---

6   Mikhail Bakhtin, *Rabelais and His World*, trans. by Helene Iswolsky (Bloomington: Indiana University Press, 1984). For an excellent introduction to Bakhtin's *oeuvre*, consult Sue Vice's *Introducing Bakhtin* (Manchester: Manchester University, 1997).

troupe. Furthermore, Sue Vice's suggestion that '[c]arnival is the opposite of a time of terror or purges' (p. 153) might also militate against considering carnival relevant to a story set in a place ruled by a military dictatorship, and, indeed, a story which, as outlined in Chapter 1, is a fictionalized account of a reality experienced by many living under dictatorial regimes. Instead, this study focuses upon the carnivalesque as a literary reflection of the reversals and transformations that occur within a society in a period of flux, change and uncertainty. It is within these parameters that the concept of a carnivalesque reading proceeds here, and such an approach is, on closer inspection, feasible not only to this text, but also very pertinent to the overall discussion of displacement in this study: the impact of the military's sudden wresting of political power is felt throughout society, as both organizations and individuals undergo an abrupt form of societal displacement. In *De amor y de sombra*, there is an underlying tension between previous roles people held in society and newer roles which have been either assumed, in the case of the military, or imposed, in the case of citizens. An example of this is Francisco Leal, one of the key figures in the text. Leal finds a job working as a photographer in a fashion magazine when the School of Psychology where he had previously worked is closed down as it is believed by the newly-installed authorities to be 'un semillero de ideas perniciosas' [*a breeding ground of pernicious ideas*].[7] This purging of professions is one of many changes noticed throughout society: as is to be discussed in greater detail in the next section, even people who previously enjoyed privileged positions in society find their lives change dramatically. For example, Beatriz Alcántara de Beltrán must convert the lower floor of her mansion into an old people's home to make ends meet, following the sudden disappearance of her husband. Alongside these sudden, visible changes in society, there is also much underground activity alluded to in the text; interestingly, and somewhat ironically, this activity is perpetrated not only by dissidents but also by members of the military, through their clandestine activities of causing citizens to *disappear*. To return to the

---

7   Isabel Allende, *De amor y de sombra*, 8th edn (Barcelona: Plaza & Janés, 1995), p. 50. Further references will appear parenthetically in the text.

example of Francisco, he continues to practise in private as a psychologist, and helps out his brother, Javier, in the poorer neighbourhoods of the city. Although superficially Francisco has accepted his enforced change of profession, he rebels against this surreptitiously by continuing to practise psychology. Throughout the text, societal displacement leads to many unorthodox combinations, confrontations and conversations between the newly-installed authorities and oppressed citizens, replicating the mixing of classes characteristic of medieval carnival. Allende uses these confrontations to examine the nature of authority and authoritarian figures in the text, as well as the subversive forms of anti-authoritarianism that emerge within the military and within the state at large. The present discussion contends that a carnivalesque reading of the text allows for these confrontations to be identified and also allows Allende to present a nuanced analysis of a superficially static society which bristles with underground activity.

To date, critical work on detecting carnivalesque features in the text has been sparse and sporadic: Wesley J. Weaver III describes Allende's presentation and combination of different narrative voices in the text as a type of 'confusión lúdica' [*playful confusion*] which, in his view, helps to 'penetra[r] en la esencia de los personajes que no se revela a veces en su propia conducta' [*penetrate the essence of characters who often do not reveal themselves through their own behaviour*].⁸ David K. Danow's *The Spirit of Carnival* does make overt reference to carnivalesque elements in *De amor y de sombra*: he identifies three main examples which seek to exemplify aspects of his own discussion of the interplay between Latin America literature and the carnivalesque.⁹ This focus of the present discussion,

---

8   Wesley J. Weaver III, 'La frontera que se esfuma: Testimonio y ficción en *De amor y de sombra y de sombra*', in *Critical Approaches to Isabel Allende's Novels*, pp. 73–81 (p. 77).
9   David K. Danow, *The Spirit of Carnival: Magical Realism and the Grotesque* (Lexington: University Press of Kentucky, 1995). Danow's examples do not significantly overlap with the thrust of the present discussion: his first example (pp. 68–70) is a description of Francisco Leal's move away from involvement in dissident activity as a teenager into a world of literature, which is used by Danow as a convenient shorthand for the way in which aspects of magical realist literature can be identified

however, is on three key aspects which are not overtly broached in Danow's excellent study of carnival and the carnivalesque: the quest for a form of eternalized youth, which highlights some surprising similarities between the aging residents of the old people's home, *La Voluntad de Dios* [*God's Will*], and the owner, Beatriz; state control and the nature of authority explored through the character of Evangelina Ranquileo and rebellious rebirths, which looks at not only the transformation of Beatriz's daughter, Irene, but also the defiant return of the *real* Evangelina Ranquileo.

Eternalized Youth? Beatriz and the Residents of La Voluntad de Dios

As with Esteban Trueba's family home in the city in *La casa de los espíritus*, the family home of two main characters in *De amor y de sombra* reflects the tensions between characters in the text. The house is owned by Beatriz Alcántara de Beltrán, a middle-class woman with aristocratic pretensions who is blind to the significant changes throughout society which have been ushered in by the military dictatorship. Since the disappearance of Beatriz's husband, Eusebio, she and her daughter Irene have found themselves in an increasingly precarious financial situation, and Beatriz decides to have the lower wing of the house converted into an old people's home. The importance of appearance, disappearance and displacement is especially relevant in relation to Beatriz, and she is obsessed with concealing any signs of change in either her appearance or lifestyle, despite the very

---

with the carnivalesque; his second example (pp. 92–3) looks at the question of transformations in Irene's life by exploring her inability to distinguish at times between dreams and reality, and his final example from *De amor y de sombra* (pp. 145–6) describes in general terms how Francisco's parents find themselves trapped in a sense of circularity, as they had left Spain during Franco's regime only to now experience a military dictatorship in their adopted homeland, which is assumed to be Chile.

obvious changes within her home and her family unit which have been triggered by her husband's disappearance. She endeavours to present a physical appearance of agelessness in order to prevent resembling her friends, who in her eyes now display an almost geographical gerontology with 'un mapa de surcos y patas de gallo en la cara, con rollos y bolsas por todas partes' (p. 17) [*a map of wrinkles and crow's feet on their faces, with folds and bulges everywhere*]. Indirectly, this desire for immutability starkly contrasts with the reality of aging which she now cannot help but witness in her own home with the elderly residents. Beatriz carefully constructs her appearance, and she seems to revel in the unnaturalness of her body:

> Lo consideraba obra suya y no de la naturaleza, porque era el producto acabado de su enorme fuerza de voluntad, el resultado de años de dieta, ejercicios, masajes, relajación yoga y avances de la cosmetología. (p. 163)

> [*She considered it a work forged by her own hand and not by nature, as it was the result of her tremendous force of will, following years of dieting, exercise, massages, yoga and the latest cosmetic procedures.*]

Her body is not merely a construction, but also a commodity, as she states that 'constituía un capital rentable, pues le proporcionaba el mayor deleite' (p. 164) [*it was a profitable source of money, as it gave her great delight*]. Her attempts to maintain this agelessness are largely successful, at least within Beatriz's frame of reference, as she travels away to enjoy the seasonal attention of her young foreign lover, Michel. Beatriz's dedication to the appearance of stasis also extends to her house, which 'mantenía dentro de lo posible la misma fachada para que desde la calle se viera tan señorial como las residencias vecinas' (p. 43) [*kept, as much as possible, the same facade so that it looked from the street as stately as neighbouring houses*]. However, despite her resolute attempts to create distance from the elderly, there is in fact a striking parallel between Beatriz and the residents: Beatriz's efforts at defying the onset of time by constructing a type of eternalized youthfulness are unwittingly replicated by the residents themselves, who escape the present by living out daily routines from their earlier years. Recollections of former glory contrast strongly with an abject present, echoing the Bakhtinian concept of *grotesque realism*.[10] A clear example is the elderly Colonel: at the beginning of the tale, it is springtime, which is suggestive of growth and renewal, but the Colonel's attempts to celebrate the arrival of spring with an imagined military parade are futile: '[f]ue interrumpido por una enfermera en uniforme de batalla, silenciosa y solapada [...] provista de una servilleta para limpiarle la baba que descendía por las comisuras de sus labios y mojaba su camisa' [*he was interrupted by a nurse kitted out in full battle gear; she approached silently and stealthily, armed with a napkin to clean the dribble that ran down the side of his mouth and dampened his shirt*](p. 14).

In direct contrast to Beatriz's treatment of the elderly residents, her daughter Irene embraces contact with them, and she is happy to spend time chatting, even when her friendliness is misconstrued by a resident who 'le colocó ambas manos sobre los senos, oprimiéndolos con más curiosidad que lascivia' (p. 16) [*placed both hands on her breasts, squeezing them more out of curiosity than lustfulness*]. Beatriz's control over her daughter and her domestic space, despite her best efforts, is slipping away. She worries that Irene's comparative neglect of her appearance may jeopardize her relationship with Captain Gustavo Morante, a key figure in the military whom Irene has known since childhood and to whom she is engaged. As Beatriz states frustratingly: '[n]o tengo ánimo para andar detrás de mi hija vigilando para que se ponga una crema en la cara y se vista como Dios manda para no espantar al novio' (p. 17) [*I just don't have the strength to be running after my daughter and checking to see she puts face cream on and dresses appropriately so as not to scare her boyfriend*]. Irene's subsequent transformation in terms of both her appearance and her growing awareness of clandestine political activity illustrates Beatriz's fundamental inability to prevent outside forces from impinging upon their lives. Beatriz is also conscious of the fragility of her control over her own domestic space. She recalls the night when her husband disappeared: on arriving home one evening with Irene, Beatriz is shocked to discover not only that her husband has disappeared but also that

---

10   For further discussion of this concept, see Katerina Clark and Michael Holquist's *Mikhail Bakhtin* (Cambridge, MA: Harvard University Press, 1984), pp. 297–9.

her house has been defiled: '[e]stupefactas, vieron entonces sobre las camas cerros de desperdicios, latas, vacías, cáscaras inmundas, papeles manchados con excrementos' (p. 44) [*shocked, they saw mountains of waste, empties, tin cans, rotting rinds and paper stained with excrement on their beds*]. Beatriz fears the worst for her husband: in her eyes, 'su ausencia no se debía a una aventura amorosa, más bien las fuerzas del orden lo habían eliminado [...] o lo tenían por error secándose en alguna prisión' (p. 44) [*he was missing not because of a love affair; instead the forces of law and order had gotten rid of him [...] or had mistakenly arrested him and had him rotting in a prison somewhere*]. She is unaware that her husband has actually left her and has not been kidnapped, the emptying out of rubbish being perhaps a ruse on Eusebio's part. Nevertheless, Beatriz is determined to keep her daughter away from the true terrors of the dictatorship, preferring to project the appearance of order despite the inner turmoil and disorder. This determination to keep up appearances and maintain the illusion of control through order is subtly echoed in the text through her description of the military as 'las fuerzas del orden' (p. 44) [*the forces of order*].

Thus, in the opening stages of the novel, the determination on Beatriz's part to maintain her daughter in a suspended state of innocence is matched by her resolute efforts to defy the passage of time by maintaining a youthful appearance, despite the private and public forms of displacement experienced. Yet even within the space of La Voluntad de Dios, Beatriz is unable to protect her daughter, and her efforts to remain forever young seem to be parodied in the text through the inhabitants of the old people's home, who have themselves returned in a sense to an eternalized form of youth through the refuge of routine. The close but innocent contact between Irene and some of the residents foreshadows Irene's move into a realm in which she becomes exposed to the full extent of the abuses that take place in the totalitarian regime. Despite Beatriz's best efforts to make time stand still, she is unable to prevent Irene's move into the world of shadows, which begins when Irene goes to cover the story of Evangelina Ranquileo.

State Control: The Case of Evangelina Ranquileo

As mentioned in the previous section, one of the key external triggers to Irene's transformation from protected daughter to committed dissident is her encounter with the teenager Evangelina Ranquileo, whose story is to be covered by Irene's magazine. Evangelina's character echoes one of the basic considerations of carnival as a blending and blurring of differences between *high* and *low*. Her mysterious trance-like states provide an example of what Bakhtin has termed 'ritual spectacle' in that they attract a large gathering of people from all echelons of society, including local peasants, religious and military figures of authority.[11] Indeed, Evangelina may be considered the carnivalesque core of the text, especially when the circumstances immediately following her birth are taken into consideration. Her adoptive mother Digna Ranquileo's earlier fear of giving birth in hospital is justified when Digna's baby is mistakenly given to another woman. Attempts to protest at the mix-up are also in vain, and she is told that 'seguramente [ella] estaba mal de los nervios y sin más trámite le inyectó un líquido en el brazo' (p. 23) [*she was certainly suffering with her nerves and without further ado they injected liquid into her arm*]. The decision by the staff to sedate Digna provides a clear example of the more generalized conflict between authorities and perceived subversives throughout the text, as well as the resolute intent on the part of authorities to institute a semblance of order and muffle any dissent, even if this leads to the denial or rejection of the voice of the individual, and actual disorder is created in the lives of citizens as a direct consequence. The hospital staff are presented as intransigent and unwilling to acknowledge the obvious physical similarities between the mothers and their respective children, while the location of the hospital at Los Riscos links it with injustice, suffering and pain, for it is subsequently revealed in the text that this town is also the location of the abandoned mine in which the disappeared, including the

---

11   Mikhail Bakhtin, *Rabelais and His World*, trans. by Helene Iswolsky (Bloomington: Indiana University Press, 1984), p. 7.

teenage Evangelina, are later buried. The combination of intrusion and exposure that Digna experiences when giving birth resembles a scene of torture and it also foreshadows the suffering that Evangelina later faces at the hands of Lieutenant Ramírez: '[d]espués de hurgar sin pedirle [a Digna] permiso en todos los orificios de su cuerpo, la hicieron dar a luz debajo de una lámpara a la vista de quien quisiera curiosear' (p. 25) [*after poking around every orifice of Digna's body without her consent, they made her give birth under a lamp in clear view of anyone interested in looking*].

Digna's mistrust of figures of authority and her inability to reason with them are also subtly reflected in the language employed in the text, with parallels established between the Health Service and the actions of savage, predatory animals:

> [Digna] [s]iempre se opuso al Servicio de Salud, que iba de casa en casa *atrapando* a los niños [...] [a]unque patalearan y ella jurara que ya habían sido tratados, de todos modos *les daba caza* y los inyectaban sin piedad. (pp. 19–20, emphasis added)

> [*Digna was always opposed to the Health Service, who went from house to house rounding up children [...] and even if the children kicked and screamed, and she swore that they had already been treated, the Health Service nevertheless* chased them down *and mercilessly doled out injections*. (emphasis added)]

The Health Service is presented as a sinister, merciless organization, a microcosmic reflection of the political authorities in the text. In an attempt to defy the various figures of authority, both mothers of the switched children make a pact in which their shared experience of motherhood and injustice is sealed:

> Desde el comienzo acordaron llamarse mutuamente comadre y dar a las criaturas el mismo nombre de pila, por si alguna vez recuperaban el apellido legítimo no tuviesen necesidad de habituarse a un nuevo apodo. (p. 35)

> [*From the very start they agreed to call each other godmother and give their daughters the same first name, so that if they should ever get back their rightful surnames they wouldn't have to get used to a new first name.*]

This switching is just one of the many instances in the text of carnivalesque role reversal, in which order is maintained through disorder. Despite the pact, Evangelina Ranquileo is never actually returned to her biological family, and she is instead presented as an enigmatic figure whose body becomes both a spectacle for the general public, when her trances begin, and later the means by which revenge is wrought by Lieutenant Ramírez, after Evangelina humiliates him. Even before her trances begin, however, Evangelina's associations with attraction and violence are apparent, particularly because of her relationship with her older adoptive brother Pradelio, who risks beatings from his father for his behaviour towards her:

> En un par de ocasiones [su padre] sorprendió a Pradelio haciéndole cosquillas, manoseándola con disimulo, besuqueándola, y para quitarle el afán de sobarla le propinó unas zurras que por poco lo despachan a otra vida. (p. 35)
>
> [*On a few occasions [his father] caught Pradelio tickling her, surreptitiously touching her, smothering her with kisses; to stop Pradelio's desire to paw her, he gave him a few good hidings that were almost the death of him.*]

Pradelio joins the army in an effort to put a stop to these dangerous games of incest, but he unwittingly informs his military superior, Lieutenant Ramírez, of his concerns about his sister's trances, which prompts Ramírez and his men to visit the Ranquileo house in order to witness the trance.[12]

Evangelina begins to experience trances from the age of fifteen; they signal a new beginning, an inexplicable and seemingly incomprehensible metamorphosis. Allende graphically describes how Evangelina is found by her mother during her first trance, in a monstrous scene of uncontrollable

---

12   Monique J. Lemaitre makes an interesting point about the behaviour of Pradelio and Evangelina, suggesting that their games are, strictly speaking, not incestuous because of the fact that Evangelina is his adoptive sister: the intransigence of the authorities and the resigned acceptance of the decision by both families have prevented them from being allowed to love each other, as 'el sistema [...] falsifica una situación incestuosa que no es sino una parodia de la construcción edípica freudiana' (p. 100) [*the system [...] has falsified an incestuous situation that is a parody of the Freudian Oedipal construct*]. The possibility of a relationship between them is actually thwarted by a combination of restrictions imposed by parental and political authorities.

destruction: she is 'de espaldas en el suelo, apoyada en los talones y la nuca, doblada hacia atrás como un arco, echando espumarajos por la boca y rodeada de tazas y platos rotos' (p. 41) [*on her back on the ground, heels and neck touching the floor, arched backwards, spewing foam from her mouth and surrounded by broken plates and cups*]. Throughout the five weeks she experiences the trances, and before her disappearance, Evangelina is taken by Digna to a variety of healers and religious figures in an attempt to seek an answer for these trances and to cure her. Digna's fear is based on the belief that 'la espuma en la boca y los ojos perdidos eran signos de Satanás' (p. 19) [*the foaming at the mouth and her absent gaze were signs of Satan*]. The conflicting attempts to cure Evangelina constitute a clash between a variety of authorities, including local, traditional wisdom and institutionalized religion. During this time, Evangelina's trances continue each day at midday, and her body rejects all the various medications prescribed, reinforcing the failure of conventional bastions of knowledge to explain what she is experiencing. The failure on the part of different authorities to resolve the enigma that Evangelina has become exposes the insufficiency of their various frames of reference to explain the situation. The confusion surrounding Evangelina's state is reinforced by the variety of requests that people ask of her during her final trance – she is asked to heal boils, prevent people from being conscripted, predict lottery numbers and bring rain. There are also strong suggestions that the trance resembles a transition into adulthood and a sexual awakening, as appears evident from the following description:

> un hondo, largo, terrible gemido la recorrió entera, como una llamada al amor [...] [e]n su rostro desfigurado se borró la expresión de niña simple que tenía poco antes y envejeció de súbito varios años. Una mueca de éxtasis, dolor o lujuria marcó sus facciones. (pp. 71–2)
>
> [*a deep, long moan coursed through her, like a call to love [...] in her disfigured face the expression of a simple child which she had shortly beforehand disappeared, and she aged suddenly by several years. A grimace of ecstasy, pain or lust marked her features.*]

Indeed, Pradelio witnesses his sister 'gimiendo en una parodia grotesca del acto sexual' [*moaning in a grotesque parody of the sexual act*], which destroys his efforts to forget the putatively incestuous games they played as 'le volvieron de golpe los calientes tormentos casi olvidados' (p. 157) [*the almost-forgotten torrid torment came back suddenly*]. Evangelina's trance, in which she is 'perdida en turbia cópula con los espíritus' (p. 73) [*lost in murky copulation with the spirits*], is interrupted by the sudden arrival of the military. Amidst the confusion caused by the indiscriminate shooting by the army officials, who fear they are under attack when they mistakenly believe the sound of pebbles falling is gunfire, Evangelina is approached by Lieutenant Ramírez. As explained in the text:

> La que tomó al Teniente Ramírez por la guerrera sin el menor esfuerzo, lo levantó en vilo y lo sacó de la casa sacudiéndolo como un estropajo, era la suave muchacha de quince años y huesos frágiles que poco antes servía harina tostada con miel bajo el porrón. (p. 75)
>
> [*It was the quiet 15-year old girl with fragile bones who shortly before was serving toasted oats with honey by the doorway who grabbed Lieutenant Ramírez by the lapels with the greatest of ease, lifted him into the air and carried him out of the house, shaking him like a ragdoll.*]

Catherine R. Perricone views the action of Evangelina as 'the complete annihilation of Ramírez's military machismo' and '[o]nly by a perverse sexual act can this affront to his machismo be undone', referring in this quotation to the return of the military later that night and Ramírez's subsequent rape and murder of Evangelina.[13] The mystique surrounding Evangelina's trances becomes replaced by the mystery surrounding her subsequent whereabouts. As a disappeared person, or *desaparecida*, Evangelina is spiritually absent, in a form of limbo. The uncertainty around whether she is alive or dead, and indeed uncertainty around all missing people is captured succinctly in a conversation between the General and the Coronel about relatives asking after the location of the *desaparecidos*:

---

13   Catherine R. Perricone, 'Iconic/Metaphoric Dress and Other Nonverbal Signifiers in *De amor y de sombra*', in *Critical Approaches to Isabel Allende's Novels*, pp. 83–96 (p. 86).

Appearance, Disappearance and Displacement

   – Preguntan por sus desaparecidos, mi General.
   – Dígales que no están ni vivos ni muertos. (p. 252)

   [– *They are asking after the disappeared, General.*
     – *Tell them they are neither dead or alive.*]

Evangelina Ranquileo's presence in the text establishes the clash between state and citizen: Ambrose Gordon suggests that '[i]t is as though the pressures and repressions of [Allende's] country were being reflected in [Evangelina]'.[14] Beyond this, there is also subtle criticism of figures and bodies of authority which find a suggested reason for Evangelina's seizures, but never an actual means of helping to stop them. The diversity of diagnoses suggested by authorities is mirrored in the variety of requests made by people who come to witness Evangelina's trances. Ultimately, the answer is never to be found for Evangelina's mysterious, uncontrollable states, as the State itself nullifies the mystery by brutally murdering her.

Enlightenment through *Endarkenment*:[15] The Transformation of Irene Beltrán

Evangelina's disappearance sparks the important changes that irrevocably alter the destiny of Irene Beltrán's life. As mentioned earlier, her mother Beatriz seeks to shield her from the horrors of the dictatorship, but she also wants her to keep up appearances so as not to lose her fiancé Gustavo

---

14   Ambrose Gordon, 'Isabel Allende on Love and Shadow', *Contemporary Literature*, 28 (1987), 530–42 (p. 537).
15   The term is borrowed from Harm de Blij's discussion of ominous shadows being metaphorically cast over the world owing to the rise of religious fundamentalism. It is employed in the present discussion to describe Irene's journey into the murky underworld of torture, death and danger. For a discussion of the original sense of the term, consult *The Power of Place: Geography, Destiny and Globalization's Rough Landscape* (Oxford: Oxford University Press, 2008).

Morante. Irene, however, gradually breaks away from her mother's protective gaze through her journalistic work and her clandestine collaboration with Francisco Leal. Irene's initial links with the military hierarchy through her engagement to Morante weaken as she becomes more involved in the search for the missing Evangelina: the slaughter of the pig one week after witnessing Evangelina's final trance appears to serve as a catalyst for the transformation in Irene. The carnivalesque spectacle of blood and death sparks a significant change in her. Indeed, the language used in the description of the slaughter of the pig is ironically echoed later in the text with reference to Irene herself. The description of the dead pig as having skin which is 'rosada y limpia como la de *un recién nacido*' (p. 107, emphasis added) [*pink and clean like* a newborn baby's (emphasis added)] subtly links with the description of Irene while she is recovering in hospital after she has been gunned down on the street; she calls for Francisco 'con la voz débil y desvalida como *un recién nacido*' (p. 234, emphasis added) [*her voice was thready and she lay there as helpless* as a newborn baby (emphasis added)]. The sacrifice of the pig, which triggers an awakening or rebirth of sorts in Irene about the true horrors of death, is in this way linked with Irene's later decision to sacrifice her life in her homeland to help expose the abuses of the dictatorship. It is noticeable that, after the discussion with Digna and the discovery of Evangelina's disappearance, Irene slowly begins her own metamorphosis: 'sus pupilas se habían tornado oscuras y tristes, del tono de las hojas secas del eucalipto […] estaba perdiendo la inocencia y ya nada podría evitar que se asomara a la verdad' (p. 110) [*her eyes became dark and sad, the hue of dried eucalyptus leaves […] she was losing her innocence and nothing could now stop her from seeing the truth*].

For Irene, the quest to find Evangelina changes her significantly: 'esa santa de dudosos milagros era la frontera ante su mundo ordenado y la región oscura donde nunca pisada' (p. 123) [*this saint of dubious miracles was the border between her ordered world and the dark region where she had never set foot*]. Irene chooses to enter the world of shadows, aided and accompanied on this journey by Francisco; her trip with him to the morgue in search of Evangelina's body is also a life-changing experience. The link between food and death, suggested earlier by the slaughtering of the pig, is again made readily apparent in the text:

> [Francisco e Irene] [v]ieron empleados *mascar su merienda sobre las mesas de autopsia*, otros escuchaban programas deportivos de la radio indiferentes a los despojos tumefactos o jugaban baraja en los depósitos del sótano donde aguardaban los cadáveres del día. (p. 112, emphasis added)
>
> [*Francisco and Irene saw the employees* eat their lunch on the autopsy tables*, while others listened to sports programmes on the radio, indifferent to the tumescent remains, or played cards in the basement morgue where the corpses from that day were waiting.* (emphasis added)]

It is as if the morgue assistants have in some way become inured to the pervasiveness of death, which contrasts starkly with Irene's experience. Irene's 'ojos desencajados' (p. 112) [*wild eyes*] seem to be at the initial shock of exposure rather than a fuller appreciation or realization of the horrors perpetrated in her country, as '[e]l ventarrón del odio la rondaba pero no llegaba a envolverla, preservada por el alto muro tras el cual la criaron' (p. 114) [*the full force of hatred stalked but did not envelope her, preserved as she was by the tall wall behind which she was raised*]. Shortly after their experience of the morgue, Francisco and Irene share their first kiss, their growing intimacy an almost instinctive response for them to the trauma of the morgue. While Irene grows closer to Francisco, she also begins to see a new and potentially more sinister side to her fiancé Captain Gustavo Morante through his association with the military: 'había dos seres diferentes en ese cuerpo atlético tan conocido. Por primera vez tuvo miedo de él y deseó que no regresara jamás' (p. 117) [*there were two different entities in that athletic body which was so familiar to her. For the first time, she was afraid of him and never wanted him to come back*]. Irene's experience of the world of shadows becomes, paradoxically a form of political enlightenment and personal *endarkenment*. Her conflicting feelings about Gustavo and Francisco find their greatest expression at night, when she links together the various forms of appearance and disappearance that have become part of her life outside of La Voluntad de Dios:

> Sentía miedo por las noches, cuando en sueños se le aparecían los cuerpos lívidos de la Morgue, [...] las filas interminables de mujeres preguntando por sus desaparecidos, Evangelina Ranquileo en camisa de dormir y descalza llamando desde las sombras y entre tantos fantasmas ajenos veía también a su padre sumergido en pantanos de odio. (p. 144)
>
> [*She was afraid at night, when the livid bodies of the morgue appeared to her in her dreams [...] the endless lines of women asking after their missing loved ones, Evangelina Ranquileo in her nightgown and barefoot calling from the shadows and, amongst so many unfamiliar ghosts, she also saw her father submerged in a reservoir of hatred.*]

Following a tip-off from Evangelina's adoptive brother, Pradelio, Francisco and Irene go to an abandoned mine in Los Riscos. They tentatively attempt to make light of the situation, convinced that nothing untoward will be found:

> Bromearon con la idea de que todo eso era un juego y trataron de contagiarse uno a otro con la creencia de que nada malo podía ocurrirles, protegidos como estaban por algún espíritu benefactor. (p. 176)
>
> [*They joked about with the idea that it was all a game and they tried to convince each other that nothing bad could happen to them and they were protected by some benevolent spirit.*]

Irene, who, at this stage of the tale is still relatively unversed in dealing with the horrors of life beyond the protective world of order and superficial appearance in which her mother had striven to maintain her, struggles to find a frame of reference for these experiences, finding the only comparable terrifying event in her background in the fairy tales of her childhood: '[e]sa noche ante el boquete de la mina, Irene volvió a sufrir esa mezcla de espanto y atracción de la época remota cuando la nana la aterrorizaba con sus fábulas' (p. 178) [*that night at the entrance to the mine, Irene once again experienced that mix of hatred and attraction like in the distant past when her nanny terrified her with stories*].

The discovery of Evangelina and the numerous other bodies buried there shocks Irene – her reaction actually mirrors Evangelina's final physical state, as Irene '[e]staba descompuesta, muda' (p. 179) [*she was in pieces, silent*]. Irene's stifled emotional reaction reflects the corporeal disintegration of Evangelina, and, as with her experience in the morgue, Irene, unable to articulate the overwhelming sense of terror she is feeling, seeks a form of Kristevian semiotic refuge to avoid the grotesque reality: '[a]unque las palabras carecían de significado para ella, demasiado impresionada para reconocerlas como su propio idioma, la cadencia de la voz [de Francisco] la arrulló consolándola un poco' (p. 180) [*although words lacked meaning for her, as she was too shocked to recognize them as her own language, the cadence of Francisco's voice lulled her and provided some consolation*].[16] Irene and Francisco travel to a shack where they make love and become further transported from the horror of the mine; they enter a private, shared space, and they implicitly endeavour to counter their horrific experience of death with a defiant celebration of life: '[n]o había espacio para otros, lejos se encontraba la fealdad del mundo o la inminencia del fin, solo existía la luz de ese encuentro' (p. 183) [*there was no room for others there; the ugliness of the world and the imminence of the end were far away – there was only the light of their encounter*].

The response of Irene and Francisco to the uncovering of Evangelina's body echoes their previous response during their visit to the morgue in that their intimacy becomes a type of bulwark against death. Their growing love serves as a means of combating the horrors they have witnessed, and within the context of the story, their night together may be construed as a carnivalesque response to horror: it is an apparently incongruous scene to place alongside the gruesome discovery of Evangelina's corpse, but one which may be viewed as a temporary, but necessary displacement of the horrors they had witnessed prior to contacting the Catholic Church, one of the remaining authorities that has not been destroyed by the military

---

16   Julia Kristeva's concept of the *semiotic*, as a form of prelinguistic communication in which the prosodic nature of language supersedes the semanticity of the words employed, is the reference here. Irene seems to recoil from the horror in this instant and retreat into a realm of protection akin to the womb. The subtle irony here may be that she finds protection not with her mother Beatriz but rather with Francisco. For further discussion of Kristeva's work see, for example, Toril Moi's *The Kristeva Reader* (London: Blackwell, 1986).

dictatorship. Their act of love-making is notably a form of temporary festivity in which the living body is celebrated.

Following on from the disclosure of the location of the bodies to the Cardinal, a commission, comprising religious and legal authorities and journalists, visits the mine. The arrival of the commission signals what could be considered the carnivalesque climax of the tale: echoes of the arrival of a variety of authorities to diagnose Evangelina's earlier condition seem to resonate here, and the horror of what they happen upon is reproduced in full here:

> un cuerpo humano de sexo femenino en avanzado estado de descomposición, cubierto con una manta oscura, un zapato, restos de pelo, huesos de una extremidad inferior, un omóplato, un húmero, vértebras, un tronco con ambas extremidades superiores, un pantalón, dos cráneos, uno completo y otro sin mandíbula, una pieza dentaria con tapaduras de metal, más vértebras, restos de costillas, un tronco con trozos de ropa, camisas y medias de diversos colores, una cresta ilíaca y varias osamentas más, todo lo cual completó treinta y ocho bolsas debidamente selladas, numeradas y transportadas a la camioneta. (p. 213)
>
> [*a human body, female, in an advanced state of decomposition, covered with a dark sheet, a shoe, hair remains, bones from a lower limb, a scapula, a humerus, vertebrae, a trunk with both upper limbs, a pair of trousers, two skulls – one complete and one lacking a jaw, a set of teeth with metal fillings, more vertebrae, remnants of ribs, a trunk with clothes in a ragged state, shirts and socks of various colours, a pelvis and several other bones, all in all it filled thirty-eight bags which were duly sealed, numbered and transported to the truck.*]

One of the most striking features of the gruesome list is the move from the identifiable, individual and integral – the body of Evangelina Ranquileo – through to the list of body parts and pieces of clothing of other people, including her father and four brothers: Ambrose Gordon perceptively notes that 'Evangelina is one of the very few disappeared who reappears' (p. 539). The list of names calls to mind the carnivalesque concept of 'dismemberment',[17] and the body parts uncovered all in a sense expose further instances of torture. As each body part is mentioned, uncovered

---

17   Vice, p. 159.

and recorded, the full extent of the horrors of the dictatorship is exposed. Each is a damning indictment of the tactics employed by the military. The seemingly excessive list provided in the text by Allende parallels the excesses of the totalitarian regime in an effort to suppress any dissidence. Attempts to alleviate the gravity of the situation when uncovering the bodies of the disappeared are unsuccessful:

> Alguien hizo la broma macabra de que si escarbaban un poco más surgirían esqueletos de conquistadores, momias de incas y fósiles de Cromagnon, pero nadie sonrió porque la pesadumbre se había instalado en todos los ánimos. (p. 213)
>
> [*Someone made a macabre joke that if they dug a little deeper they would find skeletons of Conquistadors, Inca mummies and Cro-Magnon fossils; however, nobody smiled because sorrow had taken seed in them.*]

The emphasis here is on the fact that these are actually bodies from the very *recent* past, the victims of horrors perpetrated by the *current* regime. The response of the military to the news and to the requests that relatives be given an opportunity to attempt to identify loved ones provides another carnivalesque twist. The General angrily states to the Colonel:

> Una cosa es desenterrar cadáveres y otra muy distinta exhibirlos para que todo el mundo los vea *como si esto fuera una feria*, qué se han imaginado estos pendejos, *échele tierra a este asunto*, Coronel, antes que se me acabe la paciencia. (p. 215, emphasis added)
>
> [*It's one thing unearthing corpses and quite another putting them on display for everyone to see* as if this were a show; *what were those fools thinking*, bury that business, Colonel, before I lose my patience. (emphasis added)]

The General dismisses the possibility of allowing the victims to be identified, equating such an opportunity with a sideshow. Furthermore, his suggestion that the problem be buried again implies the regime is trapped in a cycle of perpetrating acts and employing the same tactics as a means of trying to make the problem disappear. The regime is trapped in a vicious circle.

Following the discovery of the buried bodies, Beatriz notices a transformation in Irene, and mistakenly believes that she has 'peste' (p. 216) [*the plague*]. Again, however, Beatriz appears blind to the realities of death. When she reads aloud part of an article in the local newspaper, she implicitly subscribes to the opinion expressed therein: '[l]o importante es avanzar en el camino del progreso procurando cicatrizar heridas y superar animosidades, para lo cual no ayuda la rebusca de cadáveres' (p. 217) [*what is important is to move forward on the road to progress by trying to heal wounds and get over old animosities, which is not helped by this search for bodies*]. However, despite the continuing outward appearance of ignorance, Beatriz does suspect that her daughter's condition is down to something other than problems with love: 'la causa de esa alergia no era un problema amoroso, sino de otra índole' (p. 218) [*the cause of this allergy wasn't love, but something altogether different*]. Irene, in the meantime, continues on her quest to uncover the excesses of the military, and arranges to meet Sergeant Rivera. Recalling the earlier link between the sacrifice of the pig after the disappearance of Evangelina, Evangelina's imaginative reappearance is described while Rivera is eating. Irene finds it difficult not to associate the food that Rivera is eating with Evangelina's decomposing body: '[a]penas [Rivera] se llevaba algo a la boca [Irene] volvía a ver el cuerpo en descomposición' (p. 221) [*when Rivera went to put something in his mouth, Irene could once again visualize the decomposing body*]. The end of Rivera's description of how he imagines Ramírez finally killing Evangelina coincides with him 'chupando los últimos huesos del almuerzo' (p. 224) [*sucking the last few bones of his lunch*]. This becomes a key turning point in the story – shortly following their conversation, Rivera is murdered and Irene is then shot outside the magazine office and rushed to hospital.

Before Irene is shot, she meets Evangelina Flores, the real Evangelina Ranquileo, had they not been switched at birth. The growing prominence of Flores in the text also suggests a resurrection of sorts for Evangelina Ranquileo: when Flores tells her story to Irene, she is aware of having been switched at birth, and states that Ranquileo was 'la que ocupó su destino por error y murió en su lugar' (p. 227) [*the one who fulfilled her destiny by mistake and died instead of her*]. Flores is aware of the special shared bond with Ranquileo:

Appearance, Disappearance and Displacement

> [Evangelina] supo que la desaparecida era más que una hermana, era ella misma cambiada, era su vida que la otra estaba viviendo y sería su propia muerte la que Evangelina Ranquileo muriera. Tal vez en ese instante de lucidez Evangelina Flores asumió la carga que después la llevaría por el mundo pidiendo justicia. (p. 110)

> [*Evangelina knew that the missing woman was more than a sister; it was her, changed, it was her life which the other had been living and it would be her own death which Evangelina Ranquileo had experienced. Perhaps in that moment of clarity Evangelina Flores took on the role which would later take over all around the world in the search for justice.*]

After being shot, Irene hangs on to life by a thread. The description of the doctors' efforts to save her life ironically suggests that they are harming her rather than saving her, in consonance with the earlier description of medical professionals at the time of the birth of both Evangelinas:

> Le *atosigaron* de antibióticos y por último la *crucificaron* sobre una cama con el suplicio permanente de las sondas, manteniéndola sumida en la niebla de la inconsciencia para que soportara su *martirio*. (p. 231, emphasis added)

> [*They* plied *her with antibiotics and finally* crucified *her on a bed with the endless torture of the catheters, keeping her trapped deep in the fog of unconsciousness so she could tolerate her* martyrdom. (emphasis added).]

By her bedside, Francisco summons up the memory of their intimacy to comfort himself: '[e]xorcizó a la fatalidad con el recuerdo de su goce, oponiendo a las tinieblas de la agonía la luz de su encuentro' (p. 233) [*he exorcized misfortune with the memory of their pleasure, juxtaposing the darkness of dying with the light of their encounter*]. The memory of their physical relationship sustains him against the horrors of the dictatorship, and his personal and passionate response highlights the juxtaposition between their intimacy and communication and the dictatorship of silence and surreptitiousness. Beatriz, however, has no such sustenance, and the signs of weariness begin to show, albeit temporarily, in a carnivalesque metamorphosis: 'tenía la cara estragada, nada quedaba de su maquillaje y eran visibles las finas cicatrices de su cirugía plástica, sus ojos estaban hinchados, el pelo lacio de sudor y la blusa arrugada' (p. 233) [*her face was ruined; none of her makeup remained and the fine lines from her cosmetic work could be seen. Her eyes were puffy, her hair limp with sweat and her blouse creased*]. In order to escape from the hospital, Francisco and Irene must sacrifice their outer identities. Mario, a local hairdresser, visits the hospital with his 'maletín de las transformaciones' (p. 248) [*magic bag of transformative tricks*] and magically reinvents the couple's appearance: '[l]os jóvenes se miraron asombrados, sin reconocerse bajo esas máscaras, sonriendo incrédulos porque con ese nuevo aspecto casi deberían aprender a amarse desde el principio' (p. 248) [*the young people looked at each other, shocked, unable to recognize each other with those masks, smiling disbelieving because with these new appearances they would practically have to learn to love each other all over again*]. These temporary aliases are to be their passport out of the country.

Mario subsequently goes to visit Beatriz, who has discovered that her husband Eusebio had actually gone to live in the Caribbean of his own free will and had disappeared to escape, amongst other things, 'los reproches de su mujer' (p. 240) [*his wife's reproaches*]. Beatriz remains trapped in routine, 'refugiada en una elegancia de ritos y fórmulas' (p. 249) [*finding refuge in the elegance of ritual and formula*]. Mario, however, sees something altogether more grotesque when he looks at her: '[l]a imagen esbelta enfundada en seda y gamuza, le resultó engañosa, como reflejada en un espejo de feria' (p. 250) [*her svelte, suede- and silk-wrapped image looked deceptive to him, as if it was reflected in a fairground mirror*]. Indeed, despite her appearance, Mario believes she now has more in common with the elderly residents of La Voluntad de Dios than with her daughter: '[Mario] [l]a imaginó a la deriva sobre una balsa con sus ancianos olvidados y decrépitos en un mar inmóvil. Como ellos, Beatriz estaba fuera de la realidad, había perdido su lugar en este mundo' (p. 250) [*Mario imagined her adrift on a raft with the forgotten, decrepit elderly residents on an unmoving sea. Like them, Beatriz was outside reality – she had lost her place in this world*].

The combination of the testimony by Evangelina Flores and the recordings made by Irene of her conversations with Sergeant Rivera contribute to Ramírez and his men being convicted of homicide. The ruling, however, is surprisingly overturned by 'un decreto de amnistía improvisado en el último instante' (p. 254) [*a decree of amnesty improvised at the last minute*]. The anger on the part of the country's citizens is vented through the killing of a pig dressed as a general – all that is left following the public's display of outrage is 'un charco de sangre negra donde navegaban sus insignias, su quepis y su capa de tirano' (p. 254) [*a pool of black blood where his medals, cap and tyrannical cloak floated*]. The inextricable links between bloodshed and the dictatorship are again forged in the text, this time through a public spectacle that communicates the growing awareness of injustice by all citizens.

The final sacrifice made by Francisco and Irene in the text is to leave their homeland, which is a price that they have to pay for their determination to ensure that the truth about the military dictatorship is revealed. They leave their home and, now disguised, assume another shared identity, as exiles, and they 'formaban parte de esa inmensa oleada trashumante propia de su tiempo: desterrados, emigrantes, exilados, refugiados' (p. 256) [*were part of that immense wave of people moving of that time: displaced, emigrants, exiles, refugees*]. Through their actions at home and in exile, Francisco and Irene strive to ensure that the past of the *desaparecidos* is uncovered, alongside the exposure of the military government's participation. By sacrificing their future in their homeland, and by choosing exile, they help the loved ones of the *desaparecidos* to achieve a degree of reconciliation with their past, and further illustrate the abuses of authoritarianism. Irene's transformation is complete.

'¿Falsedades y contradicciones'?[18]
Carnivalesque Coherence in *De amor y de sombra*

This chapter has aimed to demonstrate that *De amor y de sombra* provides a detailed description of the abuses and excesses suffered by citizens living under a military regime. A carnivalesque reading of the text has sought

---

18   Gabriela Mora, 'Las novelas de Isabel Allende y el papel de la mujer como ciudadana', *Ideologies and Literature*, 2.1 (1987), 53–61 (p. 58).

to highlight how Allende's text pays tribute to the efforts of those who risked their own safety to expose and uncover the fate of the *desaparecidos*, and to make the past of these people an important topic in the present, thus in a sense *re-presenting* the past through its textual representation. The decision to move away from a strict testimonial documenting of Lonquén, and to introduce a very deliberate degree of *falsedad* [*falsehood*], to paraphrase Mora's comment, allows Allende to present a fictional work which nevertheless testifies to the horrors experienced by the *desaparecidos* and their loved ones throughout South America. In addition, she offers a tale of cooperation across the classes which is more important than being restricted to specific coordinates and a specific incident. By refusing to privilege the Lonquén event, Allende provides a voice for all the displaced and disappeared, unmooring the text from an exclusively Chilean context.

Characterization in *De amor y de sombra* also illustrates Allende's subtle analysis of the nature of authority: initially, Evangelina Ranquileo and Evangelina Flores are both victims of hospital authorities unwilling to accept they have made a mistake, and their lives become inextricably linked through their own direct experiences with authority and injustice. In the text, Francisco's father, Professor Leal, suggests that Ranquileo 'era sólo el producto anormal de esta sociedad desquiciada. La pobreza, el concepto del pecado, el deseo sexual reprimido y el aislamiento provocaban su mal' (p. 98) [*was merely an abnormal product of this unhinged society. Poverty, sin, repressed sexual desire and isolation caused her illness*]. Evangelina Ranquileo becomes a vehicle for the examination of the failings of figures of authority and she is, in Levine's view, 'a representation of disruptive forces in Chile'.[19] The determination on the part of military, medical and religious authorities to appropriate and interpret Evangelina according to each authority's beliefs creates a confusing, carnivalesque mix. Evangelina's trances constitute a threat to the rigidity of order, and indeed directly challenge military order through her encounter with Ramírez. As discussed earlier, the Lieutenant avenges his public display of humiliation

---

19   Levine, p. 42.

by secretly raping and murdering Evangelina: in a gruesome and grotesque echo of the scene, Allende's harrowing description of Evangelina's rape and murder calls to mind an important facet of Bakhtin's grotesque realism, that is, *degradation*: this concept draws links between 'contact with the earth' and 'the lower stratum of the body [...] relat[ing] to acts of defecation and copulation, conception, pregnancy, and birth'.[20] Evangelina's life and death are closely linked with degradation, from her birth, through to her trances, disappearance, rape, murder and crude burial. Allende's own twist on degradation is expressed in the text through Francisco and Irene's love-making, which has been argued in this chapter to act as a way of temporarily staving off the horror of the discovery of the *desaparecidos*. Furthermore, in another carnivalesque twist, the revelation of the military's role in the murder of Evangelina leads not to *degradation* for Ramírez, but rather *promotion* for his efforts.

Nevertheless, the angelic resonances in Evangelina's name also suggest otherworldliness, and, despite her violent death at the hands of the military, she becomes the catalyst for the rebirth both of her namesake, Evangelina Flores, the *real* Evangelina Ranquileo and of Irene Beltrán. While Ranquileo ultimately suffers a fate shared by many members of her biological family, the Flores', Evangelina Flores becomes a spokesperson for the abuses of both her adoptive and biological families through her testimony at the military trial. Indeed, while both Evangelinas are victims of authority, it is the actions of figures in authority that ultimately lead to the exposure of the truth: the switching at birth means that Flores has the opportunity to live and to speak out against the military, and her biological background also shows that Evangelina Ranquileo does actually live on, despite the military's attempts to silence her.

Irene's carnivalesque transformation echoes a number of issues discussed by Bakhtin in *Problems of Dostoevsky's Poetics* – as in carnival, Irene becomes an active participant in life, breaking out of the social stasis in which her mother revels and undergoes metamorphosis, initially through

20 Vice, p. 155.

her 'free and familiar contact' with the elderly residents.²¹ Her defiance of the military and her rejection of Morante illustrate her move away from childhood and the strictures of hierarchy, and her recording of Rivera's testimony provides a carnivalesque twist to the tale through her use of military tactics to expose their excesses. Her suffering and self-sacrifice suggest a further 'bringing down to earth' with the attack on her body, while the use of disguise helps to ensure a rebirth, albeit ultimately in exile.²²

Throughout the text, the putative power of the military is continually challenged: as Elías Miguel Muñoz explains, the military's voice 'es expuesta y contestada [...] por medio de los hechos no-oficiales (la mina) y el espacio social (la ciudad), y especialmente por la toma de conciencia política a la que llega Irene' [*is exposed and contested [...] through the unofficial facts (the mine), social space (the city) and especially by Irene's political awakening*].²³ The tactics employed by the military are also used against them, as mentioned in the previous paragraph, when Irene records the testimony of Sergeant Rivera and spies on him. Indeed, there is an underground network of collaboration that the military are ignorant of throughout the text: for example, one of the inhabitants of La Voluntad de Dios, Josefina Bianchi, also comes to play a key role in exposing the excesses of the military. Throughout the text she is presented as an aging, delusional character, trapped in her lost past of celebrity. However, it is the concealment of the tapes recorded by Irene that illustrates her crucial importance in helping expose the actions of the military. The military had mistakenly believed that all the residents of La Voluntad de Dios 'estaban al margen de la vida y por lo tanto también de la política' (p. 235) [*were at the fringes of life and therefore also the fringes of politics*]. Josefina's final performance has significant political impact. Irene confides in her and, beneath the apparent veneer of entrapment in a circle of celebrity, Josefina safely protects the tapes until Francisco can come to claim them:

---

21   Vice, p. 152.
22   Ibid., p. 152.
23   Elías Miguel Muñoz, 'La voz testimonial de Isabel Allende en *De amor y de sombra*', in *Critical Approaches to Isabel Allende's Novels*, pp. 61–72 (p. 62).

'lo que empezó como un juego terminó cumpliendo un propósito y las grabaciones no sólo se salvaron de la curiosidad de Beatriz Alcántara, sino también de la requisición policial' (p. 246) [*what began as a game ended up fulfilling a purpose – the recordings were not only kept away from Beatriz Alcántara's curious eyes, but also out of reach of the police search*]. In addition, Mario makes use of his skills as hairdresser and make-up artist to disguise Francisco and Irene, to cover up their present states and to ensure their safe passage out of the hospital and subsequently out of the country. He, like Josefina, though a marginal character in the text, also colludes in exposing the excesses of the military.

The military in the text, having displaced democratically elected representatives to assume power, are themselves displaced through their presentation in *De amor y de sombra*. They are parodied through their response to the pamphlet distributed by Francisco's father, Professor Leal, when they mistakenly summon the author of the text, a Russian revolutionary, Mikhail Bakunin to present himself, and through the content of the pamphlet. Within this document, 'todas esa tonterías infantiles que ocupan buena parte de su existencia y les haría parecer *payasos* si no estuviesen siempre amenazantes, todo ello les separa de la sociedad' (p. 193, emphasis added) [*all those childish acts of stupidity which take up a good part of their existence and would make them seem like* clowns *if they were not always threatening – all of this separates them from society* (emphasis added)]. This is perhaps one of the few true examples of Bakhtinian 'folk carnival humour' in the text.[24]

Allende also cleverly illustrates subversion through the presentation of a range of characters that defy military authority, though they pay dearly for their acts of insubordination. The horrific violence and attempted cover-ups perpetrated by the military are juxtaposed with the humanity and cooperation of characters such as Sergeant Rivera and the transformation of Irene's former lover, Gustavo Morante. Allende is careful to show the violent nature of the military in repressing dissent even within its own ranks, when Rivera is knocked down and killed and when Morante is shot dead. Rivera's powerful testimony plays an important part in bringing

---

24 Vice, p. 151.

Ramírez to trial, despite the later improvised amnesty. Their attempts to assert power are undermined time and again by their own actions and by the network of collaboration.

In keeping with the carnivalesque feel of the text, not all forms of authority are shown to be bad. The presentation of the Catholic Church is an interesting feature of the text: while normally portrayed as a bastion of patriarchy, it is presented in this text as a dynamic and largely positive force. Despite the changes in hierarchy through the military's appropriation of political power, the Catholic Church retains a privileged place in society. This position paradoxically appears to allow it to enjoy simultaneously a peripheral position, evidenced in the text through its underground efforts with the Vicaría de la Solidaridad [*Vicariate of Solidarity*] organization. The Godly fear that the leaders of the military maintain allows for the Catholic Church to act with relative impunity in the text, and the military's acceptance of the Church's place in society actually serves to destabilize and threaten the military's assumed position. The Catholic Church is at once marginal, central and outside the system, its carnivalesque displacement aiding the efforts to displace the military.

The rejection of maternal authority in the text, exemplified in Irene's move away from a privileged to a perilous position in society, completes her transformation in the text, while Francisco's move away from his mother Hilda allows him to move closer to Irene. Their combined efforts illustrate the power of the periphery in *De amor y de sombra*, and while, in true carnivalesque nature, their success appears temporary with the introduction of the amnesty and the fact that they have to escape the country as fugitives, the suggestion in the text is that many more will take up the fight against the dictatorship, evidenced by the public's dismembering of a pig dressed as a general towards the close of the text. The combined efforts of exiles, citizens, the Catholic Church and members of the military all serve to problematize military authority in the text, and this conflict illustrates the usefulness of a carnivalesque reading, in which subversive efforts ensure the displaced past is made present.

This reading of the text has sought to illustrate the fundamental coherence underpinning a novel that combines *amor* [love] and *sombra* [shadow]. Allende carefully contemplates the effects of internal political displacement on society, and the underground efforts to defy the newly installed dictatorial regime. While there is a groundswell of support that seeks to expose the abuses, the novel remains open-ended, a reflection perhaps of Allende's own views on her country's situation at the time of writing in the early nineteen eighties. The attempt to articulate experiences of displacement, and the interplay between language and silence are the subjects of the next chapter on *Eva Luna* and *Cuentos de Eva Luna*.

CHAPTER 4

Displacing Language: Secondary Orality and Silence in *Eva Luna* and *Cuentos de Eva Luna*

> Some people can sing; others can run; I can tell stories. Storytelling is a way of preserving the memory of the past and keeping alive legends, myths, superstitions, and history that are not in the textbooks – the real stories of people and countries.
> — ISABEL ALLENDE[1]

> If the author leaves events unexplained, the reader feels cheated. But if you explain too much, you explain away.
> — HILARY MANTEL[2]

Introduction

The carnivalesque reading of *De amor y de sombra* offered in the preceding chapter highlighted an underlying coherence to a novel which many critics had dismissed for its unhappy marrying together of regime abuses and hope. This chapter looks at the question of displacement from a linguistic perspective, and the opening epigraphs provide a useful indication of

---

1   Isabel Allende in interview with Alvin P. Sanoff, 'Modern Politics, Modern Fables', *US News & World Report*, 21 November 1988, in *Conversations with Isabel Allende*, p. 103.
2   Hilary Mantel, 'Ghost Writing', *The Guardian*, 28 July 2007, <http://www.guardian.co.uk/books/2007/jul/28/edinburghfestival2007.poetry> [accessed 18 June 2012].

the approach to this issue here: the first statement, by Allende, illustrates some of the key concerns underpinning her narrative, such as the primacy of storytelling, the crucial importance of recording and preserving the vibrant, though stifled, unofficial and often unwritten histories of people removed either geographically or socially from the mainstream and the vitality of collective memory. The importance of storytelling for Allende is traced in two texts here, that is, her 1987 novel, *Eva Luna*, and her 1989 short-story collection, *Cuentos de Eva Luna*. In relation to the overall concept of displacement, it is argued here that Allende has moved away from the national concerns of her homeland Chile, broached in the previous two chapters, into a more general exploration of place and displacement, with the issue of individuals and communities displaced from the original homelands gradually playing a greater role in her work. In these two texts, it is suggested that Allende celebrates the importance of oral language, and at the same time subverts the primacy of the written word. She achieves this by highlighting the enduring importance of oral language in a literate world in *Eva Luna*, and she maintains her focus on the struggle between the mainstream and the margins by looking at the wrestling for control of radio and television broadcasts. The contention is that while in the development of Allende's eponymous heroine literacy becomes a vital tool in her means of expression, it is nevertheless the underlying importance of a tradition of oral storytelling, explored in the present discussion through theorist Walter J. Ong's notion of *secondary orality*, that is the more crucial element in her development. It is argued that Eva's acquisition of literacy helps her to harness her talent for storytelling, seemingly inherited from her mother, Consuelo. The skill of literacy is a feature that harnesses the talent of orality.

Second, Allende also manages to explore the power of oral language, in a somewhat unconventional manner, by calling attention to what happens to individuals and communities in its absence in *Cuentos de Eva Luna*. The second epigraph in this chapter, by novelist Hilary Mantel in relation to writing ghost stories, appears to be a view shared by Allende in this collection. This part of the chapter seeks to identify the various instances and functions of silence in the collection, concentrating on four of the tales to support this stance. The conclusion considers the apparent gaps and omissions throughout *Cuentos de Eva Luna*, and argues that, through the medium of the written word, Allende ironically seeks to displace written language by omitting key pieces of information in certain tales, such as the two words whispered by Belisa Crepusculario to El Coronel in the tale 'Dos palabras' [*Two Words*]. In this way, these crucial pieces of dialogue retain their mystique by never being written down, and Allende displaces the medium of written communication by reference to the abiding importance of oral communication. These words remain part of the spoken realm of the tale.

Both *Eva Luna* and *Cuentos de Eva Luna* have already generated critical debate about language and storytelling: for example, in *Eva Luna*, Ester Gimbernat de González highlights the fundamental importance of the narrator's acquisition of literacy, and how this helps to develop the narrator's voice, arguing that '[l]a voz oral de la contadora de cuentos se amarra, se fija al sentarse la narradora y enfrentarse a la página escrita' [*the storyteller's voice becomes moored and fixed when the narrator sits down and faces the page to write*].³ Marcelo Coddou also considers Allende's approach to the importance of oral language in the text, and argues that *Eva Luna* comprises a series of layers, that is, 'lo que acontece, lo que se imagina la protagonista (que es narradora) que le acontece y, en imaginarse, al proceso de construcción y/o reconstrucción del relato de sus peripecias' [*what happens, what the protagonist (who is the narrator) imagines happens to her and, by imagining herself in these scenarios, the process of constructing and/or reconstructing the tale of her adventures*].⁴ Finally, Edna Aguirre Rehbein argues that this layered approach to plot subsequently calls into question the textual reality that is presented: '[i]ntertextuality and self-reflexivity [in the text] creates various levels of fictionalization leading

3   Ester Gimbernat de González, 'Entre principio y final: La madre/material de la escritura en *Eva Luna*', in *Critical Approaches to Isabel Allende's Novels*, ed. by Sonia Riquelme Rojas and Edna Aguirre Rehbein (New York: Peter Lang, 1991), pp. 111–24 (p. 121).
4   Marcelo Coddou, 'Dimensión paródica de *Eva Luna*', in *Critical Approaches to Isabel Allende's Novels*, ed. by Sonia Riquelme Rojas and Edna Aguirre Rehbein (New York: Peter Lang, 1991), pp. 139–49 (p. 144).

the reader to question "reality" within this fictional setting'.[5] These critics have highlighted, then, the links between language, reality and narrative in *Eva Luna*, as well as the constant slippage between fact and fiction in the novel.

Critical discussion in relation to language in *Cuentos de Eva Luna* has paid close attention to the influence of the *Thousand and One Nights*: Linda Gould Levine contends that the framework of this collection of tales 'evokes [...] a feminist connection and woman's right to appropriate words'.[6] Stephen M. Hart suggests that '[i]n their combination of fairy-tale, drama, exoticism, and romance, [the *Thousand and One Nights*] offers a perfect formula for what Allende sees as the important ingredients of a good story'.[7] Stephen Gregory is less convinced by Allende's writing and her appropriation of the *Thousand and One Nights*, and he argues that '[t]he emphasis on pleasure carries over into the stories themselves and endangers Allende's ability to articulate duly other social or political concerns'.[8] In addition, and as mentioned already in Chapter 1, *Cuentos de Eva Luna* has often been overlooked in critical discussions of Allende's work: for example, Donald L. Shaw states that the stories in *Cuentos de Eva Luna* 'seem marginal to Allende's mainstream development as a writer of fiction and as a representative of the Post-Boom', although he does suggest that the presentation of the story 'Un camino hacia el norte' ['*A Road North*'], which describes the ruthless exploitation of impoverished Latin American families by organizations purporting to offer their children a better life in the United States but who actually use these children to harvest organs, echoes in a way the committed nature of her earlier fiction.[9] The present

---

[5] Edna Aguirre Rehbein, 'Isabel Allende's *Eva Luna* and the Act/Art of Narrating', in *Critical Approaches to Isabel Allende's Novels*, pp. 179–90 (p. 180).
[6] Levine, *Isabel Allende* pp. 77–8.
[7] Stephen M. Hart, *Allende: Eva Luna and Cuentos de Eva Luna* (London: Grant & Cutler, 2003), p. 52.
[8] Stephen Gregory, 'Scheherazade and Eva Luna: Problems in Allende's Storytelling', *Bulletin of Spanish Studies*, 80 (2003), 81–102 (p. 93).
[9] Donald L. Shaw, *The Post-Boom in Spanish American Fiction* (Albany: State University of New York Press, 1998), p. 68.

discussion suggests that the collection is a key precursor to her subsequent and more concerted examinations of cultural displacement in the novels which are discussed in Chapter 5.[10]

'Ábranse las páginas sonoras del aire':[11] Secondary Orality in *Eva Luna*

The touchstone for any examination of orality, and the theoretical underpinning to this section, is Walter J. Ong's *Orality and Literacy* (1982), and a brief summary of some key points made by Ong that are relevant to the present discussion will be first offered here.[12] Ong's seminal text draws out the clear distinctions between oral cultures and literate cultures, focusing in particular on issues relating to consciousness and cognition. His in-depth analysis also explores possible textual echoes of orality in works such as Homer's *The Iliad*, and in work undertaken by ethnographers, anthropologists and linguists with oral communities still extant throughout the world.

---

10   In critical terms, Helene Carol Weldt-Basson has devoted a section of a chapter on Allende's work to the question of silence, but her focus is somewhat different to what is presented in this discussion: she argues that '[i]n contrast to Allende's novels, *The Stories of Eva Luna* rely less on agon fueled by silence and more on the use of irony and hyperbole as silent strategies to suggest a feminist reading'. While Weldt-Basson does explore a selection of stories in relation to silence, in particular the role of hyperbolic silence, the emphasis in this discussion, and the second section of this chapter, will be on the key role played by silence in relation to individuals' conflicting relationships with communities. See Weldt-Basson's 'Hyperbolic Silence: Agon and Irony in the Works of Isabel Allende', in *Subversive Silences: Nonverbal Expression and Implicit Narrative Strategies in the Works of Latin American Women Writers* (Madison, NJ: Fairleigh Dickinson University, 2009), pp. 104–37.
11   Isabel Allende, *Eva Luna*, 5th edn (Barcelona: Plaza & Janés, 1993), p. 104. Further references will appear parenthetically in the text. The translation is [*Let the sonorous pages of the airwaves open before you*].
12   Walter J. Ong, *Orality and Literacy* (London: Routledge, 1982).

He identifies a range of features common to oral narratives, including the pervasiveness of formulaic language, repetition and redundancy, all features which serve to help the audience follow the narrative. The term *orality* is not merely a synonym for *oral language*: it is, in Ong's words, '[t]hought and its verbal expression in a society where literacy is less prominent or non-existent' (p. 1). Ong describes how in primary oral or pre-literate cultures, people lived in close-knit communities and rarely moved away from these groups. The acquisition of knowledge, the preserve of the elders of each community, was gained through apprenticeship, and preserved through oral storytelling, a combination of education and entertainment often performed for the community at large. Oral cultures were, to use Ong's term, 'homeostatic' (p. 46), meaning that their oral narratives were very much related to the community in the present. With the introduction of writing, and later print, these features of communities began to change: the reification of knowledge led to a concomitant change in the position of the elders, respect for whom, in Ong's opinion, diminished significantly. The preservation of knowledge through writing, then, could be argued to have created a *dehumanizing* and perhaps even a *democratizing* of knowledge, as once people had access to books – and could read, of course – then they could access and disseminate a diverse range of knowledge. Another interesting shift can also be perceived in the move away from shared knowledge in oral communities to the possibility of acquiring knowledge through one's own personal selection of reading. Of course, Ong does not present a discussion which seeks outright to decry the demise of oral cultures; his analysis also makes extensive reference to the many advantages of print culture, such as the development of abstract, analytical thought, and the dissemination of knowledge no longer strictly bound in time and space. He also notes how in print culture the word becomes reified and fixed. Two other competing elements can also be gleaned from Ong's analysis: on the one hand, the development of a historical consciousness could be seen, with the documenting of generations replacing the homeostatic oral narratives which, as mentioned earlier, would gradually become shorn of information not deemed relevant to the culture of the time. On the other hand, the availability of knowledge also led to the possibility of change, as structured knowledge spread more rapidly and could be shared across cultures and languages.

Ong also makes reference to developments in relation to the mass media, and the apparent reintroduction of essentially oral forms of communication: he coins the term *secondary orality* in order to distinguish these forms of communication from the *primary* orality of pre- and non-literate cultures. Secondary orality is described as 'essentially a more deliberate and self-conscious orality, based permanently on the use of writing and print, which are essential for the manufacture and operation of the equipment and for its use as well' (p. 134). Secondary orality, then, is a post-literate phenomenon, which on the one hand takes advantages of the benefits afforded by the development of print culture, such as the changes in consciousness and the ability to store greater amounts of knowledge with the introduction of print, but which also displays features of the pre-literate era. The term *secondary orality*, then, makes reference to a reconfigured form of orality, rather than it being considered of lesser importance. In addition, the codification of oral language allows for feedback and commentary for those not necessarily present when, say, a speech is being given. The speech, then, to follow this example, can be recorded and in this way be preserved, reviewed and commented upon by those who had not heard it first-hand. The content of these utterances becomes in a way more durable and less evanescent in secondary orality, unmoored from its inherent spatio-temporal constraints, and becomes an extremely powerful tool for disseminating ideas, opinions and comments. Thus while technological advances such as radio and television, two frequently cited instances of secondary orality and the focus of this section, still lack the immediacy of primary oral communication, there is still the possibility of participation, and the capacity to hear and analyse speeches again.

In relation to *Eva Luna*, secondary orality is pervasive and indeed one of the few constants in the life of the eponymous heroine and her development from young girl to television scriptwriter. Two main examples may be examined in the text, that is, radio and television. Radio plays a number of crucial functions in the novel: first, it is an ambiguous medium which can serve both to promote and undermine authority. During Eva's early years with her mother, Consuelo, in the house of the eminent, though eccentric foreign scientist Professor Jones, the radio appears to be a mere adornment, a reflection of Professor Jones's general disengagement from contemporary society as he embalms bodies and works industriously on a cure for cancer:

> Allí había una radio para enterarse de las noticias, pero rara vez se encendía, sólo se escuchaban los discos de ópera que el patrón ponía en su flamante vitrola. Tampoco llegaban periódicos, sólo revistas científicas, porque el sabio era indiferente a los hechos que ocurrían en el país o en el mundo, mucho más interesado en los conocimientos abstractos, los registros de la historia o los pronósticos de un futuro hipotético, que en las emergencias vulgares del presente. (pp. 18–19)
>
> [*There was a radio to find out about the news; however, it was rarely switched on. All that could be heard were the opera records which the boss played on his resplendent gramophone. Papers never made it there either, only scientific journals, because the wise man was indifferent to what happened nationally or internationally, and was much more interested in abstract knowledge, historical records or predictions of a hypothetical future, than in the vulgar problems of the present.*]

When the Professor falls ill and is confined to his room, the atmosphere in the house changes significantly, as the servants appropriate the domestic space, and play the radio non-stop, a gesture of defiance perhaps against the Professor's determination to keep the outside world at a distance and a foretaste of how the media is used as an arena for conflict between authorities and subversives: 'pasaban el día con una radio encendida donde atronaban los boleros, las cumbias y las rancheras' (p. 53) [*they spent the day with the radio on, with boleros, cumbias and rancheras blasting out*].

Although the Professor has little use for the radio, political authorities do make use of it; following the death of the dictator, for example, the government makes a radio broadcast in an effort to restore order. As can be inferred from this, the radio can be a key way of transmitting a particular, and sometimes distorted view of the political reality of the country. Indeed, as the political situation changes in the unnamed Caribbean country, a group of students at one stage make use of radio in order to broadcast their own message of defiance against the regime: '[l]os estudiantes ocuparon los liceos y las facultades, tomaron rehenes, asaltaron una radio y llamaron al pueblo a lanzarse a la calle' (p. 166) [*students occupied secondary schools and universities and took hostages; they seized a radio station and called on*

Displacing Language

people to take to the streets]. '[L]as radios clandestinas' (p. 172) [*clandestine radios*] are also used by Eva's first love interest, and later dissident, Huberto Naranjo and his guerrilla fighters as a means of disseminating information about their efforts to free prisoners from the Santa María penal colony. The ambivalence around the use of radio by both authorities and subversives in the novel is clear when it is revealed that '[l]a lucha [de los guerrilleros] sólo era mencionada en las radios clandestinas, que daban a conocer las acciones de la guerrilla' (p. 222) [*the guerrilla fighters' struggle was only mentioned on clandestine radio stations, which broadcast all guerrilla activity*]. As Aravena, the Director of National Television, says to Rolf Carlé, '[r]ecibimos toda la información censurada, el Gobierno miente y las radios subversivas también' (p. 219) [*all the information we receive is censored; the Government lies and so do the subversive radio stations*]. Towards the end of the text, the influence of the radio is clear: 'la barahúnda que se armó en todo el país cuando las radios de la guerrilla comenzaron a difundir las voces de los prófugos lanzando consignas revolucionarias y mofándose de las autoridades' (p. 283) [*the ruckus caused throughout the country when guerrilla-controlled radio stations began to broadcast rebels' voices shouting revolutionary slogans and mocking authorities*].

For *Eva Luna*, radio also has a significant influence on her personal and professional development: initially, it is a source of much diverse information, a substitute for her late mother, Consuelo, and it serves the dual purpose of entertaining and educating her. For example, in her first meeting with Huberto Naranjo, after she has defiantly escaped from one of her many employers, she draws on radio programmes when she devises a story which she barters for food. While working alongside the cook Elvira, the radio is Eva's constant companion, and she learns songs, some rudimentary English, and follows all the *radionovelas* [*radio soap operas*]. It is, as she later reveals, her 'fuente de inspiración' [*source of inspiration*] (p. 72). The radio also serves to bring Eva and Elvira closer, as they discuss the content of the serials they listen to, or when Elvira helps to explain unfamiliar phenomena to Eva such as snow. When Eva moves on to another house, the radio also serves to bring her closer to her next mistress, a Yugoslav immigrant. The opening quotation of this section, '[á]branse las páginas sonoras del aire' (p. 104) [*let the sonorous pages of the airwaves open before you*], refers to the opening line said by the radio presenter when introducing the *radionovelas* which Eva and her mistress would listen to. Thus, radio is not merely entertaining for Eva but also a means of connecting with people and learning about the world around her. At various stages in her life, radio content and contact with people become inextricably linked, from her initial meeting with the Italian schoolteacher Melecio in La Señora's brothel through to her friendship with the prostitutes who work there. Interestingly, there is an appreciable shift in the function of the radio content here, as it is not merely assimilated by Eva here as an avid listener but significantly altered and imaginatively challenged, and the *radionovelas* become a springboard to display her gift for storytelling: '[las prostitutas] [m]e pedían que les contara la continuación de la radionovela de turno y yo improvisaba un fin dramático que nunca coincidía con el desenlace radial, pero eso no les importaba' (p. 121) [*the prostitutes asked me to tell them what was happening on the latest radionovela and I would make up a dramatic end that never tallied with the ending broadcast on the radio. They didn't mind*].

The connection between people and radio content is not as relevant during Eva's time in the village of Agua Santa. When news of the fall of the dictator is broadcast, her new Turkish employer Riad Halabí's explanation of this change in political regime in the country suggests a type of disengagement from mainstream politics in rural communities, somewhat reminiscent of Professor Jones's lack of interest in contemporary affairs. Riad explains that the political event was '[n]ada que nos importe, eso ocurre muy lejos de aquí' (p. 169) [*nothing that really matters to us – it happens far away from here*]. Despite this view, radio continues to play a key role in Eva's development: it is during her time living in Agua Santa that Eva is finally given the opportunity to learn how to read and write, helped by the private tuition offered to her by the local schoolmistress Inés. Eva explains the dramatic effect of literacy on her storytelling abilities: 'la posibilidad de escribir me permitió prescindir de las rimas para recordar y pude enredar los cuentos con múltiples personajes y aventuras' (p. 145) [*being able to write allowed me to do without mnemonic rhymes and I could make my stories more complex, with lots of characters and adventures*]. The mnemonic basis of orality, as explained by Ong, is removed, or at least rendered redundant, when she commits the stories to writing. Eva's lessons

Displacing Language 113

with Inés are also enhanced by radio content, as a picture of the world is built up for Eva:

> La señorita Inés no había salido jamás de Agua Santa, pero tenía mapas desplegados en los muros de su casa y por las tardes me comentaba las noticias de la radio, señalando los puntos ignotos donde sucedía cada acontecimiento. (p. 176)
>
> [*Inés had never left the village of Agua Santa; however she had maps all over the walls of her home and in the afternoons she chatted with me about the news on the radio, pointing out the unknown places where every event occurred.*]

On Eva's return to the city, it is noticeable that she begins to question more her original gift of oral storytelling, and in some way she feels unable to compete with what she views as the real sources of truth and wisdom:

> contar cuentos me parecía un oficio sobrepasado por los progresos de la radio, la televisión y el cine, pensaba que todo lo transmitido por ondas o proyectado en una pantalla era verídico, en cambio mis narraciones eran casi siempre un cúmulo de mentiras, que ni yo misma sabía de dónde sacaba. (p. 199)
>
> [*telling stories seemed to me like a job which was overtaken by all the advances provided by radio, television and cinema. I thought that everything broadcast on radio or shown on a screen was true, while my stories were almost always a string of lies, and I didn't even know where they came from.*]

It is significant that Eva associates radio and television with truth and progress, while somewhat naively believing that her form of oral storytelling is, by implication, false and backward. Indeed, a series of serendipitous events conspire to bring Eva into contact with people working in television, which plays a decisive role in determining the career she is to forge for herself. A chance encounter with Mimí, the new identity of her friend Melecio after undergoing gender reassignment surgery, helps to bring Eva into contact with the world of television. Mimí works as a successful actress on *telenovelas*. Again, Eva seems to lose faith with a staple from her early years, and reconsiders her previous views of *radionovelas*: 'había pasado años escuchándolos en la cocina, creyendo que eran casos verídicos y al comprobar que la realidad no era como en la radio me había sentido burlada'

(p. 234) [*I had spent years listening to them in the kitchen, believing them to be real. When I discovered that reality wasn't like what was on the radio I felt cheated*]. Mimí buys Eva a typewriter and encourages her to channel her storytelling gift into creating *telenovelas*. Eva's first committed experience of writing is significant:

> Creí que esa página me esperaba desde hacía veintitantos años, que yo había vivido sólo para ese instante, y quise que a partir de ese momento mi único oficio fuera atrapar las historias suspendidas en el aire más delgado, para hacerlas mías. (p. 234)
>
> [*I thought that page had been waiting over twenty years for me, that I had lived just for that moment, and from that moment on I wanted my only job to be catching stories that hung in the thinnest air, and to making them mine.*]

Her close friendship with Mimí grants her access to a television producer named Aravena, and she is hired to write a script for a new *telenovela* on the strength of her oral storytelling, though, rather than on a previously written script. Her involvement in mainstream political events occurs just after she is hired, through her long-standing relationship with Huberto Naranjo. She agrees to participate in the release of seven prisoners from the Santa María penal colony by using the malleable material introduced to her by her former Yugoslav mistress to fashion imitation hand grenades. The successful release provides her with the substance for her script, which she entitles 'Bolero' ['*Bolero*'] as an 'homenaje a esas canciones que alimentaron las horas de mi niñez y me sirvieron de fundamento para tantos cuentos' (p. 277) [*homage to those songs that filled my childhood years and served as a basis for so many stories*]. Eva's decision to send on the script is in direct contravention of an order by the Colonel, Tolomeo Rodríguez, who also has a romantic interest in her. She ensures that the true story of the prisoners' escape, though fictionalized through the *telenovela*, will be heard by all. Furthermore, the fact that the programme is broadcast on numerous occasions means that the story of the *guerrilleros'* success will be talked about throughout the unnamed country. The dramatizing of Eva's script through the soap opera provides a means for the truth to survive in times of censorship.

Building on her rich experiences of oral language as a child, Eva develops skills which enable her to interact and survive through her difficult childhood and adolescent years. The skills of literacy which she acquires while living in Agua Santa become a key development in her life, but she never totally rejects the principle of oral storytelling as her way of surviving, and draws frequently on her childhood memories with her mother, Consuelo, and her memories of the *radionovelas* in developing and honing her skills at oral storytelling. Mimí provides Eva with her first chance to commit to paper the stories which are in her mind, and the decision to write a script for a *telenovela* based heavily on the subversive events she has experienced and wholly participated in provides Eva with a career based on her love of storytelling. While orality forms the basis of Eva's childhood, it is secondary orality which becomes key to Eva's success in adulthood.

Silence, Communities and Communication in *Cuentos de Eva Luna*

Cuentos de Eva Luna, Allende's spin-off collection from *Eva Luna*, is framed by a prologue involving two key characters from the novel, that is, Eva Luna herself and her lover, Rolf Carlé. A memory, or perhaps memories, of shared intimacy between the lovers is recounted in an atmosphere of silent, but intense communication. The description in the prologue of the apparent differences between Carlé's way of viewing life, through photography and the still image, and Eva's textured, imaginative tales, is somewhat superficial, given that the prologue is in fact Carlé's story, an indication perhaps of Eva's storytelling influence upon him. Carlé's own important journey through failed communication and memories of his home and family is examined towards the close of the collection in 'De barro estamos hechos', one of four stories to be concentrated on in this section, which aims to illustrate the links between silence and communities in *Cuentos de Eva Luna*. Alongside 'De barro estamos hechos', this section also looks at

'Dos palabras', in relation to Belisa Crepusculario's single-handed efforts to provide a voice for silenced, rural communities apparently forgotten by the mainstream; 'Tosca' is examined in relation to Maurizia Rugieri, reinvented and renamed in the story as Tosca, and her attempted imposition of what might be called a type of cultural imperialism on the rural community where she settles, as a means of silencing her prosaic and painful past; 'Lo más olvidado del olvido' looks at two exiles who have endeavoured to silence their traumatic pasts and find a silent means of communicating this pain to each other.

'Dos palabras': Defying Local and National Silences

'Dos palabras', the opening short story, immediately establishes the links between silence and communities which feature strongly throughout the collection. Allende describes a young word-seller named Belisa Crepusculario, who has left behind her impoverished family and, after having been taught how to read and write by a local priest, is employing her skills with both the written and spoken word in order to earn a living. The crucial turning point in the story comes when Belisa is abducted and she is forced to write a speech for a prospective presidential candidate, the feared local outlaw, El Coronel [*The Colonel*].

In her everyday work, Belisa has become the means by which news travels provincially, from village to village, ensuring that local stories are voiced and shared; yet she also provides locals with an opportunity to contribute actively to this alternative communal narrative and to become part of the 'largas historias verdaderas' [*long, true stories*] which she recounts.[13] For these communities, presented in the tale at a remove from urban society, there appears to be little access to mass media, and Belisa's tales enable

---

13   Isabel Allende, *Cuentos de Eva Luna*, 8th edn (Barcelona: Plaza & Janés, 1992), p. 15. Further references will appear parenthetically in the text.

Displacing Language

local news to reach friends and relatives in distant parts of the unnamed country. Her tales recall one of Ong's key features of oral communities in that their narratives are aggregative rather than analytic. The locals gather round to hear Belisa speak:

> En cada lugar se juntaba una pequeña multitud a su alrededor para oírla cuando comenzaba a hablar y así se enteraban de las vidas de otros, de los parientes lejanos, de los pormenores de la Guerra Civil. (p. 15)

> [*In every place a small crowd gathered round to hear her when she began to talk. In this way they found out about the lives of others, of distant relatives and of the details of the Civil War.*]

Perhaps intentionally on Allende's part, the listing of events during Belisa's performances appears to privilege the local over the national, with events of most significance for the local community described before issues of national importance, in this instance, the Civil War that is taking place. This foregrounding of local over national, and of margins over mainstream, is a feature subtly present throughout the short story and even more apparent at the conclusion.

As mentioned earlier, in addition to her oratorical skills, Belisa has also developed a confident, assured command of written language. She effortlessly glides through genres, from imaginative oneiric language to base epistolary invective:

> [p]or cinco centavos entregaba versos de memoria, por siete mejoraba la calidad de los sueños, por nueve escribía cartas de enamorados, por doce inventaba insultos para enemigos irreconciliables. (p. 15)

> [*for five cents she provided verses from memory; for seven she improved the quality of dreams; for nine she wrote love letters; for twelve she invented insults for irreconcilable enemies.*]

In addition to the oral narratives she performs in each community, she also strives to provide locals with a voice at national level by penning letters to administrative bodies in the city. Indeed, while she is helping a client to draft a claim for a pension that has been denied to him, she is abducted by El Coronel's men, who have been led Belisa by his second-in-command, El Mulato [*The Mulatto*]. Belisa is tied to a horse and carried away, the disregard for her craft being represented in the tale by the men symbolically 'rompiendo el tintero' (p. 18) [*knocking over her inkwell*]. Her first encounter with the marginalized bandit, El Coronel, 'el hombre más temido del país' (p. 19) [*the most feared man in the country*], follows shortly after she regains consciousness. El Coronel explains his desire to become president and to gain the presidency by democratic means. He needs to connect at both local and national levels and to communicate a message through language, not violence. His simple request from Belisa is that she help him 'hablar como un candidato' (p. 20) [*to speak like a (presidential) candidate*]. Belisa has little option but to help, and diligently sets about crafting a carefully-worded speech. When it is revealed that El Coronel is illiterate, Belisa illustrates her resourcefulness and adaptability by reading the speech aloud to him three times to enable him to commit it to memory – yet again, she refuses to accept failure. The reaction of his henchman to the speech is enough to convince him that 'el sillón presidencial sería suyo' (p. 21) [*the presidential seat would be his*]. Belisa also gives him *dos palabras* [*two words*], his gift for this transaction, and he accepts them because of his own code of honour, and because 'no quiso ser descortés con quien lo había servido tan bien' (p. 21) [*he didn't want to be rude to somebody who had served him so well*]. Belisa whispers these words to El Coronel; crucially, his henchmen do not hear what these words are.

In the following months, El Coronel and his men embark on a country-wide presidential campaign, in many ways paralleling the journeys made by Belisa. El Coronel reconnects with the many local communities he had previously terrorized through his violent actions, and crowds surround him while he delivers his speech. Crucially he connects with both rural and urban communities, and his speech appears to resonate no matter where he goes. The transformative power of the speech is reflected in his national ratings – 'se convirtió en el político más popular' (p. 22) [*he became the most popular politician*] – and more subtly perhaps through his change of name in the story to El Candidato [*The Candidate*]. The mainstream media spread the content of the speech, and this allows the marginal El Candidato to connect with the public nationally, an example of secondary orality which was noted in the earlier discussion of *Eva Luna*. Yet, in this situation, El Coronel's increasing public popularity is contrasted with another private, surreptitious type of transformation, and one that may seriously jeopardize his chances at becoming president: in private, he becomes more introverted, and he appears fascinated by the *dos palabras* he had been given by Belisa, and also the association which these words conjure up in his mind: 'en toda ocasión en que esas dos palabras venían a su mente, evocaba la presencia de Belisa Crepusculario' (p. 23) [*every time those two words came to mind, he thought of Belisa Crepusculario*]. His henchmen perceive two clearly conflicting images of him: not merely do they see the powerful orator, but also the ever-obsessive recluse, silent and increasingly captivated by his private gift. El Mulato loyally endeavours to help his boss, but El Coronel jealously guards his words, and displays almost childish covetousness in refusing to reveal the words to his second-in-command: 'no te las diré, son mías' (p. 23) [*I'm not telling you – they're mine*]. El Coronel's men believe that his life is in danger – 'comprendieron que se le terminaría la vida antes de alcanzar el sillón de los presidentes' (p. 23) [*they understood that his life would be over before he could take the presidential seat*] – and his second-in-command, El Mulato, sets out in search of Belisa, whom he finds 'contando su rosario de noticias' (p. 23) [*recounting her rosary of news*] in a small town. Chastened by his first experience when she rejected his amatory advances with a stream of invented words he believed to be some form of curse, El Mulato respectfully allows her time to prepare for the journey back to see El Coronel. On this occasion, Belisa 'recogió su tintero' (p. 24) [*picked up her inkwell*], in stark contrast to her earlier scene when the men abducted her, 'rompiendo su tintero' (p. 18) [*knocking over her inkwell*]. When Belisa and El Coronel meet again, however, El Mulato's efforts have been in vain, as they take each other's hand at the close of the tale, the implication being that their love is of more importance than the presidential election.

Within the space of a single short story, Allende provides an array of issues relevant to language and silence: through the written word, Allende champions and celebrates the vitality of oral language, and challenges official discourse by resolutely keeping the silenced stories about, and from, the margins alive. Belisa's stories are simultaneously collective and personal, an unwritten and often unspoken history of the rural communities far removed from mainstream politics. These stories provide the local people with an opportunity to learn about friends and family geographically removed from them and to participate in a shared community, to move from the margins into an inclusive, collective rural history. Belisa manages to escape her impoverished past through language and she then empowers others to escape their own situations of poverty and silence by penning letters demanding rural people's rights. Belisa's influence on national events becomes more apparent when she writes El Coronel's presidential campaign speech, which resonates with anybody that hears it. Ultimately, however, the many instances of local silence which permeate the story finally give way towards the end to an apparently deliberate silencing of the key national event, the results of the presidential election, which Allende in a sense displaces in the text as she concentrates on the love that has blossomed between Belisa and El Coronel and never informs the reader of the outcome.

Undignified Silence in 'Tosca'

The power and impact of public performances on local communities, as exemplified in 'Dos palabras' through Belisa's tales and El Coronel's presidential speech, is also an important consideration in the short story 'Tosca'. This tale presents Maurizia Rugieri, a woman of Italian extraction, who from an early age had displayed an unwillingness to accept the status quo and is determined to forge her own path, no matter what the consequences. The opening sequence of the tale clearly illustrates this when Maurizia, during her first piano recital, ignores the praise of the president in the club where she is playing, and instead declares that '[l]o que yo quiero es ser cantante' (p. 100) [*what I want to be is a singer*]. Indeed, this juxtaposition between Maurizia's somewhat inflated sense of self and an altogether more prosaic, and at times painful, reality is pervasive throughout her life, as she endeavours to silence reality and instead to embrace a self-embroidered, fantastic version of reality. This conflict between appearance and reality, examined in the latter stages of 'Dos palabras' through the metamorphosis which El Coronel seems to undergo, creates many problems for Maurizia, and is even subtly reflected in the name she gives herself later in the tale, Tosca, which at once conjures up not only her highbrow operatic pretensions, but a harsher reality through its Spanish senses of 'coarse' or 'unrefined'. Maurizia finds herself bored with the vagaries of everyday life with her devoted, diligent husband, Ezio Longo, a man for whom '[l]e resultaba imposible expresar sus sentimientos' [*it was impossible for him to express his feelings*] and who felt that 'soportando con estoica paciencia sus extravagantes cambios de humor y sus dolencias imaginarias, compensaría las fallas de su repertorio de amante' (p. 101) [*by tolerating her extravagant mood swings and imaginary ailments with stoic patience, he would make up for his failings as a lover*]. She seeks refuge in the world of opera, and a chance meeting on a tram with a young medical student named Leonardo, who is whistling an aria from the Puccini opera *Tosca*, while on the tram, provides her with an opportunity to escape her mundane reality and seemingly share her love for opera with a kindred spirit. A lengthy, though purely platonic friendship ensues between the two, but is seriously jeopardized when Ezio, having been tipped off by a neighbour about Maurizia's new friend, follows her to a cake shop one day and violently confronts Leonardo. Maurizia refuses to talk to Ezio following this incident and, in frustration, Ezio issues her an ultimatum, telling her '[p]uedes ir con ese mequetrefe si quieres, pero no volverás a ver a nuestro hijo nunca más' (p. 104) [*you can head off with that good-for-nothing, if you want, but you'll never see our son again*].

From this point on in the narrative, the apparent freedom that Maurizia has been granted by Ezio's threat proves to be problematic, as she resolves to leave the family home and instead follow the fantasy of sharing her life with a man who supposedly shares her passions. Maurizia's pursuit of Leonardo intensifies, but it appears that her decision to follow her dreams will be fraught with many obstacles, not least when she discovers that Leonardo has left the guesthouse where he had been staying to go and work in an oil plantation without informing her. She doggedly persists in tracking Leonardo down and she harbours the dream of a dramatic reconciliation, but she is left disappointed when she is met by oil workers rather than Leonardo when she finally reaches the plantation. Throughout her time there, she continues to consider Leonardo her hero, and she forestalls any possibility of him disappointing her by inventing a series of excuses: '[s]i Leonardo Gómez daba muestras de quedarse muy atrás, ella lo atribuía a su carácter tímido y su mala salud, empeorada por ese clima maldito' (p. 106) [*if Leonardo Gómez showed any signs of lagging behind, she would put it down to his timid nature and his poor health, which had been made worse by that damned climate*]. It is perhaps ironic that in her new relationship she is echoing her husband's own behaviour of appeasement by tolerating a less than loving and fulfilling relationship.

Maurizia continues to embellish her perception of reality, employing a series of euphemisms in order to conceal the poor conditions in which they are living at the oil plantation. She struggles, however, to find a euphemism to refer to 'ese dolor animal que la doblaba en dos al recordar a su hijo' (p. 107) [*this animal-like pain which left her doubled over whenever her son came to mind*], and chooses instead not to mention him at all. Somewhat against the odds, perhaps, Maurizia and Leonardo stay together and move to Agua Santa, a village which had appeared prominently in the novel *Eva Luna* when Eva Luna moved there to live with the Turkish immigrant Riad Halabí. Maurizia uses this move as a fresh start, and a means of cementing her fantasy in a new pseudo-reality. She now renames herself Tosca definitively, and embarks on a mission of cultural imperialism, endeavouring to impose an alien culture on the local community. To a degree, she is successful in the sense that the locals embrace her performances as entertainment and call her Tosca, but there is never any true sense that the Agua Santa inhabitants have become truly engaged in opera to the extent that Tosca is; nor do they appreciate the connotations of her new, self-selected name. This is not helped, of course, by the fact that '[n]adie entendió ni una palabra del canto' (p. 108) [*nobody understood a word of the singing*]. The death of Mario, as Leonardo had been renamed by Tosca, affords her an opportunity to become enveloped in a dramatic display of mourning. In private, however, it is suggested, though never confirmed in the text, that Mario's passing means that she no longer has to 'seguir tirando de la pesada carreta de sus sueños' (p. 109) [*keep dragging around the heavy cart of her dreams*].

Displacing Language 123

The extension of a national road network to link up Agua Santa with the state brings Tosca face to face with her silenced past, when it is revealed that her husband and son own the company contracted to construct the new road. Tosca is presented with a unique opportunity to reconnect with the family she abandoned, to deal finally with the persistent undertow of guilt in relation to her son and to achieve a degree of reconciliation, perhaps, with her husband. She carefully prepares with the diligence she normally reserves for a dramatic performance, but, ominously, she finds it difficult to think of herself in anything other than operatic terms, 'como si estuviera sobre un escenario representando el momento más dramático del largo teatro que había sido su existencia' (p. 112) [*as if she were on stage, performing the most dramatic scene in the long theatre that had been her life*]. Yet at the final moment, she looks at her husband and son, as she teeters 'en la frontera entre la realidad y el sueño' (p. 112) [*on the border between dreams and reality*], and decides to walk away, choosing to seek refuge in the tragic alternative of solitude over the prosaic probability of rejection. Tosca's undignified silence confirms her unremitting self-centredness, and condemns her to a life alone, on the margins of a community of which she is never fully part.

'Lo más olvidado del olvido': The Shared Silences of the Past

'Lo más olvidado del olvido' provides a very different angle within *Cuentos de Eva Luna* on the relationship between silence and communities. The tale illustrates the limits of oral language in fully communicating shared, but silenced past experiences, and is a solemn mood piece describing an encounter between two exiles who cannot make love because of their memories of torture in a concentration camp in Chile.[14] As Linda Gould Levine notes,

---

14 While in many of Allende's stories in *Cuentos de Eva Luna* the actual setting is not made explicit, the reference to a map of Chile on the wall of the apartment in 'Lo más olvidado del olvido' seems to confirm the exiles' provenance.

this story 'pays tribute to the role that cathartic sharing has in exorcizing the demons of memory'.[15] From the opening of this compact tale, there is a strong suggestion that oral communication will actually threaten rather than enhance the intimacy the protagonists are about to share:

> Ella se dejó acariciar, silenciosa, gotas de sudor en la cintura, olor a azúcar tostada en su cuerpo quieto, como si adivinara que *un solo sonido podía hurgar en los recuerdos y echarlo todo a perder, haciendo polvo ese instante.* (p. 143, emphasis added)

> [*She let herself be caressed, silent, beads of sweat on her waist, an aroma of toasted sugar on her still body, as if she could guess that* one single sound could delve into her memories and ruin everything, reducing that moment to dust. (emphasis added)]

At first glance, the opening lines in a way appear to echo the love-making scene shared by Eva Luna and Rolf Carlé during the prologue to the collection. The unnamed protagonists here are exiles from the same country, and they strike up a conversation following a chance meeting, whereupon they speak passionately and freely about their common cultural experiences from their youth:

> de nostalgias antiguas, de cómo era la vida cuando ambos crecían en la misma ciudad, en el mismo barrio, cuando tenía catorce años, te acuerdas, los inviernos de zapatos mojados por la escarcha y de estufas de parafina, los veranos de duraznos, allá en el país prohibido. (p. 143)

> [(they spoke) of old familiar things, how life was when they grew up in the same city, the same neighbourhood, when she was fourteen, do you remember, those winters with frost-soaked shoes and paraffin heaters, those peach-filled summers, back in the forbidden country.]

Their conversation nostalgically recalls the simplicity of their youth, and their connection to the same community; their light-hearted exchange, however, seems to acquire a darker dimension through the reference to their homeland as 'el país prohibido' (p. 143) [*the forbidden country*]. Furthermore, the description of the woman's apartment seems to reflect

15   Levine, p. 81.

her marginality and perhaps failure to integrate fully into her new homeland: '[ella] [c]ompartía con otros exiliados un apartamento sórdido, en un edificio amarillo al final de un callejón lleno de tarros de basura' (pp. 143–4) [*she shared a squalid flat with other exiles, in a yellow building at the end of an alleyway filled with litter bins*].

A sense of foreboding begins to envelop the tale, and the conflict between what is said and what is thought becomes increasingly apparent: the man 'trató de amarla' (p. 144) [*he tried to love her*], but he finds himself unable to do so. A sudden chasm of incommunicability has opened up between the two, and in place of the vibrancy of their earlier conversation, 'sólo quedaban sobre la cama dos criaturas desvalidas, con la memoria ausente, flotando en el vacío terrible de tantas palabras calladas' (p. 144) [*there remained on the bed only two helpless creatures, with no memory, floating in the terrible emptiness of so many hushed words*]. Communication through language suddenly appears laboured for them both, but they nevertheless attempt to engage in conversation again, to regain the urgency of when they first met by exchanging trivial details of their new lives in exile. However, even this conversation becomes tinged with the harsh reality that they are living in a place 'donde sin embargo siempre serían forasteros' (p. 144) [*where they would nevertheless always be foreigners*].

As the man's fear begins to grow, there is a palpable sense of anxiety in everything he says: '[d]eja abierta la cortina, quiero mirarte, le mintió, porque no se atrevió a contarle su terror de la noche' (p. 145) [*leave the curtain open, I want to look at you – he lied, because he didn't dare tell her about his fear of the night*]. His fear of darkness appears to be based on how the lack of light will trigger memories, and that he could then end up 'diciendo lo que nunca se ha dicho' (p. 145). He suddenly finds that 'no pudo hablar, la voz se le quedó agarrada en el vientre, como una zarpa' (p. 145) [*he couldn't speak – his voice clung to his stomach, like a claw*]. Finally, however, he lets go, and while he 'oyó crecer el silencio en su interior' (p. 146) [*he heard the silence grow inside him*], the memory of torture and a stream of voices return to his mind, as he painfully recalls 'las voces insultando, exigiendo nombres, los gritos inolvidables de Ana supliciada a su lado, colgados de los brazos en el patio' (p. 146) [*the voices who were insulting him, demanding names from him, the unforgettable screams from Ana, who pleaded by his side, hanging by her arms in the courtyard*]. His outpouring is emotional, but not expressed through words, and the woman comforts him as he cries, with a sense of shared suffering intimated through the imagery employed: 'lo besó en la frente, le dijo llora, llora, lo tendió de espaldas sobre la cama y se acostó *crucificada* sobre él' (p. 146, emphasis added) [*she kissed his forehead, she told him to cry, laid him back on the bed and slept* crucified *on him*].

The woman's ability to empathize with the man suggests that 'ella conocía aquello que se encontraba agazapado más allá del silencio' (p. 147) [*she knew what was crouching beyond silence*], and her final act is to reveal her own scars of torture on her wrists, which she had hidden under jewellery. Finally, their earlier complicity in triviality returns in a sense as their shared experiences of torture are revealed: 'pudieron abrazarse y llorar, hambrientos de pactos y de confidencias, de palabras prohibidas, de promesas de mañana, compartiendo, por fin, el más recóndito secreto' (p. 147) [*they could embrace and cry, both hungry for pacts, secrets, forbidden words and future promises. They could share, at last, their deepest secret*]. Both share a tortured past, which they have never before articulated. This refusal to speak about their pasts is perhaps a determination not to relive those experiences as well as perhaps a desire not to recall an act of betrayal on the part of the man. Indeed, it is only through the unveiling of the woman's scars in silence that they can properly open up and share their inescapable pasts. As can be inferred from this story, Allende alludes to the perils of burying one's past, the impossibility of acquiring an adequate mode of expression to deal with a traumatic past, perhaps, and the importance of communities voicing fears and facing up to the silenced past. Their means of communication implies that language at times is unable to express the pain of their experiences.

'De barro estamos hechos': Facing Up to the Silenced Past

'De barro estamos hechos', the final story in the collection to be discussed here, continues in a similar vein to 'Lo más olvidado del olvido', with the suffering and guilt felt by the couple in the previous story being replicated in this story by Rolf Carlé, who confronts both his futility at being unable to change a situation in the present and his buried memories of a traumatic childhood in Austria. Interestingly, Allende uses the backdrop of a real event, a landslide in Colombia in 1985, and there is a strong testimonial feel to the narrative, in which there is a marked absence of hyperbole and magic realism. A combination of oral language and the subsequent inescapability of silence provide the triggers for the inner journey Carlé embarks upon. This story takes place immediately following the aftermath of the landslide; the local community had failed to heed environmental experts' warnings, which they believed 'sonaban a cuentos de viejas' (p. 266) [*sounded like old wives' tales*], and have been caught unawares by the disaster. Most of the community appear to have perished, but Carlé, and the media at large, are focusing their attention on a young girl called Azucena, a fictional projection of Omaira Sánchez from the original landslide of 1985, who has become trapped in the mud. Carlé has been assigned to the story, and his first appearance at the scene confirms, in the eyes of Eva, his apparent fearlessness: 'siempre [l]e asombró su actitud de calma ante el peligro y el sufrimiento, como si nada lograra sacudir su fortaleza ni desviar su curiosidad' (p. 268) [*she was always surprised by his calmness when faced with danger and suffering; it was as if nothing could shake his strength or deter his curiosity*].

Gradually, Carlé becomes more involved with Azucena on a personal level and less concerned with his professional responsibilities. Initially, he speaks to her 'sólo para distraerla' (p. 268) [*just to distract her*], unaware of the suffering lying ahead for both of them. The situation begins to become more desperate: each of Carlé's attempts to prise Azucena from the mud is unsuccessful, and his requests for a pump to suction away the mud surrounding her go unheeded. He is left alone with her as the night progresses, and he employs the narrative resourcefulness fostered by his lover, Eva, in an effort to keep up the spirits of the trapped young girl. In the words of Levine, 'Rolf, transformed in part by Eva's stories and the force of his own emotions, becomes a male Scheherazade of sorts, using Eva's inspiration and words to delay death.'[16] Carlé employs a mixture of memories and inventiveness in comforting Azucena: 'cuando se le agotaron los recuerdos echó mano de la imaginación para inventar cualquier cosa que pudiera distraerla' (p. 270) [*when his memories dried up he used his imagination to make up anything that could distract her*]. Eva, in the meantime, endeavours to locate a pump, but all discussions with high-ranking officials and foreign investors come to nothing. Unable to get in touch with Carlé, she becomes increasingly aware of the growing distance between them.

Carlé redoubles his efforts the following morning, always remaining by the side of Azucena. While attempting to provide solace for her, as she enters her second night trapped in the mud, Carlé begins to remember his childhood memories, triggered by the 'viejas canciones de Austria aprendidas de su madre' (pp. 273–4) [*old songs from Austria which his mother taught him*] that he sings to Azucena. Memories of his youth begin to flow relentlessly, contrasting starkly with the stasis that surrounds him: 'en esas horas revivió por primera vez todo aquello que su mente había intentado borrar' (p. 274) [*during that time he relived for the first time everything his mind had tried to blot out*]. He recalls his unhappy childhood, and the sense of fear that pervaded his early years. As he remembers his past, he is careful to avoid mentioning his traumatic experiences of burying bodies in a concentration camp, or how his father humiliated his mother.[17] While he silences these events, they nevertheless have the effect of reminding him of all the pain of his youth, and '[e]l dolor lo invadió, intacto y preciso, como siempre estuvo agazapado en su mente' (p. 274) [*an intact, precise pain pierced him, as it was always lurking in his mind*]. He identifies his psychological state with Azucena's physical state, and tries to rationalize

---

16 Levine, p. 80.
17 These events are described in detail by Allende in the second chapter of *Eva Luna*.

his actions and choices in life, coming to the realization that 'sus hazañas de periodista [...] eran un intento de mantener bajo control su miedo más antiguo' (p. 275) [*his journalistic exploits [...] were an attempt to keep his oldest fear under control*].

The President visits the scene of the natural disaster on the third day, and Carlé appeals unsuccessfully once again for a pump to help remove Azucena from the mud. As night falls, Azucena slowly deteriorates, and Carlé makes one last effort to console the young girl, saying that he 'daría cualquier cosa por estar atrapado en ese pozo en su lugar' (p. 277) [*he would give anything to be trapped in that well in place of her*]. While Eva has managed to secure a pump through her contacts, it is in vain, and Azucena passes away. The silence that follows Azucena's death forces Carlé to face up to his past, to resurrect long-forgotten incidents and to finally confront them. It helps him to deal with the trauma of the present, but it leaves him with the emotional task of resolving the trauma of his past. The unresolved conclusion to the tale in a way reflects Rolf's troubled state of mind. Eva's final words clearly indicate the journey which Carlé must still undertake: 'yo espero que completes el viaje hacia el interior de ti mismo y te cures de las viejas heridas' (p. 278) [*I hope you can complete the journey into yourself and can heal your old wounds*].

In *Cuentos de Eva Luna*, silence is pervasive in the communities that appear in the stories selected for this analysis: in 'Dos palabras', the silence that is a feature of the rural communities which Belisa visits is countered and challenged through a combination of her oral news reports, which people are invited to pay a small fee in order to contribute to, and the letters she pens on behalf of the locals in their quest to gain access to state aid. Allende subtly privileges local and personal issues over national and political matters in the tale by focusing at the conclusion on the love that has blossomed between Belisa and El Coronel rather than on the outcome of the presidential election. In 'Tosca', Maurizia Rugieri endeavours to transform herself and the local community where she decides to settle by introducing the inhabitants to operatic performances. Her performances become the means by which she attempts to silence the painful realization that she had rejected her son and husband in favour of a life with Leonardo. Ultimately she chooses to live out her days alone, after Leonardo's death, rather than to try and make peace with her family when they arrive at her village. 'Lo más olvidado del olvido' illustrates the difficulty in articulating experiences of torture, highlighting how, in silence, the exiles reveal their shared pasts of torture through their physical scars. Finally, in 'De barro estamos hechos', Rolf Carlé's efforts to forget a traumatic part of his past are shown to be ultimately futile, as the time he spends consoling the trapped and dying Azucena lead to him having to confront the past which he had sought to escape from when he left his home in Austria. Interestingly, Allende ends the collection with a story in which silence is pervasive, as the emotional wasteland in which Carlé finds himself is unromantic and unresolved. Though only four of the stories have been examined here, *Cuentos de Eva Luna* explores the challenges faced by people in becoming fully reconciled with their pasts, and the anthology also considers the dangers of endeavouring to forget the individual and collective voices of the past. Acknowledging the role of silence in the collection highlights the increasing importance in the collection of reconciliation with the past, an issue which is tackled more formally in Allende's 1991 novel, *El plan infinito*, examined in the final chapter of this discussion.

Displaced Speech? The Richness of Reticence in *Cuentos de Eva Luna*

This chapter has sought to highlight Allende's respect for storytelling, and in particular, oral storytelling, through a focus on two main issues: the application of Ong's term *secondary orality* to *Eva Luna* has demonstrated how Eva's gift for oral storytelling is filtered and honed through literacy and then reconfigured within the parameters of oral language again through the *reanimation* of her politically infused script in the *telenovela*. Her script becomes an important record of actual events, the successful escape of prisoners from the Santa María penal colony, albeit within a celluloid medium. Furthermore, as previously mentioned, the scripts in themselves become a springboard for the re-enactment of censored events through oral language, giving the events a renewed vitality and defying efforts on the part of political authorities to have these events censored. In addition, this discussion has explored the prevalence of silence in *Cuentos de Eva Luna* and noted how in a number of stories in the collection, Allende illustrates the ways in which silence impacts upon communities, from the isolated communities in 'Dos palabras', through to the individuals who have left their communities to follow their dreams, as in 'Tosca', to escape a dictatorial regime, as in 'Lo más olvidado del olvido' and to escape a traumatic past, as in 'De barro estamos hechos'.

One final issue in relation to *Cuentos de Eva Luna* merits exploration: in a number of stories, Allende seemingly neglects to provide crucial parts of the narrative. This occurs, for example, in 'Dos palabras', when neither the crucial *dos palabras* nor the presidential speech is revealed within the body of the text. Does this refusal on the part of the author to provide key information in some way weaken the power of the tale? Indeed, these textual omissions suggest that Allende is contradicting herself through this action: in a 1990 interview, for example, she had mentioned that 'the development and culmination of the story can leave no loose ends'.[18]

The apparent failure on Allende's part to allow readers to share in the magic of these elements may be deliberate, and she explains that one of her ultimate aims as a writer is to establish a platform for dialogue and communication: '[s]on muy pocos los escritores que se contemplan el ombligo hundidos en un inaccesible monólogo; la mayoría busca el diálogo, quiere comunicarse' [*very few writers spend their time navel-gazing, in an impenetrable monologue. Most seek dialogue and wish to communicate*].[19] She develops this further in another interview:

---

18   Isabel Allende, Foreword, in *Short Stories by Latin American Women: The Magic and the Real*, ed. by Celia Correas de Zapata (Houston, TX: Arte Público, 1990), p. 5.
19   Isabel Allende, 'Vamos a nombrar las cosas', in *Testimonio y documentos de la literatura chilena*, ed. by José Promis Ojeda (Santiago de Chile: Andrés Bello, 1995), pp. 291–300 (p. 294).

> I feel much better with an undetermined place and undetermined time [...] I want that place to be not my mythical place, but the reader's mythical place [...] [v]ery seldom is there a physical description of a character in my writing because I want my reader to create the character.[20]

Through Allende's omission of the transcript of the presidential speech Belisa wrote for El Coronel, she leaves it up to the reader to imagine what might have been contained in the speech. Allende paradoxically provides richness through reticence. It may be argued, then, that the apparent failure on Allende's part to include information about the *dos palabras* in the eponymous opening tale of *Cuentos de Eva Luna*, and the presidential speech therein may actually be considered a strategy on the part of the author to resist committing every element of the tale to the constraints of the story. By apparently omitting this information, Allende in a way forces the reader to imagine what these elements are.

This omission actually complements Allende's approach to oral language throughout *Eva Luna* and *Cuentos de Eva Luna*. On the one hand, she employs oral language to bridge gaps between the past and the present through, for example, Eva Luna's scripts and Belisa's oral narratives of events in local people's lives; on the other, she maintains deliberate gaps that allow for an imaginative reconfiguring of elements of her narrative. The gaps remain in the text, to be filled in by the reader. This deceptively simple tactic on Allende's part allows her to highlight the importance of oral language while also sidestepping specificity for key elements, ensuring that the events mentioned remain locked within the fictional spoken realm of each story. The framework of the written story is used as a means of celebrating oral language both overtly and covertly, and reflects a subtle subversiveness apparent within Allende's short fiction.

The final chapter of this discussion broaches the interplay between culture and displacement in the fiction written by Allende since her move to the United States, that is, *El plan infinito*, *Hija de la fortuna* and *Retrato en sepia*.

---

20   Farhat Iftekharuddin, 'Writing to Exorcise the Demons' in *Conversations with Isabel Allende*, pp. 351–63 (pp. 357–8).

CHAPTER 5

Cultural Displacement in *El plan infinito*, *Hija de la fortuna* and *Retrato en sepia*

> Típico de una cultura subdesarrollada y foránea – anotó [Samantha] sorbiendo impasible su jugo de apio.
> – ¿Cómo? – preguntó [Gregory Reeves] desconcertado.
> – Eres como esos latinos entre los cuales te criaste. Nunca debiste salir de ese barrio.[1]
>
> Tao Chi'en comprobó encantado que podía traducir las diez palabras de aquel *fan güey* y él mismo conocía por lo menos otras tantas en inglés, de modo que tal vez sería posible comunicarse.[2]

Introduction

The emphasis in this final part of the discussion is on situations of cultural displacement in three texts written by Allende since her move to the United States in 1988, that is, *El plan infinito* (1991) [*The Infinite Plan*], *Hija de la*

---

1 '*That's typical of an underdeveloped, foreign culture,*' said Samantha, slurping her celery juice coldly. '*Pardon?*' asked Gregory Reeves, worried. '*You're just like those Latinos who you were raised with. You never should have left that neighbourhood.*' Isabel Allende, *El plan infinito* (Barcelona: Plaza & Janés, 1991), p. 161. Subsequent references will appear parenthetically in the text.
2 *Tao Chi'en was delighted to discover he could translate the ten words of that foreigner and that he himself knew at least another few in English. Thus perhaps they could communicate with each other.* Isabel Allende, *Hija de la fortuna*, 3rd edn (Barcelona: Plaza & Janés, 1999), p. 201. Further references will appear parenthetically in the text.

fortuna (1999) [*Daughter of Fortune*] and *Retrato en sepia* (2000) [*Portrait in Sepia*]. In this final chapter, it is argued that the use of the United States as a new backdrop in her later fiction affords Allende the opportunity to consider in a more comprehensive way questions of cultural displacement touched upon in *Cuentos de Eva Luna*. She achieves this by introducing characters who find themselves displaced from their origins for a variety of reasons. Allende's concerted interrogation of the relationship between mainstream and margins in her earlier fiction acquires a more nuanced dimension in these three texts: for example, the challenges faced by a mainstream white family who settle in a marginal Hispanic community in Los Angeles are broached by Allende through the character of Gregory Reeves in *El plan infinito*. This discussion explores Reeves's various challenges by looking at his attempts to become integrated into the margins and the unresolved dilemmas from his childhood by drawing on Sigmund Freud's work on displacement in relation to dreams. In *Hija de la fortuna*, Englishman Jacob Todd's resolute efforts at becoming truly integrated into all levels of society in the Chilean port of Valparaiso is explored in relation to the ramifications of his rejection there. His gradual retreat from all forms of community on moving to California is coupled with his creation of a Hispanic outlaw named Joaquín Murieta, whom he writes about for local newspapers. Eliza Sommers's extensive use of mimicry in the same novel will be explored as a means for her to survive during her quest to be reunited with her lover, Joaquín Andieta. It is argued that her character becomes a commentary on cultural assimilation and her journey through the Californian wilderness in search of Andieta illustrates her resourcefulness and adaptability to a variety of cultural situations. Tao Chi'en's complex relationship with Chinese culture is explored in *Hija de la fortuna* and *Retrato en sepia* through the dichotomy of convention and contravention. This section examines his inner conflict and the ways in which he seeks to resolve the tension between his devotion to Chinese culture and his dissatisfaction with the inhuman conditions suffered by Chinese immigrant girls in the United States. Finally, Aurora del Valle's quest to uncover her multicultural past in *Retrato en sepia* will be shown to provide another nuanced examination of cultural displacement by Allende. This section looks at how Aurora manages to internalize her experiences of displacement and argues that she revels in her new-found sense of liberty and creativity, despite her rejection of a privileged role in Chilean society. Concluding comments in this chapter consider how characters from Allende's 'North American narratives' embrace a sense of displacement.[3] This approach by Allende is considered a significant departure in her fiction, and is also briefly compared with Esteban Trueba's search for societal place in *La casa de los espíritus*.

Hispanic-Stricken? Gregory Reeves and Psychocultural Displacement in *El plan infinito*

Critic Linda Gould Levine describes *El plan infinito* as a novel which 'reveals the full range of Allende's ability to capture the complexities of the human soul'.[4] Allende's exploration of Gregory Reeves illustrates the degree of psychological sophistication which is prevalent in her later fiction, and draws on both his lived experiences and his dreams in order to build up a complex picture of the angst that he suffers in this novel. Ideas developed by psychoanalyst Sigmund Freud in relation to dreams and displacement aid in understanding Allende's discussion of Reeves's distressed state. Freud uses displacement to refer to what he understood as the basic functioning of dreams and also the discourse that may be employed to describe them. Two basic patterns of dreams and texts may be ascertained: *condensation*, which combines and concentrates multiple experiences through complex images; and *displacement*, where one thing is substituted for something closely related. Subconscious elements in dreams and actions may be hidden

---

3   This term is borrowed from Philip Swanson's discussion of the three novels in 'California Dreaming: Mixture, Muddle and Meaning in Isabel Allende's North American Narratives', *Journal of Iberian and Latin American Studies*, 9 (2003), 59–67, and is employed throughout this chapter and in the conclusion.
4   Linda Gould Levine, *Isabel Allende* (New York: Twayne, 2003), p. 95.

in the subconscious, and through writing and/or therapy, repressed elements may come to light. By implication, Freud establishes a type of mutual dependence between displacement and the imagination, arguing that the imagination is 'nothing less than the essential portion of the dream-work'.[5] Freud seeks to highlight the centrality of displacement in dreaming and as one of the psyche's tools of representation, by arguing that there are often considerable discrepancies between the content and actual meaning of dreams: 'the dream is, as it were, differently centered from the dream-thoughts – its content has different elements as its central point' (p. 305). Thus, Freud implies that there is a form of de-centring or displacement at work within the dream. Furthermore, he saw dreams as a manifestation of the 'suppressed material' in people's lives, and that displacement becomes an important mechanism not only in dreaming but also in the organization of the discourse of dreams: 'the analysis [...] of dreams [...] exhibits the same processes of displacement and condensation as [the dream-work]' (p. 597). At the heart of dreams, then, there is not only an act of displacement but also a distortion of truth; the communication of dream content through writing or therapy can help to illustrate what has been repressed. In addition, displacement may equally be a feature of one's actions and not merely of one's dreams. In this sense, displacement serves as a form of defence mechanism: as Andrew Colman succinctly explains, this type of displacement is a 'redirection of emotional feelings from their original object to a substitute object related to the original one by a chain of associations.'[6] Both aspects of displacement, that is, in relation to dreams and lived experiences, coalesce in the character of Reeves, and it is here suggested that his bicultural experiences have a telling effect on him, in what may be described as *psychocultural* displacement, a conflation of Freudian ideas sketched above and a term which seeks to suggest the impact of cultural experiences as a variable in this analysis.

---

5   Sigmund Freud, *The Interpretation of Dreams* (London: Penguin, 1991), p. 121.
6   Andrew M. Colman, 'displacement *n.*', in *A Dictionary of Psychology* (Oxford: Oxford University Press, 2006), p. 264.

The opening sequences of *El plan infinito* clearly lend themselves to an analysis in relation to Freudian ideas on displacement in dreams and to the types of displacement activity which Reeves suffers at various stages of his life: in the brief prologue to the novel, Reeves's personal battle with his traumatic experiences becomes manifest in his description of a recurring nightmare. In this nightmare, he finds himself back on a term of duty as a soldier in the Vietnam War. He is the last soldier standing on a mountain top, surrounded by '[s]ombras sigilosas' [*crouching shadows*],[7] and is struggling to fend off these unfamiliar figures. Just as they reach him, Gregory suddenly awakes: '[m]i propio grito me despierta y sigo gritando, gritando' (p. 7) [*my own scream wakes me up and I keep on screaming and screaming*]. His traumatic experiences on the Vietnamese battlefields are recalled constantly on his return to the United States. He appears trapped in this nightmare, which carries over into his daily life, as he strives to discover who the 'fantasmas sin rostro' (p. 7) [*faceless phantoms*] of his dreams are.

In direct contrast with this terrifying scene is one of relative serenity, when it is revealed that Gregory Reeves is relating this nightmare, and indeed his life-story, retrospectively to an author-narrator. With the benefit of hindsight, a sense of resolution is intimated, and this revelation provides an immediate counterpoint to the menacing shadows of the prologue. Allende's text explores the various dilemmas Gregory has had to encounter in order to reach this stage of closure. The numerous experiences of loss and displacement he experiences throughout his childhood, and the new cultural milieu he finds himself in, all contribute to an increasing sense of desperation and helplessness as he grows older. Opening descriptions of a carefree youth are ominously supplanted by the proleptic suggestion of impending seismic changes in his life: '[é]se fue el único período en que Gregory se sintió seguro. La rabia empezó más tarde, cuando desapareció el padre y la realidad comenzó a deteriorarse de manera irreparable' (p. 12) [*that was the only time in his life when Gregory felt safe. His anger began later, when his father disappeared and reality began to break down irreparably*].

7   Isabel Allende, *El plan infinito* (Barcelona: Plaza y Janés, 1991), p. 7. Subsequent references will appear parenthetically in the text.

Gregory's early childhood is marked by constant movement and migration; while he travels around California in a truck with his family, his father, Charles Reeves, preaches to various groups of people on his philosophy of life, known as *El plan infinito*. Events that occur both within and outside the family unit shortly following this resettlement have an enduring and seemingly irrevocable effect on Reeves: his mother Nora, 'incapacitada para la vida práctica' [*not cut out for the practical things in life*] and whose 'mente se perdía en sueños de otro mundo' (p. 24) [*mind wandered in dreams of another world*], becomes even more distant when she lapses into a serious bout of depression after hearing about the dropping of atomic bombs in Nagasaki. His father's health deteriorates rapidly and Charles seems subsequently to descend into insanity. His sudden illness challenges the stability of the family unit, and he is forced to abandon his peripatetic proselytizing and to settle down with his family. As explained in the text, 'fue el comienzo del estropicio que acabó con la época feliz de su niñez' (p. 37) [*it was the beginning of the havoc that put an end to the happiest time in his childhood*]. The Reeves family decide to settle in a Hispanic *barrio* of Los Angeles, and, somewhat ironically, it is settling into a sedentary lifestyle which becomes most unsettling for a family which appeared to have thrived on constant movement.

Reeves struggles with this enforced domesticity, and a sense of the increasing mental and physical claustrophobia that plagues him through his adult life can be traced from these early experiences. His efforts to communicate outside the family unit are hampered by the omnipresence of the Spanish language in the *barrio*, but he gradually begins to assimilate Spanish and even uses it at one point to displace his anger at the sudden deterioration in his father's condition: 'se acurrucó [...], repitiendo chingada, chingada, como una letanía' (p. 42) [*he curled up in a ball [...] repeating fuck it, fuck it, like a mantra*]. His cultural experiences in the *barrio* leave an indelible mark on his character: on the one hand, he enjoys many positive experiences there, and later recounts as an adult that 'la música y la comida latinas quedarían para siempre unidas en su mente con la idea de amistad' (p. 46) [*He would always associate Latino music and food with the idea of friendship*]. While he admires this sense of community, and forges strong friendships with the siblings Juan José and Carmen Morales,

Cultural Displacement

he is acutely aware of the real difficulties that lie in trying to become fully integrated there:

> en el *ghetto* experimenté la desazón de ser diferente, no me integraba, deseaba ser como los otros [...] libre de las pandillas de muchachos morenos que descargaban en mí las agresiones que ellos mismos recibían de los blancos apenas asomaban las narices fuera de su barrio. (p. 55)
>
> [*in the ghetto I had the unsavoury experience of being different. I didn't belong, and wanted to be like the others [...] free from the gangs of dark-skinned boys who offloaded on me the aggression that they themselves suffered at the hands of white kids if they poked their noses outside their neighbourhood.*]

Reeves here establishes a direct connection between culture and displacement: he is the *blanco*, at once the white boy and also the target of the displaced anger felt by the local Hispanic boys.[8] Added to Reeves's difficulties in becoming a part of the local community, he again finds himself, unwittingly, to be the target of further displacement activity, when his sister, Judy, the only family member with whom he had maintained a firm relationship during this unsettling period, suddenly and inexplicably rejects him, leaving him to deal with what he describes as 'el pánico de la soledad absoluta' (p. 55) [*the panic of absolute solitude*]. Unbeknownst to Reeves at this juncture, Judy has been physically abused by their father, and her outburst appears to describe how she would have liked to address her father rather than Gregory: '¡[á]ndate al carajo y no vuelvas a tocarme en los días de tu vida!' (p. 56) [*go to hell! Don't ever touch me again for as long as you're alive!*]. For Gregory, however, such an unfathomable rejection forms part of the domestic atmosphere in which there prevails 'un misterio [...] del cual estaba excluido' (p. 59) [*a mystery ... which he was excluded from*].

As Reeves turns more towards the *barrio*, he also admits that his cultural background leaves him at a remove from fuller integration. He acknowledges this when he describes the Hispanic street gangs, stating that 'nunca podría incorporarse a ninguna; aquello también era una cuestión de raza, y enfrentarlas constituía un acto de locura' (p. 73) [*I could never*

---

8   The Spanish word 'blanco' can mean both *white (boy)* and *target*.

join any of those gangs; it was a question of race, and it would be madness to confront them]. Indeed, it is a member of one of these gangs, Martínez, who subjects Reeves to a brutal attack in the school broom cupboard. In the immediate aftermath, Gregory runs into some local fields, endeavouring perhaps to recapture the freedom and innocence of his early childhood, and retreats into the world of dreams:

> Me invade una calma profunda, se me olvida Martínez, el miedo, el dolor y el cuarto de las escobas, estoy en paz, me elevo y me voy volando con los ojos abiertos hacia el vacío sideral, me voy volando, volando con [el perro] *Oliver*. (p. 84)
>
> [*A deep calm fills me; I forget about Martinez, fear, pain and the broom cupboard. I am at peace, I rise up and fly away towards the starred emptiness with my eyes wide open. I fly away, far away, with my dog Oliver.*]

Martínez reappears briefly in Reeves's life in high school; Reeves challenges the posturing Martínez to a race against a passing train. Martínez is killed when he tries to cross in front of the train, and his death puts an end to one troubling chapter of Gregory's life.

Reeves begins to take advantage of his bicultural experiences in high school, when he becomes school president and finds he can relate to all students. Using the money bequeathed to him by his friend, the lift-operator Cyrus, Reeves relocates to Berkeley to study law. Despite the cosmopolitan backdrop of Berkeley, Gregory nevertheless experiences a sense of not belonging, yet it is not because of how he looks, but rather how he speaks: 'llegué a sospechar que me discriminaban por mi acento chicano' (p. 121) [*I began to suspect that they were discriminating against me because of my Chicano accent*]. Gregory ignores what are in truth rather isolated incidents, and he instead focuses his attention on his studies and also on finding a wife and settling down. His new, and apparently more positive dream of domestic bliss, which he believed he saw embodied in the home of the Morales family, appears doomed from the outset:

> [t]oda su vida había deseado pertenecer a un verdadero hogar, como el de los Morales, y tan enamorado estaba de aquel sueño doméstico, que decidió realizarlo con la primera mujer a su alcance, sin investigar si ella tenía el mismo plan. (p. 140)

> [*he had wanted to belong to a real home all his life, just like the Morales' home, and he was so in love with that dream of domesticity that he was determined to fulfill it with the first woman he found, without checking if she felt the same.*]

Reeves, unaware of the many problems that plague the Morales household beyond the surface appearance of intimacy and conviviality, decides to marry the self-obsessed Samantha Ernst, a woman whose focus on her physique echoes to a large degree Beatriz Alcántara de Beltrán's obsession with appearance in *De amor y de sombra*. The birth of their daughter Margaret fails to improve things between Gregory and Samantha, so he decides to enlist the services of his sister, Judy, now married with children, in the hope that she can share her maternal instincts with Samantha. However, Gregory's plan backfires spectacularly, as Judy instead uses this opportunity to reveal to him the terrible secret of her childhood experiences of abuse: 'derramó el veneno que había soportado en silencio desde aquella noche en la cual no le permitió [a Gregory] dormir junto a ella' (p. 154) [*she released the venom she had silently held in since that night when she wouldn't let Gregory sleep beside her*]. Gregory, who had felt punished as a young child by his sister's unexplained rejection of him, is yet again subjected to a shocking experience, and one which has immediate repercussions in his adult life. Judy's reasons for telling him – 'para evitar que se repita el mismo pecado de incesto en la familia' (p. 155) [*to avoid the same sin of incest being repeated in the family*] – has telling implications on Gregory, who immediately decides to give up his part-time job minding children. A perhaps more serious consequence of Judy's news, however, is that Reeves cannot display any affection toward his daughter, fearing that he may be capable of committing the same heinous act as his father:

> La confesión de su hermana erguía una muralla china entre su hija y él. Tampoco se sentía cómodo con los chicos que cuidaba en su trabajo y se sorprendía examinándose en busca de cualquier detalle revelador de una supuesta índole silenciosa heredada de su padre. (p. 157)
>
> [*His sister's confession erected a Chinese wall between his daughter and him. He didn't feel comfortable either with the children he minded at work and was surprised how he examined himself in search of any detail that would reveal an apparent silent tendency inherited from his father.*]

Unable to show affection to his daughter or to communicate with his self-absorbed wife, Gregory's dream of domestic perfection quickly degenerates into a seemingly inescapable nightmare. The prospects of escaping this scenario are bleak, with impending military service:

> Junto con el alivio de recibirse finalmente de abogado estaba la inevitable *pesadilla de ir al frente*, porque tenía un contrato con las Fuerzas Armadas y no podía seguir posponiendo el servicio. (p. 158, emphasis added)

> [*Along with the relief of finally being qualified as a lawyer was the inevitable* nightmare *of going to the front, because he had a contract with the Armed Forces and couldn't keep putting off military service.*] (emphasis added)

His wife Samantha finds an outlet for her own frustrated emotions in the frequent dinner parties which descend into naked orgies. Her inherent emotional contradictions are obvious:

> A partir de esa noche Samantha aprovechaba toda oportunidad de experimentar nuevas sensaciones en grupo, en cambio en la privacidad de la cama matrimonial seguía siendo tan fría como antes. (p. 161)

> [*From that night on Samantha took advantage of every opportunity to try new group experiences. In the privacy of her bedroom, however, she remained as cold as she had been before.*]

She presents a 'sucesión de máscaras' (p. 161) [*succession of masks*] to Reeves, and their emotional estrangement is increasingly evident. His unwillingness to participate in wife-swapping parties is naively attributed by Samantha to his upbringing in the Hispanic *barrio*, as seen in the opening epigraph to this chapter. Reeves feels an intense sense of emotional and physical isolation: '[n]o me sentía cómodo en ninguna parte' (p. 162) [*I didn't feel comfortable anywhere*]. Very quickly thereafter, Gregory escapes his troubled marriage by heading for the battlefields of Vietnam.

Reeves's experiences of war bring his internal conflicts into sharp relief: the entire sequence of events which he experiences and comments upon in Vietnam appear to take place in a surreal realm. He sees himself as one of many men who 'andan escapando de fracasos o de culpas' (p. 171) [*run*

Cultural Displacement 143

away from failure or guilt] by going to war. This escape, however, comes at a price, as he loses any sense of individuality. Gregory continues to battle with himself, and becomes both participant and detached observer of his experiences: he is engaged in 'una apuesta constante contra mí mismo, me observaba desde cierta distancia y me juzgaba con ironía' (p. 172) [*a constant battle against myself. I observed myself from some distance and judged myself with irony*]. He becomes addicted to drugs and sleeps fitfully, and becomes trapped 'en un limbo de tiempo eterno y de espacios torcidos' (p. 172) [*in a limbo of endless time and twisted spaces*]. A surprise reunion with his childhood friend Juan José Morales offers both men a brief respite from the war and an opportunity to reconnect with their shared cultural pasts and memories. However, the realities of endless warfare and the omnipresence of death continue to wear him down, and Gregory suffers a '[c]risis nerviosa' (p. 174) [*crisis of nerves*] from having to carry corpses from the battlefield. His experiences in the jungle reinforce his view of mechanization and the awareness of the erosion of individuality: '[e]n la batalla no hay que pensar, uno se transforma en una máquina de estropicio y muerte' (p. 175) [*in battle you don't have to think. You become a machine of havoc and death*].

Reeves enjoys a fleeting sense of community and belonging that he has been craving when he teaches English in a local mountain village: he reveals that '[e]ra el único lugar donde se había sentido aceptado como parte de una comunidad en casi treinta años de vida' (p. 187) [*it was the only place where he had felt accepted as part of a community in almost thirty years*]. However, this proves only to be an 'ilusoria tranquilidad' (p. 188) [*illusory peacefulness*] and Gregory falls ill. While convalescing in Hawaii, Gregory examines his path through life and contemplates his future. He is determined to ensure the life he will lead on returning to the United States bears little resemblance to other veterans' lives: '[n]o seré otro veterano en silla de ruedas, alcohólico, drogado y vencido, ya hay muchos de ellos. Seré rico, carajo' (p. 191) [*I won't be just another alcoholic, drugged-up and beaten-down veteran in a wheelchair – there's already enough of them. I'll get rich, dammit!*]. When he recovers, however, he is sent back to Saigon, much to his surprise and disappointment. Reeves survives his remaining twenty-five days in Vietnam and makes his way back to San Francisco. His resolution to embrace life appears even firmer, as he explains: '[d]e tanto ver la cara de la muerte aprendí el valor de la existencia' (p. 202) [*having seen the face of death so often, I learnt the value of existence*]. Despite this determination to follow his new dreams, he is reluctant to visit his estranged wife Samantha or to make any contact with family or relatives. His disconnection from life around him is described as stemming from an inability to return to civilian life:

> [e]n la vida civil nadie hablaba el idioma de la guerra, no existía un vocabulario para contar las experiencias del campo de batalla, pero de haberlo, de todos modos no había quien deseara escuchar mi historia, no hay interés en las malas noticias. (p. 205)
>
> [*in civilian life nobody spoke the language of war. There were no words to describe the experiences on the battlefield. Even if there were, there wouldn't be anyone who'd want to hear my story. Nobody's interested in bad news.*]

He is intensely lonely, and fears that his life from that moment on would be 'un desierto gris' (p. 206) [*a grey desert*]. Alone with his thoughts day and night, a decisive moment comes when he suffers a nightmare in which he revisits the mountain of his final Vietnam conflict, the substance of which formed part of the prologue to the novel: he is unable to stop the approaching enemies, who 'avanzaban inexorables' (p. 207) [*moved forward inexorably*]. Reeves tries to make a fresh start, burning all his possessions that remind him of the war. However, this physical purging is only half the battle, and at night, the internal conflict resurfaces for him:

> En el día lograba olvidar casi por completo, pero en las noches sufría pesadillas y despertaba bañado de sudor, con ruido de armas explotándole por dentro y visiones en rojo asaltándolo sin tregua. (p. 215)
>
> [*By day I could almost completely forget about it, but at night I had nightmares and would wake bathed in sweat. I could hear gunshot inside me and see blood-red visions endlessly assailing me.*]

Gregory's brief reunion with his childhood friend Carmen is also coloured in a sense by his experience of war; their frenzied love-making is described as an 'especie de mutual violación [...] no habían hecho el amor, sino algo que la dejó con sabor a pecado' (p. 224) [*type of mutual rape. They hadn't made love but rather something which seemed sinful*]. Indeed, despite their intimacy and long friendship, Gregory remains distant, perhaps inured to silence, as yet again memories return to haunt him:

> Le volvieron en tropel los recuerdos que procuraba mantener a raya, y sintió una profunda amargura, imposible de compartir con nadie, ni siquiera con ella en ese instante de intimidad. (p. 225)
>
> [*Memories he tried to keep at bay rushed back, and he felt a profound sense of bitterness, impossible to share with anybody, not even with her in this intimate moment.*]

Gregory is unable to communicate this sense of isolation, and is again marginalized when he visits his close friend Timothy Duane's house for dinner: '[l]o trataban con exagerada cortesía o lo ignoraban por completo, no había lugar para los combatientes fuera del campo de batalla' (p. 227) [*they treated him with exceeding politeness, or else completely ignored him. There was no place for combatants outside of the battlefield*]. However, this dinner does provide Gregory with an opportunity to meet Timothy's father, who decides to employ him in his law firm. Gregory uses his work as an excuse for losing contact with family and friends, and he becomes obsessed with material gain: 'con la misma determinación que empleó en salir vivo de Vietnam, se propuso superar los obstáculos sembrados en su camino' (p. 232) [*with the same resolve that he used to get out of Vietnam alive, he was determined to overcome the obstacles in his way*].

It is in the fourth and final part of the story that Gregory's internal conflict finally surfaces. His anguish has begun to infiltrate his daily life, and he feels that he is carrying the pain of several generations:

> mientras estaba ocupado lograba ignorar los apuros del alma, pero si le sobraban unos minutos y se encontraba quieto y en silencio, sentía una hoguera consumiéndolo por dentro, tan poderosa que estaba seguro de que no era sólo suya, la había alimentado su desaforado padre y antes de él su abuelo, ladrón de caballos, y aún antes quién sabe cuántos bisabuelos marcados por el mismo estigma de inquietud. (p. 255)

> [*while he was busy he managed to ignore the problems in his soul; however, if he had a few minutes free and was alone and silent, he felt a fire consuming him from within. The fire was so potent that he was certain that it wasn't only his, but its flames had been fanned by his wild father and, before him, his grandfather, a horse hustler, and who knows how many great grandfathers were affected by this stigma of worry.*]

Gregory's attitude is also suggested as being part of the general culture of the US in the 1980s, following the Vietnam War: it is described as 'un deseo colectivo de reivindicarse por otros medios' (p. 255) [*a collective desire for vindication through other means*]. He plummets further into debt, while his relationship with his daughter Margaret becomes purely material and perfunctory:

> Después de cada visita la devolvía con un cargamento de regalos, más apropiados para una mujer coqueta que para una colegiala impúber, y enferma por el atracón de helados y pasteles. (pp. 256–7)
>
> [*after every visit, he dropped her home with a shipment of presents, more appropriate for a flirtatious woman than for a prepubescent schoolgirl. She was sick from having gorged on so many cakes and ice creams.*]

Gregory is struggling tremendously, and he precariously hangs on to reality:

> Lo ayudaba la buena memoria para recordar cada hilo suelto de esa maraña, la buena suerte para no resbalar en un descuido y la buena salud para no morir de agotamiento como una bestia de tiro pasado el límite de su resistencia. (p. 261)
>
> [*His good memory helped him remember every loose end in that tangled mess; his good luck helped him keep out of trouble, while his good health ensured he did not die of exhaustion, like a beast of burden pushed beyond the limits of its endurance.*]

He finds love with his secretary Shanon and appears to be recovering: he makes a decisive step to establish his own law firm in San Francisco when his employer refuses to take the case of Bel Benedict and her son King, whom Gregory had befriended as a child when he travelled around with his family. His business is successful, and he exploits his bicultural background to target Hispanic clients through television advertisements. However, Reeves's dedication to work leaves him blind to Shanon's infidelity, and when he is informed of this by his secretary, Tina Faibich, '[a] Gregory el mundo se le tiñó de rojo, cogió al acusado por la solapa y se trenzó a puñetazos' (p. 280) [*Gregory's world took on a red hue; he grabbed the accused by the collar and punched him*]. However, there is an added dimension to Reeves's anger: '[f]ingió una rabia que en verdad ya no sentía, sólo por la satisfacción de humillarla, pero volvió a su lado tal como lo haría cada vez que se fuera en los meses siguientes' (p. 280) [*He feigned anger which, in truth, he did not feel. He just wanted the satisfaction of humiliating her, but he went back to her just as he would do every time he left over the course of the following months*].

Enmeshed in a world of materialism, and unable to reveal his true feelings, Reeves resorts to playing a convoluted game of pretence, rejection and acceptance. He finally decides to get divorced and leaves Shanon and his son David. Once again, work is the means by which he copes: '[s]e sumergió en el trabajo, sin tiempo ni buena disposición para trajines domésticos, se limitó a mantener vivas sus plantas' (p. 291) [*he threw himself into his work; he had no time and was unwilling to get involved in domestic chores. He just kept the plants alive*]. Carmen attempts to help him by pointing out that his clients are poor Latinos and this will not help him make money, but he reveals that '[e]ra incapaz de cerrar la puerta a quien solicitaba ayuda, tanto en la oficina como en su vida privada' (p. 294) [*he couldn't close the door on anyone who needed help, both in the office and in his private life*]. His dedication to the people from the *barrio* sends him spiralling into debt.

Added to all his professional and hidden personal problems, Reeves also has to start taking care of David, when his ex-wife Shanon decides to leave Los Angeles. Interestingly, it is Carmen who is the first to suggest that Reeves seek counselling for himself rather than for his hyperactive son. Reeves rejects the idea outright, arguing that '[s]e había criado en un medio donde esa posibilidad no se planteaba y en ese período todavía creía que los hombres deben arreglárselas solos' (p. 297) [*he had been raised in an environment where this possibility didn't exist and at that time he still believed that men should get by on their own*]. However, it is increasingly clear that Reeves is unable to cope with the various situations he is trying to juggle: 'sentía la cabeza llena de ruido, como en los peores tiempos de la guerra [...], se ahogaba como si tuviera los pulmones llenos de algodón'.

(p. 300) [*he felt his head was full of noise, like during the worst times at war … he was drowning and felt as if his lungs were full of cotton*].

When he finally starts to think about himself, he undergoes a transformation which in many ways reflects how he felt as a child when facing Martínez in the race against the train, or when he cried out after the death of a young Kansas soldier with whom he had served in Vietnam. He loses control and finally gives in to the pain:

> algo estalló en su alma, un dolor terrible clavado en el pecho y repartiéndose desde allí en ondas por el resto de su cuerpo, quemándolo, partiéndolo, rompiéndole los huesos y arrancándole la piel, perdió la capacidad de contenerse, ya no era él mismo sino ese intolerable sufrimiento, esa atormentada medusa de mar desparramándose por la habitación y llenando el espacio, una sola herida sangrante. (p. 306)
>
> [*something exploded in his soul; a terrible pain pierced his chest and spread throughout his body in waves, burning him, splitting him, breaking his bones and ripping his skin off. He could not longer contain himself; he was no longer himself but this intolerable suffering, that tortured jellyfish spilling out all over the room and filling the space, a whole, bleeding wound.*]

Reeves's transformation is immobilizing, and he experiences an immense surge of pain. Thoughts of his children spring to mind, and he wonders if he has in some way genetically passed on his anguish to them: 'acaso les había transmitido en los genes una maldición o si ellos tendrían que pagar las culpas de él' (pp. 306–7). It is only a chance phone call from Carmen that helps him escape from this labyrinth of unhealthy thoughts: '[t]ardó una eternidad en reconocer el sonido [del teléfono], darse cuenta dónde se encontraba y verse en el suelo, desnudo, mojado de orina, de vómito y de llanto, borracho, aterrorizado' (p. 307) [*It took him an age to recognize the phone ringing, to realize where he was – on the floor, nude, covered in urine, vomit and tears, drunk and terrified*].

Carmen sets about trying to do all she can to help Reeves. He receives further help from a close friend when he is introduced to Timothy Duane's fiancée Ming O'Brien, a psychiatrist. Timothy encourages him to visit her to talk about his problems. In the initial session, Ming asks Reeves to talk about a recurring dream that he experiences. He says:

> vi a mis enemigos vestidos de negro avanzando hacia mí, cientos de ellos, sigilosos, amenazadores, transparentes, mis compañeros caídos como brochazos escarlatas en el gris oprimente del paisaje. (p. 315)
>
> [*I saw my enemies dressed in black come towards me. There were hundreds of them, stealthy, threatening, transparent. My fallen comrades were like scarlet brushstrokes on the oppressive grey of the landscape.*]

Ming asks Reeves to look at the enemies' faces closely and he makes the shocking discovery that all of the enemies look like him. This realization helps him make his struggle a conscious one, and he can embark on his long journey through therapy. Five years later, he can finally understand and embrace his pain:

> Con ella pude por fin nombrar el dolor, comprenderlo y manejarlo, sabiendo que siempre estaría presente en una u otra forma, porque es parte de la existencia, y cuando esa idea echó raíces mi angustia disminuyó de manera milagrosa. (pp. 316–17)
>
> [*With her I could finally put a name to my pain, understand it and manage it, knowing that it would always be there in one way or another, as it is part of my existence. When this idea took root, my anguish lessened miraculously.*]

Gregory begins to restructure his life, but a court case brought against him by a former employee bankrupts him. With one final intervention from Carmen, now a successful jewel-seller, he can begin to pay off his debts. One of Gregory's final comments with the author-narrator explains the importance of his journey: '[c]omprendí que lo más importante no había sido sobrevivir o tener éxito, como imaginaba antes, sino la búsqueda de mi alma rezagada en los arenales de la infancia' (p. 348) [*I understood that what was most important was not surviving or being successful, as I had managed before; instead it was the search for my soul which was left behind in the sandpits of childhood*]. The unexpected discovery of love with this author-narrator, and the ability to communicate fully with her suggests he has been ultimately successful in his journey through the trauma of war and incommunicability.

Throughout *El plan infinito*, Gregory Reeves struggles to achieve a sense of identity: the shift in his early childhood from experiences of constant movement to enforced sedentariness is a mixed blessing for him, and the move into a Hispanic *barrio* leads to irrevocable changes in his life. While he greatly admires the apparent image of settled domesticity projected by the Morales family, he is largely unaware of the problems within that family. His life in the *barrio* is complicated by his background, and he becomes the target of disaffected Hispanic youths, who view Gregory's appearance there as being transgressive and worthy of punishment. His difficulties in expressing himself appear to stem from the sequential loss of contact with his family through illness, rejection and psychological displacement, yet it is interesting that Gregory never truly blames anybody other than himself for his situation, while he continues to be the target of misplaced anger in his adult life, notably during his marriages to Samantha Ernst and Shanon respectively. It is also noticeable that Gregory's displacement activities of addiction and materialism are never directed towards anybody else, and seem to be a form of self-delusion and self-destruction. Levine somewhat inaccurately suggests that, as he grows older, Gregory 'is seduced by the dominant ideological model and the promise of freedom on the other side of the barrio',[9] a view which suggests that Gregory has rejected his hybrid cultural experiences. However, his life revolves around helping marginal people, and it is to these that he consistently returns through his work in the law firm, even if this ultimately causes bankruptcy. The quest for riches is always tempered by a determination to help those from the *barrio*.

His own contributions through first-person narration highlight his problems with communicating his feelings: Cox argues that '[e]ven during the first-person sections, Gregory seems habitually unable to articulate his feelings or motives'.[10] This appears to be a deliberate ploy on Allende's part, an attempt to illustrate his internal conflict, which he cannot successfully resolve until after his therapy. Philip Swanson argues that 'Gregory Reeves's story is in many ways the story of his developing relationship with his own

---

9   Levine, p. 101.
10   Cox, p. 103.

masculinity'.[11] This is certainly borne out through his attempts to find a sense of identity, but it may be equally valid to suggest that he grapples with his understanding of ethnicity: despite being a white male, he finds it difficult to consider himself part of the mainstream, and throughout his life he finds love and acceptance in the margins. He considers the Morales family his true family; he calls Juan José his 'hermano' [*brother*] and believes that a relationship with Carmen would be akin to incest. He finds emotional understanding through the family friend Olga, and struggles with his first wife, Samantha, who believes his inability to embrace her broad concept of free love is because of his upbringing in the *barrio*. Ultimately, however, Gregory gets the help and love that he needs from the marginal communities that comprise Los Angeles: he receives financial help from the Hispanic community through Carmen and from the Chinese community through his accountant Mike Tong, while his journey through therapy is supported by the Asian woman Ming O'Brien. His relationship with the author-narrator can also perhaps be considered a relationship with the Hispanic community. His willingness to become involved with those considered marginal is a key step in escaping financial and emotional ruin.

'The Perilous Territory of Not-Belonging':[12] Jacob Todd/Freemont and the American Idyll in *Hija de la fortuna*

Allende's exploration of the links between the margins and the mainstream continues in her 1999 novel, *Hija de la fortuna*. Edward Said's above quotation is a useful starting point for an examination of the character of

11   Philip Swanson, 'California Dreaming: Mixture, Muddle and Meaning in Isabel Allende's North American Narratives', *Journal of Iberian and Latin American Studies*, 9 (2003), 59–67.
12   Edward Said, 'Reflections on Exile', in *Out There: Marginalization and Other Cultures*, ed. by Russell Ferguson, Martha Gever and Marcia Tuckers (Cambridge, MA: MIT Press, 1992), pp. 357–66 (p. 359).

Jacob Todd/Freemont in this novel:[13] throughout the text, Jacob struggles to fit in. His original efforts to become fully integrated into Chilean society are ultimately superseded by his desire to exploit language and his cultural knowledge for purely financial gain when he moves to the United States.

Jacob arrives in the Chilean city of Valparaíso on the strength of a drunken wager made back in England that he could sell three hundred Bibles anywhere in the world. Striking up a friendship with Captain John Sommers on the ship to Valparaíso, he is afforded immediate access to the marginal, though wealthy and select group of British expatriates resident there, largely because of the Sommers brothers mistaking Jacob for a Protestant missionary. On arrival, Jacob first visits the local Hotel Inglés, its false air of Britishness somewhat naively prompting him to think that 'por lo visto no tendría problemas de adaptación' (p. 25) [*apparently, he wouldn't have any problems fitting in*]. There he is introduced to John's brother, Jeremy, who has little interest in being part of the local community, and who maintains a cautious distance from locals wherever possible, because he believes that Chile is 'un país de ladrones' (p. 14) [*a land of thieves*]. Jacob's first meeting with Jeremy is representative of the general reluctance on the part of the British living there to make any efforts at social or cultural integration. They even refuse to speak Spanish, preferring instead to communicate with locals in a pidginized form of language, described as a 'jerigonza inventada por los británicos para entenderse con la servidumbre' (p. 26) [*mumbo jumbo made up by the British to make themselves understood by servants*].[14] Jacob's first formal introduction to the narrow British expatriate social circle takes place when he attends one of their frequent Wednesday-night musical gatherings hosted by

---

13   Jacob changes his surname from Todd to Freemont during the narrative. For ease of reference, he will be referred to simply as Jacob for the rest of this discussion.
14   The creation of pidgin languages, a simplified form of communication largely based on a superstrate (also known as a *lexifier*) language, was a key feature of colonizers' efforts to force slaves from various language backgrounds to work together. For further information, see Helen Thomas's *Romanticism and Slave Narratives: Transatlantic Testimonies* (Cambridge: Cambridge University Press, 2000).

Jeremy and his sister Rose Sommers, with whom Jacob becomes infatuated. However, these evenings are rather staid affairs and, judging from the numerous embarrassing incidents of broken protocol that occur, it appears as if nobody is quite sure how to behave in this situation. The expatriates inhabit a world of splendid isolation, at a remove from most people and events in Chilean society. They are described as 'una pequeña nación dentro del país, con sus costumbres, cultos, periódicos, clubes, escuelas y hospitales' (p. 23) [*a little nation inside the country, with their own customs, rites, newspapers, clubs, schools and hospitals*]. As Karen Castellucci Cox states, '[t]hough they live in Chile, they retain all the characteristics of their homeland and spurn all but the most upper-class natives.'[15] Cox's quotation makes reference to contact between the expatriates and the locals, which occurs in the *Club de la Unión* [*Union Club*], a male-dominated environment described as 'un enclave de terratenientes y políticos conservadores, donde se medía el valor de los socios por el apellido' (p. 49) [*an enclave of landlords and Conservative politicians, where the value of members was measured by surnames*]. It is this contact which helps Jacob gain privileged access to the upper classes of Valparaíso society: 'gracias a ellos se le abrieron de par en par las puertas de la próspera colonia extranjera, dispuesta a ayudarlo en la supuesta misión religiosa en Tierra del Fuego' (p. 46) [*thanks to them the doors of the prosperous foreign colony, who were willing to help him with his apparent religious mission to Tierra del Fuego, were opened wide to him*]. Jacob is automatically accepted because of his provenance and perceived reputation as a missionary, and he maintains the façade when he realizes that it is financially very beneficial to him. Unlike other British expatriates, however, Jacob is interested in trying to learn Spanish, and, through a combination of his apparent missionary work and solid linguistic skills, manages to develop a network of acquaintances from all parts of the social spectrum: '[s]e conectó con chilenos de todas clases, desde los más humildes, que conocía en sus andanzas por los barrios bajos del puerto, hasta los más empingorotados' (p. 49) [*he connected with Chileans of all classes, from the humblest, whom he met in*

---

15 Karen Castellucci Cox, *Isabel Allende* (Westport, CT: Greenwood, 2003), p. 128.

his travels through the poorer neighbourhoods by the ports, through to the richest]. Jacob's successful incorporation into all levels of society is implied by the description that 'llegó a sentirse tan cómodo en Valparaíso como si hubiera nacido allí' (p. 49) [*he began to feel as comfortable in Valparaiso, as if he had been born there*]. However, Jacob is also acutely aware that the structures of Chilean society are of little significance to him and to the other British residents there: in a conversation with Jeremy on the future of Eliza, he explains: '[s]omos extranjeros, Jeremy, apenas chapuceamos el castellano. ¿Qué nos importan las clases sociales chilenas? Nunca perteneceremos a este país' (p. 58) [*We're foreigners, Jeremy. We hardly speak any Spanish. What do Chilean social classes matter to us? We'll never belong in this country*]. The comparative irrelevance of class structure in Chile to Jacob is further reflected through his involvement in bringing together Paulina del Valle, of aristocratic stock, and nouveau riche Feliciano Rodríguez de Santa Cruz; the friendship he forges with them plays a crucial role in his bid to recover his lost reputation at a later stage of the narrative. Jacob's resistance towards social structures acquires a new dimension when he befriends young Chilean entrepreneurs, and he begins to articulate his ideas for a utopian society. He develops a friendship with Joaquín Andieta, a young worker with incendiary ideas, and, intrigued to see where he lives, Jacob follows Andieta home one night. Jacob is shocked at Andieta's squalid living conditions, and, on returning home, he finds himself 'incapaz de enfrentar el contraste entre la pobreza que acababa de dejar atrás y esos salones con muebles de cuero y lámparas de cristal' (p. 73) [*unable to deal with the contrast between the poverty which he had just left behind and those living rooms with leather furniture and glass lamps*]. It is at this stage in the novel, as Jacob appears to be developing a social conscience and is becoming aware of the pervasive socioeconomic inequality in Valparaíso, that there is an abrupt shift, when news breaks that Jacob has been siphoning funds from the missionary coffers for personal use. All links he had previously enjoyed with privilege and power are immediately severed as his fraudulent activity is exposed and his social displacement is immediate:

Cultural Displacement

> Se terminaron para él las tertulias de los miércoles en casa de los Sommers y nadie en la colonia extranjera volvió a invitarlo; lo eludían en la calle y quienes tenían negocios con él, los dieron por concluidos. La noticia del engaño alcanzó a sus amigos chilenos, quienes le sugirieron discreta, pero firmemente, que no apareciera más por el *Club de la Unión* si deseaba evitar el bochorno de ser expulsado. (p. 70)

> [*The Wednesday evening gatherings in the Sommers's house ended for him. Nobody in the foreign colony invited him out again. They avoided him on the street and anybody who had business with him considered their business over. The news of his deceit reached his Chilean friends' ears. They suggested discreetly, but firmly, that he should not turn up again at the Club de la Unión if he wanted to avoid the shame of being ejected.*]

Despite his previous success at moving between the British and Chilean worlds, he is immediately shunned and displaced from his previous position of privilege. Jacob is merely left with the solace of his friendships with Joaquín, Feliciano and Paulina. His apparent ability to resist the impositions of social structures is futile as he descends into a world of alienation and alcoholism, until he finally accepts the offer to travel back on John Sommers's ship to England, where he feels that he can 'perderse en la muchedumbre' (p. 80) [*get lost in the crowd*]. Unable to cast off the shackles of financial scandal even on returning to England, or to further his dream of a utopian society there, Jacob accepts an invitation by Feliciano to reestablish and reinvent himself in San Francisco. Drawing on his linguistic strengths, which had won over so many in Chile, and encouraged them to contribute to his putative missionary work, Jacob chooses to become a journalist, and to document the developing multicultural landscape of California. In this fractious atmosphere, Jacob is drawn to the ethnic struggles there and grows interested in an elusive bandit named Joaquín Murieta, who may or may not be his former Chilean acquaintance Joaquín Andieta.[16] The true identity of the bandit is never revealed in the text, and, for Jacob, this is of little consequence, given that Jacob never actually meets any bandit. Instead, he fashions an imaginative, pan-Hispanic composite, and he thrives on the unexpected financial success the stories he writes about this

---

16   Jacob never directly alludes to this in the novel; this suggestion is based upon Eliza's search for Joaquín Andieta in California.

outlaw brings him. As Jacob himself notes, 'buscando el anonimato estaba encontrando la celebridad' (p. 323) [*while searching for anonymity he was finding celebrity*]. However, the impact of his work is telling: 'sus artículos sensacionalistas habían creado un héroe para los hispanos y un demonio para los yanquis' (p. 372) [*his sensationalist articles had created a hero for the Hispanic community and a villain for the Yankees*]. Though conscious of the dangerous possibility of being exposed once again for fraudulent activity, Jacob persists in developing this persona, and has even plotted out an alternative means of exploiting this fictive fabrication, should his lies ever be exposed; he plans to write a novel. Once again, Jacob's lack of interest in perceived social boundaries is evident, but this situation is now markedly different from his time in Valparaíso because of the reactions from different ethnic groupings. Jacob travels through California, and documents local people's descriptions of the bandit. Again, he employs his linguistic skills to great effect:

> La misma fervorosa elocuencia que años antes empleaba en Chile para describir a unos indios patagones en Tierra del Fuego, donde nunca había puesto los pies, ahora le servía para sacar de la manga a un bandolero imaginario. (p. 377)

> [*The same feverish eloquence which years before he had used in Chile to describe indigenous Patagonians in Tierra del Fuego, where he had never set foot, was now being used to create magically an imaginary bandit.*]

He is also aware of the changes this creation is having upon his own personality, and appears in the imaginative projection of rebelliousness constituted by Murieta:

> El embuste de las misiones en Valparaíso había quedado atrás, pero ahora estaba fraguando otro y sentía, como antes, que su creación se apoderaba de él e iba sumiéndose irrevocablemente en sus propias flaquezas. (p. 394)

> [*The lie about the missions in Valparaiso had been left behind; now he was forging a new one and he felt, like before, that his creation was taking control of him and he was gradually becoming trapped by his own foibles.*]

Jacob revels unexpectedly in the Californian wastelands, and this apparently less than idyllic landscape is extremely profitable. Yet he begins to become 'embrollado en su retórica' (p. 395) [*embroiled in his own rhetoric*], and his journalism is never submitted to close scrutiny. This transformation seems to be beyond his control; he becomes more removed from reality, and he finds refuge in his imaginative creation. He exploits his cultural experiences in Chile to trace the ethnic fault lines of the burgeoning California, but he surrenders his own identity in the process. However, Jacob does not try to expose the true story, and instead rather cowardly hides behind his successful creation: 'no tenía valor para hacerlo. El prestigio se le había ido a la cabeza y andaba mareado de celebridad' (p. 395) [*he hadn't the heart to do it. Prestige had gone to his head and he was dizzy from his celebrity status*]. As is explained concisely in the sequel to *Hija de la fortuna*, *Retrato en sepia*, articles such as those written on Murieta by Jacob 'acabaron por darle bien ganada fama de embustero' (p. 54) [*ended up giving him the well-earned reputation of being a liar*]. He has not been chastened by his experience in Chile and continues to exploit his cultural knowledge for purely personal gain, and to engage in further fraudulence. He pays little or no heed to the dangerous effects his writing has on flaring the passions of both locals and immigrants. In his quest to belong, he ends up inhabiting a financially rewarding, though socially isolating territory of non-belonging, as his misappropriation of cultural knowledge displaces him once again into a profitable but solitary utopia.

Eliza's Cop(y)ing Strategies: Mimicry in *Hija de la fortuna*

The challenges of integration faced by Jacob Sommers and the experience of cultural displacement are also significant discussion points in relation to Eliza Sommers in *Hija de la fortuna*. In 'Of Mimicry and Man', cultural theorist Homi K. Bhabha explores the idea of mimicry within colonial discourse, and describes it as a resemblance that is partial, 'almost the same, but not quite'.[17] David Huddart explains Bhabha's concept of mimicry as 'an exaggerated copying of language, culture, manners, and ideas'.[18] Homi Bhabha offers a variety of perspectives on the interconnection of mimicry, authority and subversion in colonial contexts which may be usefully applied to Eliza Sommers in *Hija de la fortuna*. While Bhabha's work is chiefly concerned with colonial and postcolonial situations, the relationship between power and mimicry enters into contexts which depend upon maintaining dominant and subordinate relations. In essence, Bhabha argues that, at one level, mimicry is a reflection of the dominant discourse's insistence upon a clearly recognizable other in keeping with its expectations and the accommodation to its strategies of those under its authority. Yet at another level, mimicry becomes a secret form of insubordination and of difference which threatens the views of those in authority. In Bhabha's eyes, then, mimicry is a reminder to the dominant discourse of an 'other' 'that is almost the same, but not quite' (p. 381). For Bhabha, the ambivalence of mimicry does not rupture the dominant discourse but rather brings about a degree of uncertainty which renders the subjected as a 'partial' or 'incomplete' presence, primarily because of a lack of recognition on the part of the dominant but also because they represent a challenge to the way these dominant groups endeavour to appear natural or normal. Thus the success of authoritative discourse is largely dependent upon the creation of partial or incomplete subjects who reflect what the discourse desires of them but signify a constant rejection of it. Subjects of colonial discourse inhabit a space in which overtly or covertly authority and power are mocked. This section explores how Eliza Sommers successfully exploits this concept of mimicry to survive, gain independence, explore gender and adapt to the cultural dilemmas and cultural displacement she encounters in *Hija de la fortuna*.

From the earliest descriptions of Eliza's background, there is a type of narrative jostling for a claim on her past between the identifiably (neo)colonial British and the indigenous: clear discrepancies can be seen between the

---

17   Homi K. Bhabha, 'Of Mimicry and Man: The Ambivalence of Colonial Discourse', in *The Location of Culture* (London: Routledge, 1994), pp. 85–92 (p. 89).
18   David Huddart, *Homi Bhabha* (London: Routledge, 2006), p. 57.

embellished tale of her apparently serendipitous arrival, offered by her adoptive mother, the British expatriate Miss Rose Sommers, and the more prosaic reality of Eliza's ostensibly calculated abandonment on the Sommers' doorstep which is recounted by the indigenous household servant, and in a sense her second adoptive mother, Mama Fresia. Eliza's formative years are greatly coloured by this tacit conflict between her two maternal substitutes, and she receives, and indeed greatly benefits from, two very divergent forms of education offered by each of her adoptive mothers: on the one hand, Miss Rose endeavours to raise her 'en los sólidos principios de la fe protestante y el idioma inglés' (p. 12) [*in the solid principles of the Protestant faith and the English language*], while on the other, Mama Fresia provides an altogether earthier education, with magical tales, herbal remedies and bilingual communication in a combination of Spanish and the indigenous language Mapuche. Mimicry is a cornerstone of the lives led by Eliza's adoptive parents, the siblings Jeremy and Rose Sommers in postcolonial Chile: Miss Rose strives to foster Eliza's outward appearance as a quintessentially Victorian girl, wholly immersed in an edifying environment saturated with high culture, including piano lessons and intensive private home schooling. Jeremy's life is also miserably mired in mimicry: for example, he attempts to have a house built which would reflect the architectural styles of London, but his efforts fall hopelessly short, and the house he shares with his sister ends up being more accurately described as an 'adefesio' (p. 12) [*eyesore*]. Furthermore, even Jeremy's choice of attire is driven by the seasons of the Northern Hemisphere, and he resolutely tolerates the relative absurdity and inconvenience of doing this in a country of the Southern Hemisphere, dressing in winter clothes during the stifling summer heat and in lighter clothes during the bitter winter months. Eliza is acutely aware of the pervasiveness of mimicry in her environment, and she even toys briefly with the idea of imitating Jeremy's attitude: she innocently believes that his 'actitud desganada [...] era signo de fortaleza interior' (p. 53) [*apathy ... was a sign of inner strength*]. Expectations that Eliza successfully mimic what she is being taught by the Sommers are high; failure to achieve this would lead to her being expelled from the house and sent to the local orphanage, as Rose menacingly suggests to a disobedient Eliza at one stage. In a sense, then, Eliza appears trapped in her adoptive parents' skewed, imperfect projection of an English home away from home, and in an artificial family set-up: as is revealed, Eliza 'vivía en el mundo cerrado de la casa de sus benefactores, en la ilusión eterna de no estar allí, sino en Inglaterra' (p. 54) [*lived in the hermetic world of her benefactors' house, in an endless illusion of not being there [in Chile], but in England instead*].

Eliza presents an outward image of compliance, dutifully accomplishing the tasks expected of her in becoming a groomed and grounded Victorian girl. And yet, within this apparently static and stifling model of mimicry, Eliza carves out a space for herself in which to thrive emotionally and intellectually: on one occasion, her mimicry is perhaps too successful (and closer to Bhabha's notion of mimicry as exaggeration) when she adds to the confusion that prevails during Jacob Todd's first visit to the house by embarrassingly deciphering Rose's euphemistic description of her as a 'protegida' (p. 33) [*protégée*] in the following way: '[s]i me porto mal, me mandan donde las monjas' (p. 33) [*If I misbehave, I'll be sent to the orphanage (run by nuns)*]. Eliza succeeds in reacting against the supposed strictures of her Victorian education in numerous ways, illustrating her masterful moulding of mimicry to meet her requirements: for example, she enjoys learning how to cook by Mama Fresia's side, much to the annoyance of Miss Rose. Eliza's mimicry, however, is rarely, if ever, an exact replica: following the guidance of Mama Fresia, she later finds recipes from friends which '*mejoraba* en su cocina' (p. 84, emphasis added) [she improved upon *in her kitchen* (emphasis added)]. Indeed, it is revealed that Eliza '[p]oseía una rara vocación culinaria' (p. 21) [*had a truly rare culinary calling*], moving beyond culinary mimicry effortlessly and excelling, when it is explained that 'había elevado la costumbre local de intercambiar guisos y postres a la categoría de arte' (p. 84) [*she had raised the local custom of making stews and desserts to an art form*].

As Eliza grows, the malleability she finds within mimicry develops through the control of the domestic space within the house. She appears to have an uncanny ability to control space and almost render herself invisible: 'poseía el raro don de volverse invisible a voluntad, perdiéndose entre los muebles, las cortinas y las flores del papel mural' (p. 55) [*she had the rare gift of becoming invisible at will, disappearing amongst the furniture, curtains and flowers on the wallpaper*]. During her first meeting with Joaquín

Andieta, her adoptive father's employee, she displays all her resourcefulness: 'aprovechó su facultad de tornarse invisible y pudo observarlo a su antojo' (p. 92) [*she took advantage of her ability to become invisible and could watch him just as she pleased*]. Eliza's subsequent fling with Andieta is conducted in the back rooms of the residence, unbeknownst to Jeremy, Miss Rose or Mama Fresia. Everybody seems baffled by Eliza's ability to appear to be there yet not always be seen:

> daba la impresión de estar en varios lugares al mismo tiempo, confundiendo a todo el mundo, o bien nadie podía recordar dónde o cuándo la habían visto y justamente cuando empezaban a llamarla, ella se materializaba con la actitud de quien ignora que la están buscando. (pp. 123–4)
>
> [*She gave the impression of being in several places at once, confusing everybody; nobody could quite remember where or when they had seen her and just when they began to call for her, she would turn up, pretending not to know that she was being looked for.*]

Her sense of social and physical in-betweenness – part of the Sommers family, yet not part of it – is reinforced through her adopting the role of an interpreter, owing to her multilingual background: for instance, she intercedes when Mama Fresia goes to visit an ailing Jacob Todd, and is later rewarded for her efforts by Jacob, when he safely and surreptitiously deposits her back in the Sommers's residence after she gets lost at a religious procession. Eliza constantly moves between roles, and these skills are to become a key factor on her later journey.

On discovering she is pregnant by Joaquín, Eliza resolves to be reunited with him in California: aged just sixteen, she enlists the help of Mama Fresia and the recently arrived Chinese practitioner, Tao Chi'en, to stow away on the *Emilia*, rather than face the possibility of being sent to England by the Sommers in order to have her child there. She draws on her experiences of mimicry in the Sommers's house and leaves them a forged letter from the Chilean aristocratic del Valle family, with whom a tenuous link had been established by Jeremy Sommers for purely commercial convenience. The letter suggests Eliza has apparently been invited to stay with the del Valle family on their country estate. Through this last act of pretence in

Valparaíso, Eliza manages to buy herself sufficient time to escape to sea before Rose and Jeremy can discover the truth.

A new sense of enforced mimicry is forged in the text from this point on: first, Eliza must undress in front of Tao Chi'en, and in a sense say goodbye to her recognizably feminine self: 'iba perdiendo [...] los contactos con la realidad conocida y entrando inexorablemente en la extraña ilusión que sería su vida en los próximos años' (p. 170) [*she was gradually losing [...] contact with reality as she knew it and entering inexorably into the strange illusion that was to be her life for the following years*]. Eliza's voyage is fraught with difficulties, however: she has to explain to Tao Chi'en that she is pregnant, and then suffers a miscarriage. On arrival in California, Eliza leaves the boat dressed as a deaf-mute Chinese boy, the putative brother of Tao Chi'en. Eliza enters a completely new phase of masculine mimicry in her quest to find Joaquín. Another significant difference experienced by Eliza in her new form of mimicry is the fact that she must remain silent: her inability to communicate is a real shock, and is compounded by her bewildering experience of the Chinese district of Little Canton: 'fue como trasladarse a otro planeta, no entendía una sola palabra y le parecía que todo el mundo estaba furioso, porque gesticulaban a gritos' (p. 253) [*it was like being transported to another planet; she couldn't understand a word, and she thought that everybody was angry, because they were gesturing and shouting*]. Even her visit to the Chilean district is challenging, as, because of the fact that she is dressed as a Chinese boy, she is unable to interact freely and must hide her Chilean accent: 'iba desesperada en su papel de muchacho sordomudo y tonto' (p. 261) [*she was desperate in her role as a deaf and dumb boy*]. While Eliza is still forced to remain largely silent, she tellingly begins to use some of her earlier skills to become integrated, echoing the sense of mimicry with a difference which she displayed in the Sommers's household: for example, she briefly works alongside Tao in his work as a physician, and draws on an earlier skill, adapting it for a new purpose: 'aprendió a coser carne humana con la misma tranquilidad con que antes bordaba las sábanas de su ajuar' (p. 264) [*she learned to sew human flesh with the same ease as she had embroidered sheets for her trousseau*]. Her interpreting skills are employed once again when she travels with Tao, and this gives her an opportunity to speak Spanish once again. Frustrated by her inability to find

Cultural Displacement 163

Joaquín, Eliza leaves Tao behind in Sacramento, and she travels on through California. She assumes a new guise, presenting herself as Elías Andieta, Joaquín's putative brother. She once again highlights her chameleonic versatility, blending into the background or adapting, where necessary, in order to cope with the different places she visits and the different groups, mostly of men, with whom she travels:

> Aprendió a imitar el acento mexicano y peruano a la perfección, así se confundía con uno de ellos cuando buscaban hospitalidad. También cambió su inglés británico por el americano y adoptó ciertas palabrotas indispensables para ser aceptada entre los gringos. (p. 301)
>
> [*She learned to imitate the Mexican and Peruvian accents perfectly, and in this way could be mistaken for one of them when she and Tao looked for somewhere to stay. She also changed her British accent to an American one and adopted some choice swearwords to gain acceptance amongst the gringos.*]

The apparently carefree way Eliza moves through the Californian wastelands, however, belies her psychological battle with her unconscious: her masculine mimicry leads to her questioning her gender, and she agonizes over whether she is a 'mujer vestida de hombre, hombre vestido de mujer o una aberración de la naturaleza' (p. 303) [*a woman dressed as a man, a man dressed as a woman, or an aberration of nature*]. Alongside this, she must continually remind herself of her distant experiences with Joaquín, and she frequently draws on their love letters to ensure what they shared was real, and not 'un infundio de su imaginación' (p. 307) [*a product of her imagination*]. Nevertheless, Eliza continues to move on, and despite losing some money on a wager, manages to recoup some of her losses by offering bilingual writing services in English and Spanish to miners. The sudden arrival of Joe Rompehuesos's travelling brothel to the town presents Eliza with an opportunity to travel further and earn money. This unique group comprises the formidable androgynous figure of Joe Rompehuesos [*Joe Bonecrusher*], a woman who accepted her fate as 'haber nacido hombre en cuerpo de mujer' (p. 327) [*having been born a man in a woman's body*], the reformed gargantuan criminal Babalú el Malo [*Babalú the Bad*], a young adopted indigenous boy called Tom Sin Tribu [*Tom No Tribe*] and four prostitutes, who in their own ways found that working and living with Joe 'era lo más parecido a una familia que tenían' (p. 328) [*was the closest thing to a family which they had*]. While working and travelling with this intriguing family grouping, Eliza once again makes an unexpected use of a skill acquired during her youth, by playing the piano for evening entertainment: 'pudo ganarse el sustento en un burdel transhumante, finalidad que jamás pasó por la mente de Miss Rose cuando se empeñaba en enseñarle el sublime arte de la música' (p. 20) [*she managed to earn a living in a travelling brothel, something that never would have crossed Miss Rose's mind when she went to such efforts to teach her the sublime art of music*]. Eliza remains in her disguise as Elías Andieta, and some of her co-workers mistakenly think that she is in fact a young homosexual man because of her appearance, mannerisms and physical slightness. This creates no problems for her, however, and indeed she is praised for her apparent display of virility, when she chops off the gangrenous fingers of a local bandit. In performing this action, she uses knowledge attained in her formative years, in this instance drawing on prayers learnt from Mama Fresia and, for the first time, also puts into practice knowledge she has assimilated from working as an assistant for Tao Chi'en.

Eliza's memory of Joaquín begins to fade, as thoughts of Tao Chi'en begin to populate her dreams. At the same time, she works and becomes closer to Tao Chi'en, employing her linguistic and general communicative skills to assist him: 'había aprendido los rudimentos necesarios de chino para comunicarse a un nivel primario, el resto lo improvisaba con pantomima, dibujos y unas cuantas palabras de inglés' (p. 406) [*she had learnt the basics of Chinese to be able to communicate functionally – the rest she made up with a mixture of pantomime, drawings and some English*]. Eliza grows ever closer to Tao Chi'en and assists him in his dangerous efforts to rescue the Chinese slave girls, or *sing song girls*. As the memory of Joaquín fades, the desire to rediscover her femininity grows more intense. Initially she is afraid of having 'perdido por el camino su condición de mujer para convertirse en un raro ente asexuado' (p. 426) [*lost along the way her womanhood and turned into a strange asexual being*], but this fear dissipates, and it is subsequently revealed that the fear of being forever trapped mimicking masculinity, an ability which has enabled her to survive on her journey to find Joaquín, is much greater: 'el terror de verse otra vez en tales circunstancias fue más fuerte que el ímpetu de la juventud' (p. 427) [*the horror of being in such a situation again was stronger than the impetus of youth*]. Her return to femininity is associated with the pain she has endured through her quest for Joaquín, but she slowly begins to rediscover her body and work through her fears, as her reflection is first of 'una mujer casi desconocida' (p. 428) [*an almost unrecognizable woman*]. She finally dresses once again in women's clothes, and tenaciously forces a type of begrudging reconciliation with her female self: 'con cada prenda que se ponía iba conquistando sus dudas y afirmando su deseo de volver a ser mujer' (p. 433) [*with every piece of clothing she put on she gradually conquered her fears and affirmed her desire to become a woman again*]. She casts aside her meandering mimicry and wholly embraces her femininity.

Accompanied by Tao, Eliza has two photos taken; one with Andieta's love letters, a final snapshot of her past prior to destroying them, and one without them. These photographs capture the subtle, but significant difference, when Eliza leaves the memory of Andieta behind and chooses to embrace femininity and a life with Tao. Her final words of '[y]a estoy libre' (p. 439) remain ambiguous within the context of *Hija de la fortuna*, but nevertheless affirm her acceptance of being a woman.[19]

Mimicry, then, plays a crucial role in Eliza's exploration of self in *Hija*: as Bhabha explains, 'mimicry must continually produce its slippage, its excess, its difference.'[20] Eliza's subservient, compliant front conceals her subversive nature throughout the text: mimicry becomes a displacement of roles and transposition of skills, showing her recovered adaptability follow-

---

19 Of course, any confusion within the parameters of *Hija de la fortuna* are cleared up in *Retrato en sepia*, when it is revealed that Eliza stands there 'hasta que estuvo bien segura de que no era el hombre a quien ella había perseguido durante años' (p. 61) [*until she was completely sure that it wasn't the man she had been pursuing for years*]. Allende also perhaps unwittingly misquotes Eliza's final words from Hija, paraphrasing 'Ya *estoy* libre' (p. 439, emphasis added) as 'Ya *soy* libre' (p. 61, emphasis added). Both translate into English as *I am now free*.
20 Homi K. Bhabha, 'Of Mimicry and Man: the Ambivalence of Colonial Discourse', in *The Location of Culture*, pp. 85–92 (p. 86).

ing enforced episodes of loss. Nelly Martínez suggests that Eliza 'embodies freedom because she subverts cultural prescriptions by drawing upon the concrete circumstances of her own experience'.[21] This is true, but Eliza does more than this, by blurring the distinctions between high and low culture, gender and ethnicity, employing mimicry always with a difference in order to illustrate the problematics of convention, cultural imperialism and cultural exchange. Eliza's stated freedom at the close of the novel is a deliberate move away from mimicry, as she has begun to accept herself, her gender and her new situation.

Convention and Contravention: Tao Chi'en and Chinese Culture in *Hija de la fortuna* and *Retrato en sepia*

The character of Tao Chi'en provides another perspective on cultural displacement. This section explores Tao's characterization through the dichotomy of convention and contravention, and contends that Tao Chi'en's development and variety of experiences illustrate the clash between a determination to adhere to cultural precepts and his own experiences of multiculturalism which complicate and call into question this determination.

From the opening section of *Hija de la fortuna*, the clash between Tao's views and experiences is brought into sharp relief. In a conversation between the adult Tao and Eliza in San Francisco, Tao attaches great importance to his family line: 'podía recitar los nombres de todos sus antepasados, hasta los más remotos y venerables tatarabuelos muertos hacia más de un siglo' (p. 14) [*he could recite the names of all his ancestors – even the most remote and venerable great-grandfathers who had died over a century before*]. This initial impression of Tao is somewhat contradictory, however,

---

21 Nelly Martínez, 'Isabel Allende's Fictional World: Roads to Freedom', in *Isabel Allende Today: An Anthology of Essays*, ed. by Rosemary G. Feal and Yvette E. Miller (Pittsburgh, PA: Latin American Literary Review, 2002), pp. 51–73 (p. 65).

when background information provided on Tao's formative years reveals significant discrepancies between his respect for his cultural heritage and his actual experiences of rejection: as a child, he is merely named El Cuarto Hijo [*The Fourth Son*] and, owing to his position in the family as fourth son, is sold off to a group of passing merchants. Tao's first direct intervention in determining the path of his own life occurs when he saves the life of one of these merchants during an ambush; he is rewarded for his knowledge of local remedies and their medicinal properties with an apprenticeship under a *zhong yi*, a traditional Chinese healer.

It is through this apprenticeship in Canton that Tao begins to gain a fuller appreciation and understanding of Chinese culture. In addition, he is given the resonant, polysemous name of Tao, suggesting a new direction to his life, and the surname of his master, Chi'en. Within this period of apprenticeship in Canton, Tao acquires a sense of identity and a love for knowledge. He learns the precision of written Chinese and a selection of its spoken dialects: '[p]or propia iniciativa Tao Chi'en decidió dominar mandarín y cantonés, porque el dialecto de su aldea resultaba muy limitado' (p. 183) [*on his own initiative, Tao Chi'en decided to become fluent in Mandarin and Cantonese, because his village dialect was very limiting*]. During his apprenticeship he also experiences firsthand the effect of cultural differences, and how his *zhong yi* feels shamed by the colonial influence of the British. The cultural affront following the humiliating defeat by the British in the Opium War and the subsequent Treaty of Nanking leads to Tao's master committing suicide, and it is on this occasion when Tao's survival tendencies and flexibility towards the rigours of his own culture are first glimpsed in the text. Despite being given the surname of his master, Tao was never formally adopted, and thus has no rights to inheritance; his first act of cultural disobedience involves filching a small amount of money prior to leaving his master's house and heading to Hong Kong to begin practising as a physician there, while others scramble to take all of his master's remaining possessions. He acknowledges his limited options prior to leaving Canton definitively and the family life he could possibly return to in the countryside:

Nada lo llamaba en esa dirección, ni siquiera las obligaciones filiales con su padre y sus antepasados, que recaían en sus hermanos mayores. Necesitaba irse lejos, donde no lo alcanzara el largo brazo de la justicia china. (p. 189)

[*Nothing called him in that direction, not even the filial obligations to his father and forefathers – this was the duty of his elder brothers. He needed to go far away, where the long arm of Chinese justice could not reach him.*]

His move to Hong Kong brings him into contact with foreigners, or *fan güey*, for the first time, and he is surprised both by their gestures and features. His comments suggest the sense of difference he feels: 'de haberse atrevido los hubiera tocado para comprobar si esos seres grandes y sin ninguna gracia eran realmente humanos' (p. 193) [*if he had dared he would have touched them to see if those big, graceless beings were really human*]. Despite Tao's initial reservations, he resolves to explore further: spurred on by his love of knowledge and his awareness of the presence of the British in Hong Kong, Tao begins to learn English. He also befriends an English doctor, Ebanizer Hobbs, and they share their different experiences of medicine, although they do not practise each other's respective medical methods. Even from the outset, the problems with cultural differences, which form a significant part of Tao Chi'en's life, are in evidence, and their friendship must remain a secret: '[s]e juntaban casi en secreto, porque de haberse conocido su amistad, arriesgaban su reputación' (p. 203) [*they met up almost in secret, because if their friendship had been discovered, both would have risked their reputations*].

Despite the increasing flexibility in Tao's relationship with his culture, he remains determined to find a wife with 'lirios dorados' (p. 192) [*golden lilies*]; that is, with small, delicate feet due to the Chinese custom of footbinding for women: 'no pensaba conformarse con menos y vivir para el resto de sus días con una esposa de pies grandes y carácter fuerte' (pp. 192–3) [*he didn't plan on settling for less and living out the rest of his days with a wife who had big feet and a strong character*]. His apparent privileging of physical attributes over personal qualities is again evidenced by his narrow views of women as 'criaturas de trabajo y reproducción [...] o bien objetos caros de decoración' (p. 204) [*creatures of work and reproduction [...] or even expensive objects of decoration*]. However, Tao begins to revise this after

Cultural Displacement 169

his love affair, marriage and premature loss of his wife Lin. Though Lin has the aesthetically appealing feature of the *lirios dorados*, she is fragile and sickly, and she dies shortly after giving birth to a stillborn child. Even the combined medical knowledge of Tao and Ebanizer cannot prevent her premature death.

In the depths of depression, Tao finds it difficult to focus on his profession and begins to lose his reputation quickly. While eking out a living as a doctor at the docks, Tao is shanghaied onto a boat named Liberty, bound for Valparaiso, Chile. Forced to work as a chef, Tao has the time to develop a broader perspective on life and culture: '[s]u primera sorpresa fue descubrir que China no era el centro absoluto del universo' (p. 217) [*his first surprise was to discover that China was not the absolute centre of the universe*]. He comes to recognize cultural differences and the interplay between power and violence, which will later influence greatly his life and work in California: 'había otras culturas, más bárbaras, es cierto, pero mucho más poderosas' (p. 217) [*there were other cultures; more barbaric, yes, but much more powerful*].

Tao meets Eliza during his brief time in Valparaiso, and reluctantly agrees to stow her away on the *Emilia* ship bound for California, where on this occasion he is willingly being employed as a chef. Despite his initial reservations, Tao grows fonder of Eliza and admires her determination to be reunited with Joaquín; indeed, on arrival in California, 'la idea de desprenderse definitivamente de ella le producía una mezcla de tremendo alivio y de incomprensible ansiedad' (p. 240) [*the idea of leaving her forever produced in him a mix of tremendous relief and incomprehensible anxiety*]. He feels in some way obliged to help the ailing Eliza: '[e]staba atrapado, al menos hasta que ella estuviera más fuerte, se conectara con otros chilenos o diera con el paradero de su escurridizo enamorado' (p. 257) [*he was trapped, at least until she was feeling stronger, met other Chileans or came upon the whereabouts of her elusive lover*]. He travels north with her to Sacramento, convinced by Eliza to stay on and practise medicine there. His thirst for knowledge about indigenous culture there prompts him to speak to locals, and he is aided in his efforts by Eliza: 'Eliza y Tao Chi'en se sentaban con ellos en un círculo en torno a un hueco [...] [d]espués fumaban, conversando en una mezcla de inglés, señales y las pocas palabras en la lengua nativa que habían aprendido' (pp. 266–7) [*Eliza and Tao Chi'en sat with them in a circle around a hollow [...] afterwards they smoked, conversing in a mix of English, signs and the few words of their native language which they had learnt*]. Tao's friendship with Eliza grows: 'le sorprendía que con Eliza pudieran compartir el humor, a pesar de los tropiezos ocasionales del idioma y las diferencias culturales.' (p. 269) [*he was surprised how he could share a laugh with Eliza, despite the occasional linguistic gaffe and the cultural differences*]. In Tao's eyes, despite different cultural backgrounds, they share a great deal. Their circumstances begin to change, when Eliza decides to head north, dressed as a cowboy, while Tao decides to settle in Sacramento. More of his countrymen have begun to arrive in the United States, which is a mixed blessing for him: he makes the acquaintance of another Chinese healer and he can begin to share his knowledge, not only of medicine but also of his own life experiences. Chastened by his experience with Lin, Tao advises his colleague to search for 'una esposa sonriente y sana, todo lo demás no importa' (p. 348) [*a smiling, healthy wife – nothing else matters*]. Tao, however, struggles to communicate his experiences of love and loss to his colleague, despite his evident linguistic prowess: '[t]rató de explicárselo a un amigo, pero se enredó en el lenguaje, sin palabras en su vocabulario para expresar ese tormento' (p. 349) [*he tried to explain it to his friend, but he got tangled up in language. He didn't have the vocabulary to explain his torment*]. At the same time, there is also the establishment of *tongs*, Chinese gangs, in both Sacramento and San Francisco, where Tao next decides to live. Tao moves to Chinatown in San Francisco and he is surprised at how similar it is to China: 'la ilusión de encontrarse en el Celeste Imperio era perfecta' (p. 354) [*the illusion of being in the Celestial Empire was perfect*]. Outside of Chinatown, however, he is attacked by three people and he decides to change his appearance, mindful that such a change will make it difficult for him to return home to China: by cutting his queue 'probaba el propósito de no volver a China e instalarse de firme en América, una imperdonable traición al emperador, la patria y los antepasados' (pp. 367–8) [*he was proving that he planned never to return to China and instead settle for good in America, which was an unforgivable betrayal of the Emperor, the homeland and his ancestors*].

Despite this apparent rejection of a return to China, Tao is in many ways still as close to his culture, its conventions and restrictions while in San Francisco: he notes that '[e]l gobierno de los americanos nada controlaba entre los chinos, que vivían en su propio mundo, en su lengua, con sus costumbres y sus antiquísimas leyes' (p. 378) [*The American government didn't control anything amongst the Chinese, who lived in their own world, with their language, their customs and their age-old laws*]. The distance he has covered and the multicultural diversity he has been exposed to appear irrelevant as Tao 'se encontró de nuevo prisionero de las costumbres, las jerarquías y las restricciones de sus tiempos en Cantón' (p. 379) [*was once again a prisoner of customs, hierarchies and the restrictions of his time in Canton*]. He witnesses the gross inequalities in how Chinese women are treated and resolves to do what he can to address this. His work brings him directly into contact with women who remind him of his sister.

For protection, Tao decides to join one of the local *tongs*, conscious of the fact that 'lo que sucedía en el barrio quedaba confinado a sus calles. Nada de recurrir a la policía, ni siquiera en caso de vida o muerte; los conflictos se resolvían dentro de la comunidad' (p. 379) [*what happened in the neighbourhood remained within its streets. There was no running to the police, not even if it was a question of life or death. Conflicts were resolved within the community*]. Tao becomes drawn into the world of prostitution through his work as a *zhong yi*, and he is called to attend to sick and dying women: while working with these women, he is assailed by the memory of his sister: 'los maullidos de las *sing song girls* lo perseguían, recordándole a su hermana' (p. 380) [*the meowing of the sing song girls pursued him, reminding him of his sister*]. This memory determines a significant part of Tao's future, as he decides to do all within his power to help these women, and he is ably assisted in these endeavours by Eliza. He notes that these women have been silenced, and it takes him a long time to earn their confidence. They have been denied access to their culture and act 'como si hubiera[n] perdido el uso del lenguaje' (p. 386) [*as if they had lost the use of language*]. In order to save some of these women from this world, they will have to accept a type of perpetual cultural displacement, away from China: 'algunas no volvían a hablar en su lengua ni a ver otro rostro de su raza' (p. 411) [*some would never speak their language again, nor see another face of a person from their race*]. This sacrifice is required by them to ensure their survival.

In *Retrato en sepia*, Tao redoubles his efforts to help these women. At this stage, Tao and Eliza have married, and have two grown-up children, Lucky and Lynn. Lynn passes away in childbirth, and Tao decides to bring up Lynn's daughter, Lai Ming (Aurora), in Chinatown. Although the Chinatown *tongs* are aware of the work that Tao has been engaged in for over twenty years, his reputation and the largely insignificant effect of his efforts on their profits mean that he is contravening the rules of *tong* culture, but only to a minor extent:

> Mientras Tao Chi'en no acudiera a las autoridades americanas, actuara sin bulla y salvara a las chicas una a una, en una paciente labor de hormiga, podían tolerarlo, porque no hacía mella en los enormes beneficios del negocio. (p. 58)
>
> [*As long as Tao Chi'en didn't go to the American authorities, acted without a fuss and saved the girls one by one, working patiently like an ant, they could put up with him; this was because he didn't make a dent in the business's enormous profits.*]

However, Tao decides to involve figures of authority from outside the Chinese community, and San Francisco police proceed to conduct a series of raids in Chinatown. Lucky fears there will be severe repercussions for his father, whom he believes has committed 'una imprudencia irreparable' (p. 331) [*an irreparable foolish act*]. His fears are confirmed when he is attacked one night while out walking with his granddaughter and severely beaten. Tao is left close to death but, crucially, it is not a 'violent murder', as described by Susan E. Carvalho.[22] This distinction is important because, although the *tongs* have seen fit to punish Tao for contravening the laws by which they abide, it is actually Tao who makes the decision to die, in conjunction with his wife, Eliza. He survives the attack and regains the power of speech, but he is left permanently paralyzed. Tao and Eliza's complicity means that Tao 'no debió explicar nada, porque sabía que su mujer haría lo indispensable para ayudarlo a morir con dignidad, tal como lo haría él

---

22   Susan E. Carvalho, *Contemporary Spanish American Novels by Women: Mapping the Narrative* (Woodbridge: Tamesis, 2007), p. 76.

por ella' (p. 338) [*he didn't have to explain anything, because he knew that his wife would do whatever necessary to help him die with dignity, just as he would have done the same for her*]. In agreement with Eliza, Tao says goodbye with one final act of defiance.

Throughout both texts, Tao illustrates his love of knowledge and growing appreciation of multiculturalism. He settles in Chinatown but lives there with an outsider, Eliza, and he dresses in the way he pleases. His ability to embrace other cultures is coupled with an increasing dissatisfaction with many strictures within his own culture. The violent attack perpetrated by members of a local *tong* suggests initially that Tao has been punished within his community for his actions and suffers a type of internal retribution. Nevertheless, Tao's decision to die and the fulfilling of his final wish that his body be brought back to China by Eliza convey his continual ambivalence towards Chinese culture and his resistance to the most restrictive aspects of his background. Tao maintains his respect for Chinese culture, but chooses to act outside its strictures and to control the direction of his life and, ultimately, his death.

Culture *in Camera*: Aurora's Quest for Cultural Exposure in *Retrato en sepia*

This section explores Aurora's quest to uncover hidden aspects of her cultural background, and focuses on how she represents a unique form of cultural displacement. This is illustrated through the contrast between her appearance and her thoughts. The adult Aurora, who narrates the story, explains from the outset her situation of displacement. Aurora's complex cultural heritage combines English, Chinese and Chilean ancestry, but her appearance defies this complexity. As Cox explains, '[h]er Hispanic features [...] hide her Asian background and [subsequently] aid her transition into

Chilean society'.²³ At the age of five, Aurora finds herself suddenly removed from her home in Chinatown to live in Paulina's loftier mansion in Nob Hill. Her enforced departure from her home is left unexplained and the young Aurora is greatly troubled.

The narrative switches forward to the adult Aurora. She refers to a picture from her life in Chinatown, before her grand-mother's decision to 'borrar mis orígenes' (p. 109) [*erase my origins*]. She struggles to remember the circumstances of the picture and admits that 'no reconozco a la niña de ese único retrato' (p. 109) [*I don't recognize the girl in the only portrait that exists*]. Alongside the gaps in her past, Aurora is haunted by a recurring nightmare and an inability to decipher its meaning; in this nightmare, she is walking along, accompanied, and then a group corner her and her companion: '[n]os acorralan, nos empujan, nos tironean, nos separan; busco la mano amiga y encuentro el vacío. Grito sin voz, caigo sin ruido y entonces despierto con el corazón desbocado' (p. 111) [*they corner us, push us, pull at us, keep us apart. I look for a friendly hand and find emptiness. I shout voicelessly, fall noiselessly and then wake with my heart in my mouth*]. As can be inferred, Aurora believes this nightmare to be part of a lost memory, and she must embark on what becomes a frustrating quest to understand these nightmares and perhaps consequently discover her origins. As Linda Gould Levine correctly notes: '[m]emory for Aurora is more than the desire to preserve the past; it is the pressing need to identify the landscape of a past [...] her quest is more difficult [...] because she can rely neither on invention nor objective materials to fill in the gaps.'²⁴

One of the main challenges for Aurora is that her pain and anguish are internal and less obvious: as she states, '[l]a mía [marca] no se ve, pero existe' (p. 112) [*my marks can't be seen, but still exist*]. She even revisits her recurring nightmare, 'tratando de penetrar las capas de misterio que lo envuelven a ver si descubro algún detalle, hasta entonces desapercibido, que me dé la clave de su significado' (p. 111) [*trying to penetrate the layers of mystery around it to see if I can find out anything, that I might have missed*

---

23   Cox, p. 158.
24   Levine, p. 157.

beforehand, that would give me the key to its meaning]. Within this context, photography becomes Aurora's creative reaction to the nightmare which resists definition. Referring to the days following the nightmare, she explains that 'mis mejores fotografías han sido tomadas en días como ésos' (pp. 113–14). It is through photography that she can endeavour to make visible what is often hidden or obscured: 'puede revelar los secretos que el ojo desnudo o la mente no captan, todo desaparece salvo aquello enfocado en el cuadro' (p. 114) [*it can reveal the secrets that the naked eye or the mind cannot capture; everything disappears except for what is in focus in the picture*].

Aurora recalls her early experiences in Paulina's house, and her sense of apprehension at being in such a formidable house. She escapes from the mansion, and makes her way back to Chinatown. However, the atmosphere there is threatening and unwelcoming, and she is saved by the intervention of her Uncle Lucky and deposited back in Paulina's house. This incident is one of the contributing factors towards Paulina's decision to return to Santiago. This return home for Paulina also constitutes Aurora's first visit to the site of one of her cultural backgrounds. When she arrives, she speaks 'una mezcolanza de chino, inglés y español' (p. 159) [*a mixture of Chinese, English and Spanish*]. Paulina chooses to keep Aurora's Chinese heritage concealed: '[p]ara protegerme del rechazo ocultó cuidadosamente la existencia de mi cuarto de sangre china' (p. 161) [*to protect me from rejection, she carefully hid the existence of my quarter-Chinese blood*]. Aurora begins to achieve a gradual sense of stability, and, mirroring Eliza's young experiences in the Sommers' residence in San Francisco, appropriates the domestic space: '[t]omé el edificio entero por asalto, no dejé vericueto sin explorar ni rincón sin conquistar.' (p. 174) [*I took control of the entire building; I didn't leave a nook unexplored or a corner unconquered*].

It is perhaps somewhat surprising that one of the first places in which the recovery of her Chinese heritage begins to take place is actually in Santiago. Her encounter with her dying father, Matías, is a crucial step towards discovering about her maternal grandfather Tao Chi'en. The effects on Aurora are telling:

Bastó que mencionara su nombre completo y me dijera que era un chino alto y guapo, para que mis recuerdos se desencadenaran gota a gota, como lluvia. Al ponerle nombre a esa presencia invisible que me acompañaba siempre, mi abuelo dejó de ser una invención de mi fantasía para convertir en un fantasma tan real como una persona de carne y hueso. (p. 214)

[*The mere mention of his full name and that he was a tall, handsome Chinese man were enough for my memories to flood back, drip by drip, like rain. When I put a name to that invisible presence that was always by my side, my grandfather was no longer a figment of my imagination, but now a ghost as real as a person of flesh and blood.*]

Although the reference to Tao unleashes a stream of repressed memories for Aurora, she receives no further information, and is instead matched with, and later marries a respectable young Chilean man who is renamed Diego Domínguez for the purposes of Aurora's story: she explains that 'no es su verdadero nombre, lo he cambiado en estas páginas porque todo lo referente a él y su familia debe ser protegido' (p. 243) [*it isn't his real name. I've changed it in these pages because everything that refers to him and his family has to be protected*]. She moves with her new husband and his family to their country estate of Caleufú but feels trapped there in its intellectually stultifying atmosphere. Despite the façade of marriage and satisfaction, Aurora finds herself even further removed from her quest to understand her past. She concedes that Diego led an independent life, and was like a ghost to her. Emotional and geographical distance separates the couple considerably: 'había un silencioso abismo entre ambos y mis intentos de intercambiar ideas o averiguar sobre sus sentimientos se estrellaban contra su obstinada vocación de ausente' (p. 270) [*there was a silent chasm between us. My efforts to exchange ideas or find out about his feelings crashed against his obstinate vocation of being absent*].

In Caleufú, however, Aurora finds a sense of freedom through her creative outlets of photography, reading and writing. While still troubled by efforts to understand the fullness of identity which she feels has been denied to her, she explores and grows. She discovers that her husband has been unfaithful to her with his sister-in-law, but remains silent out of love and respect for Diego's dying mother, Doña Elvira. Indeed, it is her friendship with Elvira which sustains her: 'Elvira tenía la virtud de centrarme y de aplacar la ansiedad que a veces me estrangulaba' (p. 286) [*Elvira centred me and calmed me down when my anxiety, at times, choked me*].

The news of Paulina's impending death provides Aurora with an opportunity to return to Santiago. Paulina's subsequent death signals the return of Aurora's maternal grandmother, Eliza, and a fuller sense of identity is gradually revealed for Aurora. As Aurora explains, Eliza 'me dio las piezas que faltaban para armar el rompecabezas de mi existencia' (p. 319) [*gave me the missing pieces to complete the jigsaw of my existence*]. On seeing Eliza, Aurora spontaneously utters the Chinese term for grandmother, *Oi poa*, and this kinship term triggers the next stage of Aurora's rediscovery of her lost Chinese heritage after having previously learned Tao's name from her father, Matías. She learns of her own Chinese name, Lai-Ming, and Eliza explains why she had been sent to live with Paulina: 'era necesario sacar a la criatura de Chinatown algunas horas al día para americanizarla' (p. 327) [*you had to take the girl out of Chinatown for a few hours a day to Americanize her*]. Both grandmothers had striven to save Aurora from the trauma and the heartache of recalling the attack, the shadows of her nightmares being the men that had encircled her and Tao Chi'en during the attack. Their efforts to ensure that Aurora enjoyed the full benefits of total integration in society perhaps unwittingly fail to take into account the traumatic effects and subsequent emotional upheaval felt by this uprooting.

The character of Aurora allows Allende to explore interesting aspects of cultural displacement, given her Hispanic features and the fact that she was brought up for her first five years of her life in Chinatown. For example, her appearance facilitates her integration into Chilean society, similar to the way in which Eliza's disguise grants her the freedom to move through California in search of Joaquín. Yet while for Eliza her journey is liberating, Aurora's journey is inhibiting. The advantages for Aurora of photography are numerous: as Susan Carvalho explains, the camera 'grants not only geographical mobility but sovereignty over places, as Aurora is finally able, camera in hand, to map her own world'.[25] Aurora decides to embrace

---

25   Carvalho, p. 78.

her past, and to accept her apparently marginal situation in Chilean society as a wife who has abandoned her husband, owing to the freedom and independence it offers her.

Conclusion: Embracing Displacement

The five examples selected from Allende's North American narratives provide a mosaic of cultural displacements; however, all five illustrate the contrast between external appearance and inner turmoil, and through a combination of place and displacement Allende endeavours to resolve these dilemmas. In *El plan infinito*, Reeves's unresolved family issues, which stem from his childhood, later overlap with his experiences of war in Vietnam; his exasperating relationship with his two wives, his daughter, Margaret, a drug addict and his hyperactive son, David, all appear to reflect his troubled mind. His ultimate recognition of himself is aided through therapy, and he appears to become reconciled with his hybrid cultural background towards the close of the text. In *Hija de la fortuna*, Jacob Todd's integration into the expatriate British community and later all echelons of Valparaíso society is founded on a fundamental misunderstanding; that is, that he has arrived as a missionary. The question of scruples appears to be superseded in Jacob's mind by a desire for wealth when he recognizes the influence of his persuasive oratorical skills and the many advantages of pursuing this pastoral persona. Social place appears of little consequence to him, as he interacts freely throughout Valparaíso society, but the exposure of his fraudulent identity and activities quickly reveals the reliance he had on social contacts. Jacob finds himself swiftly divested of the social position he had enjoyed, and he returns briefly to England, cherishing the idea of creating a utopian society, but he fails to find people reliable enough to join him in his endeavour. Somewhat paradoxically, the surprising success he achieves when he moves to California in a way provides him with the utopia he dreamed of, as he prefers to exploit rather than explode the myth of Joaquín Andieta. His apparent place in society is again irrelevant here, as his secret meetings with the marginal bandit are purely a product of his imagination. Jacob draws on his range of cultural experiences, but solely for financial gain. However, the impact of his writing is telling, as ethnic tensions are stoked through his lies. Underneath the patina of success enjoyed by Jacob are layers of uncertainty. He re-emerges from the shame experienced in Valparaíso, ostensibly championing the cause of the marginal through his narrative weaving together of a random selection of characteristics in order to fashion a pan-Hispanic outlaw. His success helps fuel rage and his hero becomes reductive rather than creative, mirroring paradoxically Jacob's own experience of self. His anger at experiences of displacement ultimately leaves him isolated.

Eliza's experiences of cultural displacement are very different to those of Jacob: while she exploits her cultural knowledge, she does so in an effort to be reunited with Joaquín. She engages in a form of cultural syncretism, mixing high and low culture, as well as indigenous and imposed. Eliza's escape from the strictures of her upbringing in Valparaíso allows her to witness up close the developing society of Gold Rush California from the relative invisibility of a male persona, in a region where females are scarce. She tires of this self-imposed temporary gender reassignment, and ultimately rediscovers her true sense of self and her love for Tao. Levine notes interestingly that 'Eliza utilizes her female skills – piano playing and cooking – to survive economically as a male'.[26] Cox maintains that Tao and Eliza form 'a new kind of hybrid that represents the unorthodox, multicultural land to which they have arrived'.[27] However, Cox's concluding statement to her discussion of *Hija de la fortuna* needs to be qualified: Tao and Eliza settle in Chinatown, a place in which Eliza remains a foreigner, and through his actions, Tao alienates himself culturally, if not geographically. By retaining Eliza's surname of Sommers rather than Tao's Chinese surname for their children, they also endeavour to ensure that their children will be able to integrate into mainstream American society. Carvalho somewhat unfairly

---

26   Levine, p. 140.
27   Cox, p. 137.

views Eliza's characterization as it develops in *Retrato en sepia* as being merely bound up in duty to husband and adoptive mother: she believes that 'once those to whom [Eliza] is obligated are dead, she is finally free to resume her earlier course as a nomad'.[28] Yet it is patently clear that the obligations to both Tao and Miss Rose complement her nomadic spirit through the experience of renewed travel. Eliza's desire for union is not contradicted by her desire to travel, as Tao's spirit accompanies her on her journeys, after his passing.

Third, Tao's own experiences of cultural displacement allow Allende to present a complex situation in which Tao is bound to his culture but becomes increasingly dissatisfied with its inflexibility. Carvalho suggests that 'Tao Chi'en and Eliza are limited as transgressive characters', and she cites their behaviour in public and their desire to Americanize their children.[29] However, throughout much of his life Tao struggles to accept monocultural restrictions, and, in marrying Eliza and acquiring American citizenship, he illustrates his ambivalence towards his home culture and his willingness to transgress, whatever the consequences. As Levine succinctly suggests, Tao's 'ability to open himself to new experiences leads to his fascination with western medicine and the egalitarian relationship between husbands and wives that he observes in California, both of which are antithetical to the values of his Chinese heritage'.[30] Further, he defies the Mafia-like authorities of the *tongs* in order to offer the young Chinese females the opportunity to defy restrictions imposed by his culture and the *tongs* by forging a new life for themselves outside of China and, crucially, outside of Chinatown. Levine expresses surprise at Tao's final act in the plot: '[g]iven Tao Chi'en's ability to find meaning in life, regardless of the stage, his decision to end his life is somewhat surprising,' though she concedes that 'his death marks his absence from the physical world only.'[31] As explained earlier in the discussion of Tao, his death is defiant rather

28 Susan E. Carvalho, *Contemporary Spanish American Novels by Women: Mapping the Narrative* (Woodbridge: Tamesis, 2007), p. 77.
29 Ibid., p. 83.
30 Linda Levine, *Isabel Allende*, p. 148.
31 Ibid., p. 163.

than defeatist, and his act is consonant with his determination to respect his culture, but to transgress when these cultural strictures are deemed harmful or restricting.

Finally, in the presentation of Aurora and her private anguish, Allende shows the ambiguous nature of cultural displacement by presenting a character displaced from her original culture, but forever denied access to it through a combination of factors, in particular her own appearance. Her recovery of a sense of identity and independence completes the picture of her past yet she is permanently displaced because of her unwillingness to remain within a loveless marriage. As María Inés Lagos states, 'as a married woman who has abandoned her husband, [Aurora] lives in a social limbo'.[32] Aurora acknowledges that '[v]ivo en el limbo de las "separadas", donde van a parar las infortunadas que prefieren el escarnio público a vivir con un hombre que no aman' (p. 112) [*I inhabit the limbo of 'separated wives', a place where all those unfortunate women who prefer public shame to living with a man who they don't love end up*]. Cox suggests that 'Aurora turns to an art medium that offers irrefutable evidence of reality',[33] but this is not completely true, for it is Iván Radovic, the man who becomes Aurora's lover in *Retrato en sepia*, who spots the closeness between Diego Domínguez and his sister-in-law in a photograph. Furthermore, Aurora's self-portraits do not manage to capture the internal strife and struggles she suffers. However, her outward position of being trapped in a social limbo equally fails to capture the sense of inner freedom she celebrates. As mentioned in Chapter 1, María Cinta del Ramblado-Minero argues that 'the trajectory of Aurora is a repetition of the experience of previous characters, from the original ones in *La casa de los espíritus*, to Aurora's own maternal grandmother, Eliza, in *Hija de la fortuna*'.[34] She foregrounds the issues

---

32   María Inés Lagos, 'Female Voices from the Borderlands: Isabel Allende's *Paula* and *Retrato en sepia*' in *Isabel Allende Today*, ed. by Rosemary G. Feal and Yvette E. Miller (Pittsburgh, PA: Latin American Literary Review, 2002), pp. 112–27 (p. 120).
33   Cox, p. 157.
34   María de la Cinta Ramblado-Minero, *Isabel Allende's Writing of the Self: Trespassing the Boundaries of Fiction and Autobiography* (Lewiston, NY: Edwin Mellen, 2003), p. 177.

of 'love and heterosexual romance' in establishing the parallels between female characters in Allende's fiction. However, the cultural dimension seems to contradict this assertion considerably: to use Eliza and Aurora, for example, there are clear cultural differences that call into question this relatively reductive view of both characters: it is true that both find expression and independence while enjoying a relationship with Tao and Iván Radovic, respectively. Yet, this apparent similarity fails to incorporate significant factors in both lives: Eliza and Aurora at the end of *Retrato en sepia* find themselves in significantly different situations, Eliza widowed and a nomad, and Aurora, separated from her husband but secretly enjoying her relationship with Radovic and revelling in her creative independence. The cultural dimension to both characters further calls into question the view that their experiences are repetitions: Eliza journeys away from home in search of love, explores cultural diversity and encounters freedom in the process. Her ultimate sense of perpetual displacement is geographical rather than cultural, however, and she is accompanied by her husband, Tao, her spiritual guide who remains as close as ever. Aurora ends *Retrato en sepia* also aware that she must endure a sense of perpetual cultural displacement because of the fact that she lacks Chinese physical features. Again, it is the spirit of her grandfather Tao that comforts her, along with the secret love affair she conducts with Radovic. The significantly different cultural conundrums female characters face through Allende's *oeuvre* call into question the statement that their journeys are merely reconfigured repetitions of one journey.

The unsettling experience of displacement and the various ways in which a cultural past can be integrated into a new situation are explored extensively through Allende's North American Narratives. Her three novels illustrate concerns such as belonging, identity, culture and displacement. Allende appears to celebrate the embracing of difference and displacement through these characters, which contrasts strongly with the extensive efforts made by Esteban Trueba back in *La casa de los espíritus* to escape a sense of societal displacement. The characters of her North American Narratives examined here all find a sense of place through displacement; Gregory Reeves's understanding of self requires a willingness to recognize the enemy within rather than the supposed enemies in the *barrio* or on the battlefields of Vietnam. His support from the margins brings an important sense of resolution. From the opening sections of *Hija de la fortuna*, Jacob Todd/Freemont is presented as a conflicted figure who never reveals the true reasons for his actions. Although he is initially mistaken for a missionary, he never explains how he is really only in Valparaíso on the strength of a wager, and his lies continue even when he is disgraced by the revelation of his fraudulent activities. Gold Rush California is a boon for Jacob, but not because of the presence of gold: Jacob makes his fortune through the composite bandit to whom he pretends to have exclusive access. Jacob's imaginative creation seems to consume him towards the end of the text, and he seems again displaced from society. Eliza Sommers embarks on her journey in search of Joaquín Andieta and appears to end up living a life of constant displacement following the death of her partner Tao, whose spirit accompanies her on her nomadic journeys. Finally Aurora's outward social displacement is contrasted with her sense of freedom away from a loveless marriage. This freedom allows her to concentrate fully on her passions of photography and her hidden relationship with Iván Radovic. The desire for place in society becomes a distant echo in Allende's later fiction.

The conclusion offers some final comments on the fiction examined here and tentatively seeks to locate Allende's fiction in a broader framework.

Conclusion

In this journey through a selection of Isabel Allende's fiction – from 1982 to 2000 – displacement is shown to be an abiding feature of her work, and is one which serves to foreground the depth and diversity within her corpus of writing. In Chapter 2, *La casa de los espíritus* concentrates on Esteban Trueba's desperate quest to achieve material, social and political success at any cost. There is a clear correlation between geographical and social displacement in Trueba's determination to regain the role in society which his family has lost. Ideas from the field of Development Studies illustrate here the many failings in Trueba's approach to dealings with the local community of Las Tres Marías, and expose the marginality which is a constant throughout his life, despite his apparent successes. His inability to connect with local habitants, however, is a microcosmic representation of Trueba's strong sense of displacement in the novel. He fails to recognize the importance of community, and his ultimate eviction of the campesinos from the estate is a clear indication of his rash responses to what he sees as perceived threats. His growing awareness and ultimate acceptance of his diminished role in society is a liberating experience for him, affording him licence to attempt some reconciliation with his estranged family. His final pleading with Tránsito Soto to secure the release of his closest family member, his grand-daughter Alba, reveals Trueba's real dependence on the margins and this humbling experience serves as Allende's way of meting out a form of justice within the novel.

In Chapter 3, ideas from Mikhail Bakhtin's discussion of medieval carnival and the carnivalesque also highlight the pervasiveness of societal displacement in *De amor y de sombra*. The focus is now on displacement at a national level, and the effects of the newly installed military on all aspects of society are explored in this novel. A carnivalesque reading evinces the underlying coherence of a novel which seeks to expose abuses perpetrated by the dictatorial regime and also to displace these abuses, in a sense, with a tale of the love which blossoms in adversity between Irene Beltrán and Francisco Leal and a more general tale of dissidence which cuts across age, gender, class and sexuality.

In Chapter 4, the narrative shift in Allende's fiction from an identifiably Chilean – and national – milieu occurs in *Eva Luna* and continues in *Cuentos de Eva Luna*. Issues of language and communication are especially prevalent in these works, and the approach to these works illustrates how Allende presents the latent power of oral language, while also alluding to the difficulties faced in articulating experiences of loss and dislocation. This analysis also demonstrates the centrality of *Cuentos de Eva Luna* in any analysis of Allende's fiction; the short stories become a proving ground for her ideas on cultural displacement and the conflict between individuals and communities, which are more fully articulated in her subsequent works.

The final chapter of this discussion sees Allende return to her roots by using Chile as one of a series of backdrops in both *Hija de la fortuna* and *Retrato en sepia*. The emphasis on displacement in this analysis is clearly cultural. Allende explores a series of scenarios in which her characters leave their homelands and subsequently suffer a crisis of identity as they struggle to reconcile their cultural experiences from their youth with their new cultural milieux.

Allende closes a narrative circle in writing *Retrato en sepia* because of the links between this novel and *La casa de los espíritus*. However, the narrative journey back to Chile in *Retrato en sepia* is more than just a return to her homeland, as it also brings the narrative journey Allende's fiction has taken into sharper focus. A brief comparison between some aspects of *Retrato en sepia* and *La casa de los espíritus*, as seen briefly in the conclusion to Chapter 5, is instructive: Aurora, at the close of *Retrato en sepia*, rejects privilege and status, in stark contrast to Esteban Trueba, whose life was driven by the quest for social status. It may even be more apposite to compare and contrast Aurora with Alba from *La casa de los espíritus*: Aurora and Alba share a similar sense of marginality at the close of their respective novels. However, while for Alba, the quest to discover and record her family's history is a key concern, for Aurora the past seems to be of less consequence for her, once she has deciphered her nightmares.

Aurora appears more content to face the future without a privileged role in society but with independence, a successful career and relationship.

In *Retrato en sepia*, and indeed in all her fiction, Allende uses displacement as a springboard for discussion on a range of issues: the conflict between the mainstream and margins is probed from a variety of angles, and the subtleties of subversive activity appear time and again. By using displacement as a point of departure, Allende's fiction can be seen to be open-ended and multi-layered. Indeed, very few, if any, of her fictional works examined here seem to finish on a note of resolution, and it is this feature which highlights the dynamism in her writing. There is a striking modernity to her later fiction, which, while set in the later nineteenth century and early twentieth century, broaches issues of considerable relevance in the twenty-first century, such as cultural integration, assimilation and the consequences of geographical displacement on one's relationship with one's homeland.[1]

Aurora's situation at the end of *Retrato en sepia* highlights the evolution in Allende's fiction while at the same time complicating efforts to answer adequately the question of where to place Allende's fiction in relation to other recent Latin American fiction. In fact, in an introduction to essays on English-language American fiction produced in the 1990s, Jay Prosser identifies a series of features which are strikingly apparent in much

---

1 There remains much investigation to be completed in relation to Isabel Allende's work, which is beyond the immediate scope of this discussion. One especially interesting area would be the exploration of how the voices of characters who experience cultural displacement are rendered in their respective languages: the challenges of rendering John, Miss Rose and Jeremy Sommers in English would be an interesting starting point for an examination of how translators constantly tread the fine line between fidelity to the source text and innovation in the target text. Translation Studies theorist Jeremy Munday's recent analysis of Latin American writing in English illustrates the increasing interest in issues of translation and identity, and the lexical and syntactic choices made by Allende's translator, Margaret Sayers Peden, would make an especially interesting area of analysis in relation to this type of cultural back-translation. For further information, see Jeremy Munday, *Style and Ideology in Translation: Latin American Writing in English* (London: Routledge, 2008).

of Allende's fiction:[2] to take *Retrato en sepia* as an example, in this text, which primarily focuses on Aurora's discovery of her multicultural ethnicity, Allende also tackles key issues of increasing importance in the United States, such as the relationship with the past, the horrors of warfare, the challenges of multicultural diversity and the influence of the media on ethnic tensions. While of course none of these questions is the preserve of English-language studies in the United States *per se*, Allende's focus on these issues may be due in part to the environment in which she is living and writing. In addition, the experience of displacement is shown to be problematic, rather than merely a positive experience: Aurora is resigned to accepting the fact that the choices she makes – such as leaving her husband – and her physical appearance – the fact that she has Westernized features – means that she will be forever socially displaced.

Indeed the very parameters of Latin American fiction continue to be debated: as Juan E. De Castro has explained, 'how the Latin American space is constituted and what is meant by Latin America is clearly in turmoil.'[3] Allende's relocation to the United States has inevitably brought her into constant contact not merely with emigrants from the various countries of Latin America, but also second- and third-generation descendants from all over the world who seek to find a means of becoming integrated into the mainstream of the United States. Displacement in her fiction highlights the question of integration as an on-going process, and is never fully resolved, even for later generations. It is displacement that is one of the true constants in her fiction, and the characters that populate her North American narratives definitely appear to embrace the reality of experiences of displacement, be they geographical, social, linguistic or psychological.

---

2   Jay Prosser, 'Introduction' in *American Fiction of the 1990s: Reflections of history and culture*, ed. by Jay Prosser (New York: Routledge, 2008), pp. 1–14. Prosser deals with transnational borders, race cathexes, historical narratives, sex images and postmodern technologies. While postmodern technologies are not, strictly speaking, of direct relevance to *Retrato en sepia*, it is noticeable that many of the other general characteristics outlined by Prosser are applicable to this text.

3   Juan E. De Castro, *The Spaces of Latin American Literature: Tradition, Globalization, and Cultural Production* (New York: Palgrave, 2008), p. 139.

The dynamism within Allende's fictional world illustrates that her work remains a rich and fertile terrain for exploration, and this study has sought to highlight the benefits of not merely reading, but also rereading her work closely.

Allende uses displacement as a means of deftly exploring issues of key relevance to her own life, to the past and present of Latin America, and indeed to societies everywhere. She delicately balances personal and national concerns with public and international ones, and uses the space of literature in which to examine issues which are at once timely and timeless. Rereading her works of fiction through the prism of displacement unlocks the sophisticated subtleties that underpin her writing, and challenges views that her work is merely formulaic and repetitive in nature.

Bibliography

Primary Sources

Allende, Isabel, *Afrodita: cuentos, recetas y otros afrodisíacos* (Barcelona: Plaza & Janés, 1997)
——, *Cuentos de Eva Luna*, 8th edn (Barcelona: Plaza & Janés, 1992)
——, *De amor y de sombra*, 8th edn (Barcelona: Plaza & Janés, 1995)
——, *El cuaderno de Maya* (Barcelona: Plaza & Janés, 2011)
——, *El plan infinito* (Barcelona: Plaza & Janés, 1991)
——, *Eva Luna*, 5th edn (Barcelona: Plaza & Janés, 1993)
——, *Hija de la fortuna*, 3rd edn (Barcelona: Plaza & Janés, 1999)
——, *La casa de los espíritus*, 12th edn (Barcelona: Plaza & Janés, 2004)
——, *La isla bajo el mar* (Barcelona: Plaza & Janés, 2009)
——, *La suma de los días* (Barcelona: Plaza & Janés, 2007)
——, *Mi país inventado* (Barcelona: Areté, 2003)
——, *Paula* (Barcelona: Plaza & Janés, 1994)
——, *Retrato en sepia* (Barcelona: Plaza & Janés, 2000)

Interviews

Allende, Isabel, Foreword, in *Short Stories by Latin American Women: The Magic and the Real*, ed. by Celia Correas de Zapata (Houston, TX: Arte Público, 1990)
——, 'Magical Romance/Magical Realism: Ghosts in US and Latin American Fiction', in *Magical Realism: Theory, History, Community*, ed. by Lois Parkinson Zamora and Wendy B. Faris (Durham, NC: Duke University Press, 1995), pp. 407–550
——, 'Vamos a nombrar las cosas', in *Testimonio y documentos de la literatura chilena*, ed. by José Promis Ojeda (Santiago de Chile: Andrés Bello, 1995), pp. 291–300

―――, 'Modern Politics, Modern Fables', interview with Alvin P. Sanoff, *US News & World Report*, 21 November 1988, in *Conversations with Isabel Allende*, revised edn, ed. by John Rodden (Austin: University of Texas Press, 2004), p. 103

―――, 'Self-Portrait in Sepia', interview with Cristen Reat, in *Conversations with Isabel Allende*, revised edn, ed. by John Rodden (Austin: University of Texas Press, 2004), pp. 281–90

―――, 'Magical Feminist', interview with Jennifer Benjamin and Sally Engelfried, in *Conversations with Isabel Allende*, revised edn, ed. by John Rodden (Austin: University of Texas Press, 2004), pp. 185–99

―――, 'An Overwhelming Passion to Tell the Story', interview with Jennifer Benjamin and Sally Engelfried, in *Conversations with Isabel Allende*, revised edn, ed. by John Rodden (Austin: University of Texas Press, 2004), pp. 115–30

―――, *The Guardian*, 14 April 2008, Section G2, p. 14, <http://www.guardian.co.uk/theguardian/2008/apr/14/features.g2> [accessed 23 July 2008]

Secondary Sources

Álvarez-Rubio, Pilar, *Metáforas de la casa en la construcción de identidad nacional: Cinco miradas a Donoso, Eltit, Skármeta y Allende* (Santiago: Cuarto Propio, 2007)

André, María Claudia, 'Breaking through the Maze: Feminist Configurations of the Heroic Quest in Isabel Allende's *Daughter of Fortune* and *Portrait in Sepia*', in *Isabel Allende Today*, ed. by Rosemary G. Feal and Yvette E. Miller (Pittsburgh, PA: Latin American Literary Review, 2002), pp. 74–91

Antoni, Robert, 'Parody or Piracy: The Relationship of *The House of the Spirits* to *One Hundred Years of Solitude*', *Latin America Literary Review*, 32 (1988), 16–28

Armitt, Lucie, *Contemporary Women's Fiction and the Fantastic* (London: Macmillan, 2000)

Assal, Munzoul, 'Rights and Decisions to Return: Internally Displaced Persons in Post-war Sudan', in *Forced Displacements: Whose Needs are Right?* ed. by Katarzyna Grabska and Lyla Mehta (Basingstoke: Palgrave Macmillan, 2008), pp. 139–58

Bakhtin, Mikhail, *Problems of Dostoevsky's Poetics* (Minneapolis: University of Minnesota Press, 1984)

―――, *Rabelais and His World*, trans. by Helene Iswolsky (Bloomington: Indiana University Press, 1984)

Bammer, Angelika, ed., *Displacements: Cultural Identities in Question* (Bloomington: Indiana University Press, 1994)
Berman, Marshall, *All That Is Solid Melts into Air: The Experience of Modernity* (London: Verso, 1983)
Bhabha, Homi K., *The Location of Culture* (London: Routledge, 1994)
Bloom, Harold, 'Introduction', in *Isabel Allende*, ed. by Harold Bloom (Philadelphia, PA: Chelsea House, 2003), pp. 1–3
Burkholder, Mark A., and Lyman L. Johnson, *Colonial Latin America*, 5th edn (New York: Oxford University Press, 2003)
Campos, Rene, '*La casa de los espíritus*: mirada, espacio, discurso de la otra historia', in *Los libros tienen sus propios espíritus*, ed. by Marcelo Coddou (Mexico: Universidad Veracruzana, 1986), pp. 21–8
Carvalho, Susan E., *Contemporary Spanish American Novels by Women: Mapping the Narrative* (Woodbridge: Tamesis, 2007)
Cavallo, Ascanio, Manuel Salazar and Oscar Sepúlveda, *La historia oculta del régimen militar: Chile 1973–1988* (Santiago de Chile: Grijalbo, 1997)
Centre on Housing Rights and Evictions (COHRE), 'One World, Whose Dream? Housing Rights Violations and the Beijing Olympic Games', <http://www.cohre.org/store/attachments/One_World_Whose_Dream_July08.pdf> [accessed 9 July 2012]
Chambers, Robert, 'Paradigm Shifts and the Practice of Participatory Research and Development', in *Power and Participatory Development*, ed. by N. Nelson and S. Wright (London: Intermediate Technology, 1998), pp. 30–42
Chernin, Kim, *Everywhere a Guest, Nowhere at Home: A New Vision of Israel and Palestine* (Berkeley, CA: North Atlantic Books, 2009)
Chinese Government, 'Briefing on the relocation project for Olympic venues', <http://en.beijing2008.cn/news/official/preparation/n214253222.shtml> [accessed 4 July 2012]
Clark, Katerina, and Michael Holquist, *Mikhail Bakhtin* (Cambridge, MA: Harvard University Press, 1984)
Coddou, Marcelo, '*La casa de los espíritus*: De la historia a la Historia', in *Los libros tienen sus propios espíritus*, ed. by Marcelo Coddou (Mexico: Universidad Veracruzana, 1986), pp. 5–22
——, 'Dimensión paródica de Eva Luna', in *Critical Approaches to Isabel Allende's Novels*, ed. by Sonia Riquelme Rojas and Edna Aguirre Rehbein (New York: Peter Lang, 1991), pp. 139–49
Colman, Andrew M., 'displacement *n.*', in *A Dictionary of Psychology* (Oxford: Oxford University Press, 2006), p. 264

Cox, Karen Castellucci, *Isabel Allende: A Critical Companion* (Westport, CT: Greenwood, 2003)
Danow, David K., *The Spirit of Carnival: Magical Realism and the Grotesque* (Lexington: University Press of Kentucky, 1995)
Davies, Lloyd, *La casa de los espíritus* (London: Grant & Cutler, 2000)
De Beistegui, Miguel, *Thinking with Heidegger: Displacements* (Bloomington: Indiana University, 2003)
De Blij, Harm, *The Power of Place: Geography, Destiny and Globalization's Rough Landscape* (Oxford: Oxford University Press, 2008)
De Castro, Juan E., *The Spaces of Latin American Literature: Tradition, Globalization, and Cultural Production* (New York: Palgrave, 2008)
De González, Ester Gimbernat, 'Entre principio y final: La madre/materia de la escritura en *Eva Luna*', in *Critical Approaches to Isabel Allende's Novels*, ed. by Sonia Riquelme Rojas and Edna Aguirre Rehbein (New York: Peter Lang, 1991), pp. 111–24
Desai, Vandana, and Robert B. Potter, *The Companion to Development Studies*, 2nd edn (London: Hodder Education, 2008)
De Toro, Fernando, 'El desplazamiento de la literatura y la literatura del desplazamiento. La problemática de la identidad', in *Cartografías y estrategias de la 'postmodernidad' y la 'postcolonidad' en Latinoamérica: 'Hibridez' y globalización* (Madrid: Iberoamericana, 2006), pp. 417–38
Donoso, José, *La desesperanza* (Barcelona: Seix Barral, 1986)
Eakin, Marshall C., *The History of Latin America: Collision of Cultures* (New York: Palgrave Macmillan, 2007)
Falconer, Helen, 'Colouring the Family Album', *The Guardian*, 17 November 2001, <http://www.guardian.co.uk/books/2001/nov/17/fiction.isabelallende> [accessed 15 June 2012]
Feal, Rosemary G., and Yvette E. Miller, eds, *Isabel Allende Today* (Pittsburgh, PA: Latin American Literary Review, 2002)
Foreman, P. Gabrielle, 'Past-On Stories: History and the Magically Real, Morrison and Allende on Call', *Feminist Studies*, 18 (1992), 369–88
Freud, Sigmund, *The Interpretation of Dreams* (London: Penguin, 1991)
Glickman, Nora, 'Los personajes femeninos en *La casa de los espíritus*', in *Los libros tienen sus propios espíritus*, ed. by Marcelo Coddou (Mexico: Universidad Veracruzana, 1986), pp. 54–60
Gordon, Ambrose, 'Isabel Allende on Love and Shadow', *Contemporary Literature*, 28 (1987), 530–42
Gregory, Stephen, 'Scheherazade and Eva Luna: Problems in Allende's Storytelling', *Bulletin of Spanish Studies*, 80 (2003), 81–102

Hall, Leslie, *The Cambridge Introduction to Jacques Derrida* (Cambridge: Cambridge University Press, 2007)
Hart, Patricia, '"Magic Books" and the Magic of Books', in *Isabel Allende*, ed. by Harold Bloom (Philadelphia, PA: Chelsea House, 2003), pp. 5–22
Hart, Stephen M., *Allende: Eva Luna and Cuentos de Eva Luna* (London: Grant & Cutler, 2003)
——, 'Magical Realism in the Americas: Politicised Ghosts in *One Hundred Years of Solitude*, *The House of the Spirits*, and *Beloved*', *Journal of Iberian and Latin American Studies*, 9 (2003), 115–23
——, '*The House of the Spirits* by Isabel Allende', in *The Cambridge Companion to the Latin American Novel*, ed. by Efraín Kristal (Cambridge: Cambridge University Press, 2005), pp. 270–82
Houe, Poul, 'Place and Displacement in Kierkegaard – Place and Displacement of Kierkegaard', *Edda*, 97 (1997), 358–63
Huddart, David, *Homi Bhabha* (London: Routledge, 2006)
Human Rights Watch, <http://www.hrw.org> [accessed 20 October 2012]
Iftekharuddin, Farhat, 'Writing to Exorcise the Demons', in *Conversations with Isabel Allende*, revised edn, ed. by John Rodden (Austin: University of Texas Press, 2004), pp. 351–63
Jenkins, Ruth Y., 'Authorizing Female Voice and Experience: Ghosts and Spirits in Kingston's *The Woman Warrior* and Allende's *The House of the Spirits*', *Melus*, 19 (1994), 61–73
Jorgenson, Beth, '"Un puñado de críticos": Navigating the Critical Readings of Isabel Allende's Work', in *Isabel Allende Today*, ed. by Rosemary G. Feal and Yvette E. Miller (Pittsburgh, PA: Latin American Literary Review, 2002), pp. 128–46
Karrer, Wolfgang, 'Transformation and Transvestism in Eva Luna', in *Critical Approaches to Isabel Allende's Novels*, ed. by Sonia Riquelme Rojas and Edna Aguirre Rehbein (New York: Peter Lang, 1991), pp. 151–64
Konchar Farr, Cecilia, and Jaime Harker, eds, *The Oprah Affect* (Albany: State University of New York Press, 2008)
Kristal, Efraín, ed., *The Cambridge Companion to the Latin American Novel* (Cambridge: Cambridge University Press, 2005)
Lagos, María Inés, 'Female Voices from the Borderlands: Isabel Allende's *Paula* and *Retrato en sepia*', in *Isabel Allende Today*, ed. by Rosemary G. Feal and Yvette E. Miller (Pittsburgh, PA: Latin American Literary Review, 2002), pp. 112–27
Latham, Don, 'The Cultural Work of Magical Realism in Three Young Adult Novels', *Children's Literature in Education*, 38 (2007), 59–70

Lemaitre, Monique J., 'Deseo, incesto y represión en "De amor y de sombra"', in *Critical Approaches to Isabel Allende's Novels*, ed. by Sonia Riquelme Rojas and Edna Aguirre Rehbein (New York: Peter Lang, 1991), pp. 97–107

Levine, Linda Gould, *Isabel Allende* (New York: Twayne, 2003)

Lindsay, Claire, *Locating Latin American Women Writers: Cristina Peri Rossi, Rosario Ferré, Albalucía Angel, and Isabel Allende* (New York: Peter Lang, 2003)

McCallister, Richard, 'Nomenklatura in *La casa de los espíritus*', in *Critical Approaches to Isabel Allende's Novels*, ed. by Sonia Riquelme Rojas and Edna Aguirre Rehbein (New York: Peter Lang, 1991), pp. 21–36

McClennen, Sophia A., *The Dialectics of Exile: Nation, Time, Language, and Space in Hispanic Literatures* (West Lafayette, IN: Purdue University Press, 2004)

McElroy, Ruth Ann, 'Spirits at the Border, Migration and Identity in Contemporary African- and Latin-American Women's Fiction' (unpublished doctoral thesis, Lancaster University, 1997)

Mantel, Hilary, 'Ghost Writing', *The Guardian*, 28 July 2007, <http://www.guardian.co.uk/books/2007/jul/28/edinburghfestival2007.poetry> [accessed 18 June 2012]

Marcos, Juan Manuel, and Teresa Méndez-Faith, 'Multiplicidad, dialéctica y reconciliación del discurso en *La casa de los espíritus*', in *Los libros tienen sus propios espíritus*, ed. by Marcelo Coddou (Mexico: Universidad Veracruzana, 1986), pp. 61–70

Martínez, Nelly, 'Isabel Allende's Fictional World: Roads to Freedom', in *Isabel Allende Today: An Anthology of Essays*, ed. by Rosemary G. Feal and Yvette E. Miller (Pittsburgh, PA: Latin American Literary Review, 2002), pp. 51–73

Marting, Diane E., 'Dangerous (To) Women: Sexual Fiction in Spanish America', in *Narrativa Femenina en América Latina: Prácticas y Perspectivas Teóricas*, ed. by Sara Castro-Klarén, pp. 197–220

Meyer, Doris, '"Parenting the Text": Female Creativity and Dialogic Relationships in Isabel Allende's *La casa de los espíritus*', in *Isabel Allende*, ed. by Harold Bloom (Philadelphia, PA: Chelsea House, 2003), pp. 31–42

Mohan, Giles, and Kristian Stokke, 'Participatory Development and Empowerment: The Dangers of Localism', *Third World Quarterly*, 21 (2000), 247–68

Moi, Toril, *The Kristeva Reader* (London: Blackwell, 1986)

Moody, Michael, 'Entrevista con Isabel Allende', *Discurso literario*, 4.1 (1986), 41–53

Mora, Gabriela, 'Ruptura y perseverancia de estereotipos en *La casa de los espíritus*', in *Los libros tienen sus propios espíritus*, ed. by Marcelo Coddou (Mexico: Universidad Veracruzana, 1986), pp. 71–8

——, 'Las novelas de Isabel Allende y el papel de la mujer como ciudadana', *Ideologies and Literature*, 2.1 (1987), 53–61

Munday, Jeremy, *Style and Ideology in Translation: Latin American Writing in English* (London: Routledge, 2008)

Muñoz, Elías Miguel, 'La voz testimonial de Isabel Allende en *De amor y de sombra*', in *Critical Approaches to Isabel Allende's Novels*, ed. by Sonia Riquelme Rojas and Edna Aguirre Rehbein (New York: Peter Lang, 1991), pp. 61–72

Nelson, Alice A., *Political Bodies: Gender, History, and the Struggle for Narrative Power in Recent Chilean Fiction* (Lewisburg, PA: Bucknell University Press, 2002)

Ong, Walter J., *Orality and Literacy* (London: Routledge, 1982)

Otero, José, 'La historia como ficción en "Eva Luna" de Isabel Allende', *Confluencia*, 4 (1988), 61–7

Oviedo, José Miguel, *Historia de la literatura hispanoamericana 4. De Borges al presente* (Madrid: Alizana, 2001)

Perricone, Catherine R., 'Iconic/Metaphoric Dress and Other Nonverbal Signifiers in *De amor y de sombra*', in *Critical Approaches to Isabel Allende's Novels*, ed. by Sonia Riquelme Rojas and Edna Aguirre Rehbein (New York: Peter Lang, 1991), pp. 83–96

——, 'Allende and Valenzuela: Dissecting the Patriarchy', *South Atlantic Review*, 67 (2002), 80–105

Prosser, Jay, 'Introduction', in *American Fiction of the 1990s: Reflections of History and Culture*, ed. by Jay Proffer (New York: Routledge, 2008), pp. 1–14

Ramblado-Minero, María de la Cinta, *Isabel Allende's Writing of the Self: Trespassing The Boundaries of Fiction and Autobiography* (Lewiston, NY: Edwin Mellen, 2003)

Rehbein, Edna Aguirre, 'Isabel Allende's Eva Luna and the Act/Art of Narrating', in *Critical Approaches to Isabel Allende's Novels*, ed. by Sonia Riquelme Rojas and Edna Aguirre Rehbein (New York: Peter Lang, 1991), pp. 179–90

Reisz, Susana, 'Estéticas complacientes y formas de desobediencia en la producción femenina actual: ¿Es posible el diálogo?', in *Narrativa Femenina en América Latina: Prácticas y Perspectivas Teóricas*, ed. by Sara Castro-Klarén (Madrid: Iberoamericana, 2003), pp. 331–49

Richardson, Harry W., Peter Gordon and James E. Moore, eds, *Natural Disaster Analysis After Hurricane Katrina: Risk Assessment, Economic Impacts and Social Implications* (Cheltenham: Edward Elgar, 2009)

Rodden, John, *Conversations with Isabel Allende*, revised edn (Austin, TX: University of Texas, 2004)

——, 'Technicolored Life', *Society*, March/April 2005, 62–5

Rodríguez, Ana Patricia, '"Did Isabel Allende Write This Book for Me?": Oprah's Book Club Reads *Daughter of Fortune*', in *The Oprah Affect*, ed. by Cecilia Konchar Farr and Jaime Harker (Albany: State University of New York Press, 2008), pp. 189–210

Rojas, Mario A., '*La casa de los espíritus* de Isabel Allende: un caleidoscopio de espejos desordenados', in *Los libros tienen sus propios espíritus*, ed. by Marcelo Coddou (Mexico: Universidad Veracruzana, 1986), pp. 83–90

Rojas, Sonia Riquelme, and Edna Aguirre Rehbein, eds, *Critical Approaches to Isabel Alende's Novels* (New York: Peter Lang, 1991)

Said, Edward, 'Reflections on Exile', in *Out There: Marginalization and Other Cultures*, ed. by Russell Ferguson, Martha Gever and Marcia Tuckers (Cambridge, MA: MIT Press, 1992), pp. 357–66

Saona, Margarita, *Novelas familiares: figuraciones de la nación en la novela latinoamericana contemporánea* (Rosario: Beatriz Viterbo, 2004)

Shaw, Donald L., *The Post-Boom in Spanish American Fiction* (Albany: State University of New York Press, 1998)

Skármeta, Antonio, *El baile de la victoria* (Barcelona: Planeta, 2003)

Stavans, Ilan, 'Do you remember?', *The Times*, 5 October 2001, <http://www.timesonline.co.uk/tol/incomingFeeds/article766336.ece> [accessed 18 June 2011]

Swanson, Philip, 'California Dreaming: Mixture, Muddle and Meaning in Isabel Allende's North American Narratives', *Journal of Iberian and Latin American Studies*, 9 (2003), 59–67

——, 'Tyrants and Trash: Sex, Class and Culture in *La casa de los espíritus*', in *Isabel Allende*, ed. by Harold Bloom (Philadelphia, PA: Chelsea House, 2003), pp. 109–32

——, 'Magic Realism and Children's Literature: Isabel Allende's *La Ciudad de las Bestias*', in *A Companion to Magical Realism*, ed. by Stephen M. Hart and Wen-Chin Ouyang (Woodbridge: Tamesis, 2005) pp. 168–80

——, 'Z/Z: Isabel Allende and the Mark of Zorro', *Romance Studies*, 24 (2006), 265–77

Sznajder, Mario, and Luis Roniger, *The Politics of Exile in Latin America* (Cambridge: Cambridge University Press, 2009)

Thomas, Helen, *Romanticism and Slave Narratives: Transatlantic Testimonies* (Cambridge: Cambridge University Press, 2000)

Umpierre, Luz María, 'Unscrambling Allende's "Dos palabras": The Self, the Immigrant/Writer, and Social Justice', *MELUS*, 27 (2002), pp. 129–36

United Nations Refugee Agency, *Colombia: Internal Displacement – Policies and Problems*, <http://www.unhcr.org/refworld/docid/44bf463a4.html> [accessed 7 September 2012]

Vice, Sue, *Introducing Bakhtin* (Manchester: Manchester University Press, 1997)

Villa, Marta Inés, 'Políticas públicas sobre el desplazamiento forzado en Colombia: Una lectura desde las representaciones sociales', in *Las migraciones en América Latina: políticas, culturas y estrategias*, ed. by Susana Novick (Buenos Aires: Catálogos, 2008), pp. 229–48

Weaver, Wesley J., 'La frontera que se esfuma: Testimonio y ficción en *De amor y de sombra*', in *Critical Approaches to Isabel Allende's Novels*, ed. by Sonia Riquelme Rojas and Edna Aguirre Rehbein (New York: Peter Lang, 1991), pp. 73–81

Weiss, Thomas G., and David A. Korn, *Internal Displacement: Conceptualization and its Consequences* (London: Taylor & Francis, 2006)

Welden, Alicia Galaz-Vivar, 'Chile en el discurso referencial de *La casa de los espíritus*', in *Narrativa Hispanoamericana Contemporánea: Entre la vanguardia y el posboom*, ed. by Ana María Hernández de López (Madrid: Pliegos, 1996), pp. 265–77

Weldt-Basson, Helene Carol, *Subversive Silences: Nonverbal Expression and Implicit Narrative Strategies in the Works of Latin American Women Writers* (Madison, NJ: Fairleigh Dickinson University Press, 2009)

Williams, Raymond Leslie, *The Twentieth Century Spanish American Novel* (Austin: University of Texas Press, 2003)

——, *The Columbia Guide to the Latin American Novel Since 1945* (New York: Columbia University Press, 2007)

Zamora, Lois Parkinson, and Wendy B. Faris, eds, *Magical Realism: Theory, History, Community* (Durham, NC: Duke University Press, 1995)

Zapata, Celia Correas, *Isabel Allende: Vida y espíritus* (Barcelona: Plaza & Janés, 1998)

Index

Allende, Isabel *passim*
  memory and writing 14
  originality of work 3–4, 6
  place 132
  storytelling 103
  writers 131
Allende, Salvador 18
André, María Claudia 30
Antoni, Robert 19n42
Assal, Munzoul 11n21

Bakhtin, Mikhail 22, 71, 73, 80, 97
Bammer, Angelika 9, 15
Bangladesh 39
Berman, Marshall 62
Bhabha, Homi K. 157–8, 160, 165
Bloom, Harold 5–7
Bolivia 12
bosque de los pigmeos, El [*Forest of the Pygmies*] 31
Burkholder, Mark A. 38n7

Campos, René 37
carnival and carnivalesque
  definition 73–4
  degradation 97
  dismemberment 90
  disorder 22
  folk humour 99
  high and low 80
  metamorphosis 93
  mixing of classes 75
  role reversal 82
Carvalho, Susan E. 172, 177, 179–80
Catholic Church 89, 100

Cavallo, Ascanio 21n43
Centre on Housing Rights and Evictions 10n19
Chambers, Robert 45–6
Chernin, Kim 11n21
Chile 12–13, 18, 32, 123
Ciudad de las Bestias, La [*City of the Beasts*] 31, 32
Clark, Katerina 78n10
Coddou, Marcelo 66–7, 105
Colman, Andrew 136
Colombia 12, 127
community 8, 104, 143
  British 152, 178
  Chinese 151, 171–3
  Hispanic 134, 138, 151, 156
  local 35, 38–40, 49, 112, 116–19, 122, 127, 129, 131, 185
  and multinationals 11
  oral 107, 117
  shared 120
condensation 135–6
Cox, Karen Castellucci 72, 150, 153, 173, 179, 181
Cuaderno de Maya, El [*Maya's Notebook*] 32

Danow, David K. 75
Davies, Lloyd 18, 54, 66, 67
de Beistegui, Miguel 15n35
De Blij, Harm 85n15
De Castro, Juan E. 188
De González, Ester Gimbernat 105
Derrida, Jacques 16n36
Desai, Vandana 38n5

desaparecido [disappeared person] 21–2, 84, 95, 96
Development Studies 20, 35, 38–40, 185
   decentralization 39
   exterior knowledge 46
   participatory development 39–40, 45–6
   social capital 40, 50
   social networks 40, 52–3, 56
   visualization 39–40, 48
displacement
   definition 9–10
   development-induced displacement 10
   and Development Studies 38
   dreams 135–6
   external 11, 16
   globalization 15
   identity 15
   internal 10, 54
   internally displaced persons (IDPs) 10, 11–12
   psychocultural 136
Donoso, José 13
Dorfman, Ariel 13
dreams
   Cuentos de Eva Luna 117, 121–3, 131
   De amor y de sombra 76n9, 88
   El plan infinito 134, 135–8, 140, 142, 144, 148
   Hija de la fortuna 155, 164

Eakin, Marshall C. 12n25
endarkenment 85n15, 87
Escobar, Arturo 41
exile 15, 123

Falconer, Helen 4
Freud, Sigmund 134, 135–7

García Márquez, Gabriel 19

Glickman, Nora 36
Gómez, Juan Vicente 23
Gordon, Ambrose 85, 90
Gordon, William 16, 27
Gregory, Stephen 106
grotesque realism 78

Hall, Leslie 16n36
Hart, Patricia 66
Hart, Stephen M. 18, 65n17, 106
Heidegger, Martin 15n35
Holquist, Michael 78n10
Houe, Poul 15n35
Huddart, David 158
Human Rights Watch 11n22

Iftekharuddin, Farhat 132n20
Inés del alma mía [*Inés of my Soul*] 31
isla bajo el mar, La [*The Island Beneath the Sea*] 31, 32
Israel 11

Johnson, Lyman L. 38n5
Jorgenson, Beth 4

Karim, Mahbabul 39
Kierkegaard, Søren 15n35
Kingston, Maxine Hong 18
Korn, David A. 10n18
Kristal, Efraín 5
Kristeva, Julia 89n16

Lagos, María Inés 181
Lemaitre, Monique J. 72–3, 82n12
Levine, Linda Gould 29, 72, 96, 106, 124, 128, 135, 150, 174, 179, 180
Lindsay, Claire 5, n5

McClennen, Sophia 15
Mantel, Hilary 103, 104
Mapuche tribe 12

Marcos, Juan Manuel 68
Martínez, Nelly 166
matrilineality 44, 66
memory
    and Allende 14
    Cuentos de Eva Luna 115, 117–18, 124–5
    De amor y de sombra 93
    El plan infinito 146
    Eva Luna 104
    Hija de la fortuna 164–5, 171
    La casa de los espíritus 20, 43, 66
    Retrato en sepia 174
Méndez-Faith, Teresa 68
metamorphosis 82, 86, 93, 97, 121
Meyer, Doris 66
Mi país inventado 12, 16–17, 31
Mohan, Giles 39–41
Moody, Michael 21n43
Mora, Gabriela 37, 68, 72, 95n18, 96
Morales, Evo 12
Morrison, Toni 18
Munday, Jeremy 187n1
Muñoz, Elías Miguel 98

Ong, Walter J. 26, 40n9, 104, 107–8, 112, 117, 130
Orality and Literacy 107–8
Otero, José 23n44
Oviedo, José Miguel 68

Perricone, Catherine R. 84
Pinochet, Augusto 13, 18
Potter, Robert B. 38n5
Problems of Dostoevsky's Politics 97
Prosser, Jay 187–8
Putnam, Robert 40

Ramblado-Minero, María de la Cinta 4, 7, 181–2
Raymont, Peter 13n28

Rehbein, Edna Aguirre 105–6
reino del Dragón de Oro, El [*Kingdom of the Golden Dragon*] 31
Rodden, John 14–15, 28
Rodríguez, Ana Patricia 7n12
Rojas, Mario 37
Roniger, Luis 12n25

Said, Edward 151–2
Salazar, Manuel 21n43
Saona, Margarita 43n11
secondary orality 26, 109
Sepúlveda, Oscar 21n43
Shaw, Donald L. 106
silence
    Cuentos de Eva Luna 26, 107n10, 115, 119–20, 123, 126, 127, 129–30
    De amor y de sombra 93, 97
    Eva Luna 26
    Hija de la fortuna 171
    El plan infinito 145, 171
Skármeta, Antonio 13
Stavans, Ilan 3–4
Stokke, Kristian 39–41
subversion
    De amor y de sombra 21–2, 75, 80, 99, 100
    La casa de los espíritus 5, 54, 63
    Eva Luna 110–11, 115
    Hija de la fortuna 158, 165
Sudan 11
suma de los días, La [*The Sum of Our Days*] 31, 32
Swanson, Philip 32, 63, 66, 135n3, 150–1
Sznajder, Mario 12n25

Thomas, Helen 152n14

Venezuela 16, 23
Vice, Sue 74, 90n17
Villa, Marta Inés 12

violence
- *La casa de los espíritus* 36–7, 54, 59
- *Cuentos de Eva Luna* 118
- *De amor y de sombra* 82, 99
- *Hija de la fortuna* 169

Weaver, Wesley J., III 75

Weiss, Thomas G. 10n18
Weldt Basson, Helene Carol 107n10
Winfrey, Oprah 7n12

Zapata, Celia Correas 25n45
Zapatistas 41
Zorro 31

Hispanic Studies: Culture and Ideas

Edited by
Claudio Canaparo

This series aims to publish studies in the arts, humanities and social sciences, the main focus of which is the Hispanic World. The series invites proposals with interdisciplinary approaches to Hispanic culture in fields such as history of concepts and ideas, sociology of culture, the evolution of visual arts, the critique of literature, and uses of historiography. It is not confined to a particular historical period.

Monographs as well as collected papers are welcome in English or Spanish.

Those interested in contributing to the series are invited to write with either the synopsis of a subject already in typescript or with a detailed project outline to either Professor Claudio Canaparo, Department of Iberian and Latin American Studies, School of Arts, Birkbeck College, 43 Gordon Square, London WC1H 0PD, UK, c.canaparo@sllc.bbk.ac.uk, or to Peter Lang Ltd, oxford@peterlang.com.

Vol. 1   Antonio Sánchez
         Postmodern Spain. A Cultural Analysis of 1980s–1990s Spanish Culture. 220 pages. 2007.
         ISBN 978-3-03910-914-2

Vol. 2   Geneviève Fabry y Claudio Canaparo (eds.)
         El enigma de lo real. Las fronteras del realismo en la narrativa del siglo XX. 275 pages. 2007.
         ISBN 978-3-03910-893-0

Vol. 3   William Rowlandson
         Reading Lezama's *Paradiso*. 290 pages. 2007.
         ISBN 978-3-03910-751-3

Vol. 4   Fernanda Peñaloza, Jason Wilson and Claudio Canaparo (eds)
           Patagonia. Myths and Realities. 277 pages. 2010.
           ISBN 978-3-03910-917-3

Vol. 5   Xon de Ros
           Primitivismo y Modernismo. El legado de María Blanchard.
           238 pages. 2007.
           ISBN 978-3-03910-937-1

Vol. 6   Sergio Plata
           Visions of Applied Mathematics. Strategy and Knowledge.
           284 pages. 2007.
           ISBN 978-3-03910-923-4

Vol. 7   Annick Louis
           Borges ante el fascismo. 374 pages. 2007.
           ISBN 978-3-03911-005-6

Vol. 8   Helen Oakley
           From Revolution to Migration. A Study of Contemporary Cuban and
           Cuban-American Crime Fiction. 200 pages. 2012.
           ISBN 978-3-03911-021-6

Vol. 9   Thea Pitman
           Mexican Travel Writing. 209 pages. 2008.
           ISBN 978-3-03911-020-9

Vol. 10   Francisco J. Borge
           A New World for a New Nation. The Promotion of America in Early
           Modern England. 240 pages. 2007.
           ISBN 978-3-03911-070-4

Vol. 11   Helena Buffery, Stuart Davis and Kirsty Hooper (eds)
           Reading Iberia. Theory/History/Identity. 229 pages. 2007.
           ISBN 978-3-03911-109-1

Vol. 12   Matías Bruera
           Meditations on Flavour. *Forthcoming.*
           ISBN 978-3-03911-345-3

Vol. 13   Angela Romero-Astvaldsson
         La obra narrativa de David Viñas. La nueva inflexión de *Prontuario*
         y *Claudia Conversa*. 300 pages. 2007.
         ISBN 978-3-03911-100-8

Vol. 14   Aaron Kahn
         The Ambivalence of Imperial Discourse. Cervantes's *La Numancia*
         within the 'Lost Generation' of Spanish Drama (1570–90).
         243 pages. 2008.
         ISBN 978-3-03911-098-8

Vol. 15   Turid Hagene
         Negotiating Love in Post-Revolutionary Nicaragua. The role of love
         in the reproduction of gender asymmetry. 341 pages. 2008.
         ISBN 978-3-03911-011-7

Vol. 16   Yolanda Rodríguez Pérez
         The Dutch Revolt through Spanish Eyes. Self and Other in historical
         and literary texts of Golden Age Spain (c. 1548–1673). 346 pages. 2008.
         ISBN 978-3-03911-136-7

Vol. 17   Stanley Black (ed.)
         Juan Goytisolo. Territories of Life and Writing. 202 pages. 2007.
         ISBN 978-3-03911-324-8

Vol. 18   María T. Sánchez
         The Problems of Literary Translation. A Study of the Theory and
         Practice of Translation from English into Spanish. 269 pages. 2009.
         ISBN 978-3-03911-326-2

Vol. 19   Aino Linda Rinhaug
         Fernando Pessoa. A Ludicrous Self. *Forthcoming.*
         ISBN 978-3-03911-909-7

Vol. 20   Ana Cruz García
         Re(de-)generando identidades. Locura, feminidad y liberalización en
         Elena Garro, Susana Pagano, Ana Castillo y María Amparo Escandón.
         259 pages. 2009.
         ISBN 978-3-03911-524-2

Vol. 21   Idoya Puig (ed.)
          Tradition and Modernity. Cervantes's Presence in Spanish
          Contemporary Literature. 221 pages. 2009.
          ISBN 978-3-03911-526-6

Vol. 22   Charlotte Lange
          Modos de parodia. Guillermo Cabrera Infante, Reinaldo Arenas,
          Jorge Ibargüengoitia y José Agustín. 252 pages. 2008.
          ISBN 978-3-03911-554-9

Vol. 23   Claudio Canaparo
          Geo-epistemology. Latin America and the Location of Knowledge.
          284 pages. 2009.
          ISBN 978-3-03911-573-0

Vol. 24   Jesús López-Peláez Casellas
          "Honourable Murderers". El concepto del honor en *Othello*
          de Shakespeare y en los "dramas de honor" de Calderón.
          321 pages. 2009.
          ISBN 978-3-03911-825-0

Vol. 25   Marian Womack and Jennifer Wood (eds)
          Beyond the Back Room. New Perspectives on Carmen Martín Gaite.
          336 pages. 2011.
          ISBN 978-3-03911-827-4

Vol. 26   Manuela Palacios and Laura Lojo (eds)
          Writing Bonds. Irish and Galician Contemporary Women Poets.
          232 pages. 2009.
          ISBN 978-3-03911-834-2

Vol. 27   Myriam Osorio
          Agencia femenina, agencia narrativa. Una lectura feminista de la obra
          en prosa de Albalucía Ángel. 180 pages. 2010.
          ISBN 978-3-03911-893-3

Vol. 28   *Forthcoming*

Vol. 29   Soledad Pérez-Abadín Barro
           Cortázar y Che Guevara. Lectura de *Reunión*. 182 pages. 2010.
           ISBN 978-3-03911-919-6

Vol. 30   Gonzalo Pasamar
           Apologia and Criticism. Historians and the History of Spain,
           1500–2000. 301 pages. 2010.
           ISBN 978-3-03911-920-2

Vol. 31   Victoria Carpenter (ed.)
           (Re)Collecting the Past. History and Collective Memory in Latin
           American Narrative. 315 pages. 2010.
           ISBN 978-3-03911-928-8

Vol. 32   Geneviève Fabry, Ilse Logie y Pablo Decock (eds.)
           Los imaginarios apocalípticos en la literatura hispanoamericana
           contemporánea. 472 pages. 2010.
           ISBN 978-3-03911-937-0

Vol. 33   Julian Vigo
           Performative Bodies, Hybrid Tongues. Race, Gender, Sex and
           Modernity in Latin America and the Maghreb. 391 pages. 2010.
           ISBN 978-3-03911-951-6

Vol. 34   Heike Pintor Pirzkall
           La cooperación alemana al desarrollo. Factores condicionantes de su
           transformación en la década de los noventa y su impacto en América
           Latina. 374 pages. 2010.
           ISBN 978-3-0343-0107-7

Vol. 35   Arturo Casas and Ben Bollig (eds)
           Resistance and Emancipation. Cultural and Poetic Practices.
           419 pages. 2011.
           ISBN 978-3-0343-0160-2

Vol. 36   *Forthcoming*

Vol. 37   Guillermo Olivera
          Laboratorios de la mediatización. La experimentación con materiales
          mediáticos, la teoría y la crítica cultural argentina, 1965–1978.
          364 pages. 2011.
          ISBN 978-3-0343-0201-2

Vol. 38   Guy Baron
          Gender in Cuban Cinema. From the Modern to the Postmodern.
          334 pages. 2011.
          ISBN 978-3-0343-0229-6

Vol. 39   Claudio Canaparo
          El imaginario Patagonia. Ensayo acerca de la evolución conceptual del
          espacio. 576 pages. 2011.
          ISBN 978-3-0343-0287-6

Vol. 40   Inmaculada Murcia Serrano
          Agua y destino. Introducción a la estética de Ramón Gaya.
          220 pages. 2011.
          ISBN 978-3-0343-0251-7

Vol. 41   Bill Richardson
          Borges and Space. 266 pages. 2012.
          ISBN 978-3-0343-0246-3

Vol. 42   *Forthcoming*

Vol. 43   Ann Frost
          The Galician Works of Ramón del Valle-Inclán. Patterns of Repetition
          and Continuity. 241 pages. 2010.
          ISBN 978-3-0343-0242-5

Vol. 44   Milagros López-Peláez Casellas
          What About the Girls? Estrategias narrativas de resistencia en la primera
          literatura chicana. 265 pages. 2012.
          ISBN 978-3-0343 0264-7

Vol. 45   Bill Richardson and Lorraine Kelly (eds)
           Power, Place and Representation. Contested Sites of Dependence and
           Independence in Latin America. 268 pages. 2012.
           ISBN 978-3-0343-0710-9

Vol. 46   Patricia D'Allemand
           José María Samper. Nación y cultura en el siglo XIX colombiano.
           177 pages. 2012.
           ISBN 978-3-0343-0288-3

Vol. 47   *Forthcoming*

Vol. 48   Emilio Rosales
           Baroja. La novela como laberinto. 163 pages. 2012.
           ISBN 978-3-0343-0774-1

Vol. 49   Kristine Vanden Berghe
           Las novelas de la rebelión zapatista. 171 pages. 2012.
           ISBN 978-3-0343-0779-6

Vol. 50   William Rowlandson
           Borges, Swedenborg and Mysticism. 267 pages. 2013.
           ISBN 978-3-0343-0811-3

Vol. 51   Elena Rodríguez-Guridi
           Exégesis del "error". Una reinterpretación de la praxis de escritura en
           Libro de la vida, *Novelas ejemplares* y *Desengaños amorosos*.
           175 pages. 2013.
           ISBN 978-3-0343-0817-5

Vol. 52-53 *Forthcoming*

Vol. 54   Mel Boland
           Displacement in Isabel Allende's Fiction, 1982–2000.
           212 pages. 2013.
           ISBN 978-3-0343-0932-5